The Rules of the Game in the Global Economy: Policy Regimes for International Business

Second Edition

The Rules of the Game in the Global Economy: Policy Regimes for International Business

Second Edition

Lee E. Preston
University of Maryland

Duane Windsor
Rice University

Kluwer Academic Publishers
Boston / Dordrecht / London

Distributors for North America:
Kluwer Academic Publishers
101 Philip Drive
Assinippi Park
Norwell, Massachusetts 02061 USA

Distributors for all other countries:
Kluwer Academic Publishers Group
Distribution Centre
Post Office Box 322
3300 AH Dordrecht, THE NETHERLANDS

Library of Congress Cataloging-in-Publication Data
Preston, Lee E.
    The rules of the game in the global economy : policy regimes for
international business / Lee E. Preston, Duane Windsor.
        p.   cm.
    Includes bibliographical references and index.
    ISBN 0-7923-9887-4. -- ISBN 0-7923-9888-2 (pbk. : alk. paper)
    1. International economic relations. 2. International economic
integration.   3. International business enterprises.
4. International cooperation.   I. Windsor, Duane.   II. Title.
HF1412.P74   1997
338.8'8--dc21   97-1578
                                                                    CIP

Printed on acid-free paper.

Printed in the United States of America

To our wives
Patricia L. Preston
and
Sandra S. Windsor

Summary Table of Contents

Contents

CONTENTS

List of Figures and Tables

PREFACE

The subject of this study is the way that firms, industries, and nations organize their relationships with one another in order to engage in international business. To the casual observer, the processes of buying and selling, borrowing and lending, investing and receiving investment returns may seem much the same, whether they occur within a single country or between and among businesses in different political jurisdictions. In fact, however, business contacts between firms or individuals in different countries are significantly different from their domestic counterparts. Not only do international buyers and sellers, borrowers and lenders, investors and earnings recipients often use different languages and currencies, they also frequently operate under different basic rules governing contracts, accounting practices, and dispute-settlement arrangements; and they are subject to different tax systems. Most important, they may require explicit permission, or at least facilitating arrangements, from their respective governments in order to engage in any economic contact whatsoever. It may well be that, as Adam Smith believed, there is "a certain propensity in human nature ... to truck, barter, and exchange one thing for another" (1776, vol. 1, p. 17); but the fact is that most important markets and business relationships do not simply appear and evolve as natural phenomena. In fact, they are created by human effort and are highly organized, and international business relationships are the most highly organized of all.

This study combines themes and topics from two major fields of knowledge, international relations (a branch of political science) and international business. However, it differs significantly from the mainstream literature in both of them. The international relations and international political economy literature is primarily theory-focused and state-centered; its principal emphasis is on the relationships among governments. Even when concerned with business-related topics, it gives little attention to the internal dynamics of industries and business enterprises.

The international business literature is, of course, typically enterprise- or industry-centered, but its treatment of the surrounding policy environment is typically descriptive, institutional, and static. It gives little attention to the origins and evolution of the various policy regimes governing international business operations, the connections among such regimes, or the role of business interests in the shaping of them. It is our intention here to bridge the gap between these two literatures, to emphasize the importance of business and other economic actors in the creation and development of regimes, and to analyze the policy environment of international business from a dynamic and evolutionary perspective. The importance of fundamental efficiency considerations, in contrast to normative considerations (as in much of the political science literature) and profit motivations (as in the business literature), is stressed throughout.

Since initial work on the first edition of this study was first undertaken, more than a decade ago, the environment of international business has greatly changed. At that time, the Union of Soviet Socialist Republics (USSR) was a large and sometimes troublesome international economic actor, and its collection of satellite states, organized into the Council for Mutual Economic Assistance (CMEA, or COMECON), offered an interesting contrast to the liberal economic regimes that were developing elsewhere in the world. Now the USSR is no more, and the former members of the CMEA are clamoring to join global trade and investment systems based on liberal principles. They are also eager to collaborate with, or even to join, evolving regional economic integration systems such as the European Union (EU) or Asia Pacific Economic Cooperation (APEC). In addition, new international arrangements such as the World Trade Organization (WTO) and the North American Free Trade Association (NAFTA) have come into being, and the overall pace of economic globalization may be accelerating.

Some readers of the 1992 edition of this study have suggested that it failed to emphasize strongly enough the fact that many of the important business and economic regimes created during the post–World War II era are currently encountering difficult pressures, are undergoing significant changes, and may even be in danger of collapse. We acknowledge that there are many evidences of strain in, for example, the postwar monetary exchange and free trade regimes and in many areas of international environmental protection. However, we support our belief in the continuing importance of the contemporary set of regimes (and particularly the importance of the underlying forces that have brought them into being and still determine their evolution and effectiveness) with two observations:

First, most of the current controversies are about the *specific features* of individual regimes, not about whether or not some system of mutually acceptable understandings and behaviors should or will be maintained, or what its principal purposes should be. For example, establishment of the WTO in 1994, as successor to the 1947 General Agreement on Tariffs and Trade (GATT), reflected widespread recognition of many problems within the evolving liberal trade regime. WTO mechanisms are intended to provide new, more flexible, and more effective means of dealing with these concerns. The eagerness of officials and executives in, for example, China to become participants in this new regime says a great deal about its importance as a focus of global policy development.

Second, even as some regimes, such as the fixed-exchange rates currency regime originally embodied in the International Monetary Fund (IMF), have weakened, others have appeared and grown stronger. The evolution of the European Community (EC 12) into the European Union (EU 15) and of GATT into the WTO, creation of the North American Free Trade Area, and some results of the 1992 Rio de Janeiro Earth Summit are examples of this countertrend.

We share the view reflected in the important twenty-two volume series of studies sponsored by The Brookings Institution under the overall title *Integrating National Economies: Promise and Pitfalls,* that the international arrangements that have evolved during recent decades "reflect a new threshold in global economic relations and in the relations between governments and their citizens" (Lawrence, Bressand, and Ito, 1996, p. 14). The notion of these authors that international economic contacts will be increasingly modulated through "clubs" of various kinds (industry-specific, functional, and regional) and perhaps ultimately harmonized through a global "club of clubs" is strongly consistent with our own analysis.

For these reasons, we believe that the notion that international business is increasingly governed by a complex system of multilateral regimes remains accurate, even though the detailed characteristics of specific regimes are subject to change over time. Our purpose in this analysis is to show what international regimes are like, why they have become numerous and important, and how they become adapted to changing circumstances. Our case studies of individual regimes are intended to explain their emergence and evolution over several decades, to point out similarities and differences among them, and, where possible, to indicate likely patterns of evolution for the future. With all modesty, we should note that prediction in this field is a soft art at best and that a study of this sort is not the place to look for news about the latest current developments, which continue to occur even after a manuscript has been sent to the printer.

In preparing this revised edition, we have tried to accomplish the following specific objectives:

- Update all data and tables and include more recent developments and examples, wherever possible and appropriate.
- Give specific attention to the evolution of new institutional arrangements, such as the European Union, NAFTA, and WTO.
- Increase emphasis on the importance to business and economic activity of environmental regimes as reflected in the issues raised at the 1992 Earth Summit in Rio de Janeiro and related developments.
- Reorganize some sections of the text, including the elimination of one chapter, the rearrangement of materials within and among others, and the introduction of a separate chapter on telecommunications and services.
- Revise the text throughout to correct errors and ambiguities and to clarify our intended meaning.

P.1 STRUCTURE OF THE ANALYSIS

Part I of this book sets forth the basic framework of concepts and data underlying our analysis. In chapter 1, we identify the three major types of linkages (trade, investment, and enterprise) that account for the strong and increasing *interdependence* of actions and interests within the global economy (cf. Dunning, 1993); and we characterize as "rules of the game" the *international policy regimes* that have come into being to facilitate and mediate these interdependencies. Chapter 2 examines some of the theoretical issues and controversies concerning the concept of international policy regimes and explains in detail the way in which this concept will be used in our case studies in part II. Chapter 3, the final chapter in part I, documents the evolution of a truly global economy, an economy in which remote and varied parts are intimately linked to form a dynamically functioning whole that is the environment for contemporary international policy regimes. Our necessarily brief and selective synthesis of this complex material inevitably runs the risk of oversimplification; its purpose, however, is not exhaustive factual coverage but analytical presentation of major trends and relationships.

The chapters in part II present integrative case studies of six major types of international policy regimes: global policy developments taking place within the United Nations (UN) system; regional and other associative systems (with emphasis on the EU and NAFTA); and important functional regimes for trade, payments, and foreign investment, for sea and air transport, for telecommunications and services, and for environmental protection. Each of these case studies is based on an extensive survey of the relevant literature, consultation with experts, and careful integration and synthesis of material from diverse sources. The purpose of the case studies, taken together, is to provide empirical evidence of the nature and impact of regimes, the similarities and differences among them, and other forces contributing to their creation and evolution over time. These case studies are intended to be both of interest in themselves and of value as illustrations and applications of the more general and theoretical arguments made in part I. Our inclusion of environmental regimes is intended to emphasize their key similarities and differences as compared to the major business and economic regimes, and also the critical connections and interactions among regimes of all types that affect international business operations. (Environmental regulation is also covered, albeit briefly, in the recent survey of the institutions of international economic integration included in the Brookings series, cf. Kahler, 1995, especially pp. 72–77.) The epilogue deals with frontier issues likely to receive increased attention in international negotiations. Tax harmonization and corrupt business practices receive special emphasis.

P.2 DATA AND DOCUMENTATION NOTE

This study uses various kinds and sources of data and documentation. The reader should take note that all such material, both reported here and in the original sources, must be used with caution. International and comparative data, often estimates at best, are notoriously unreliable and sometimes even contradictory. For example, the reported volume of outbound UK investment going to the US is never the same as the volume of inbound investment reaching the US from the UK, and the discrepancy between the two is unstable in both amount and direction from one time period to the next. In addition, analysts and experts often make different interpretations, or even outright errors, in their use of the same data or the explanation of the causes, meaning, and impact of specific developments. We believe that the data and interpretations presented here are accurate for their intended purposes and that errors or discrepancies that might be pointed out are not of sufficient importance to affect the overall thrust of the analysis.

P.3 TERMINOLOGICAL NOTE

The language of analysis for international business and policy is not yet standardized, and the terminology suggested by some analysts inevitably strikes others as artificial and unhelpful. It has been our intention here to keep the use of technical terms and academic jargon to a minimum. Even so, it seems wise to clarify the precise meaning that we attach to certain commonly used terms.

We use the term *enterprise* to refer to any managerial organization through which economic activity is carried out. An enterprise may be owned and controlled by private individuals, by national states or other governments, or in some other or combined fashion; and an enterprise may be organized as a corporation or in some other legal form within its home jurisdiction. These distinctions of ownership and legal form may, or may not, be significant in explaining the behavior and influence of enterprises in the international environment. The appearance of new types of enterprises (for example, joint ventures, networks, and strategic alliances) that do not fit into conventional categories may be of special importance.

Business activities are *international* whenever they involve enterprises based in two or more national jurisdictions and hence require crossborder contacts of one sort or another. Many purely domestic enterprises are regularly involved in *international business* (e.g., sales, purchases, and/or loans to or from enterprises in other countries). Individual national governments regularly make policies with respect to the *international* aspects of business operations taking place entirely within their own borders. Multinational business relationships arise when participants from more than two (and, as a rule, potentially many) national jurisdictions are simultaneously involved. A *multinational enterprise* (MNE) is one in which substantial amounts of activity are carried out within and among several different national jurisdictions; again, such enterprises may be organized and owned in many different ways, and such differences may or may not be important for any particular analytical purpose. *International policies* involve understandings and agreements among actors (governments, enterprises, or others) representing or based within different national jurisdictions about matters of mutual interest. Although such policies can be *bilateral* (i.e., involving relations between two countries), most of the significant policy arrangements affecting business involve several, possibly very many, different jurisdictions and hence can be termed *plurilateral, multilateral,* or, more generally, *multinational.* It is important to remember that *multinational policies* may relate to industries, such as international air transport, that (at least for the present) contain no or very few *multinational enterprises.*

Acknowledgments

Many sources of support, both intellectual and financial, were acknowledged in the preface to the first edition. Here, in addition to repeating our thanks to all of them, we must make special mention of Martin Dresner, who took responsibility for updating and revising our study of international sea and air transport regimes (chapter 7); Kenneth L. Conca, who contributed to the revision of our study of environmental regimes (chapter 9); and the helpful guidance received from published reviews of the first edition by John Mahon (1993) and S. Prakash Sethi (1994).

References

Dunning, John H. 1993. *The Globalization of Business: The Challenge of the 1990s.* London: Routledge.

Kahler, Miles. 1995. *International Institutions and the Political Economy of Integration.* Washington, DC: Brookings Institution.

Lawrence, Robert Z., Albert Bressand, and Takatoshi Ito. 1996. *A Vision for the World Economy: Openness, Diversity, and Cohesion.* Washington, DC: Brookings Institution.

Mahon, John F. 1993. *Business and Society*, vol. 32, no. 1 (Spring), pp. 59–63.

Sethi, S. Prakash. 1994. *Journal of International Business Studies*, vol. 25, no. 2 (Second Quarter), pp. 404–409.

Smith, Adam. 1776. *An Inquiry into The Nature and Causes of The Wealth of Nations.* Edwin Cannan, ed. Chicago: University of Chicago Press.

I THE CONTEXT OF INTERNATIONAL POLICY REGIMES

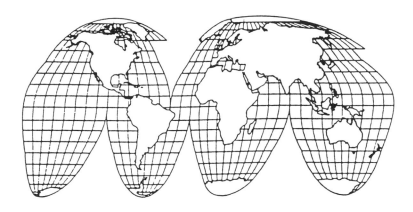

1

COMPLEX LINKAGES IN
THE GLOBAL ECONOMY

During the half century since World War II, the international economy has evolved from a collection of national units, loosely tied together through various economic and political relationships, into a truly "global" system, an interdependent network of trade, investment, and development processes that touches nearly all parts of the world. In the course of this evolution, many poor countries have become richer and more active on the international scene, while advanced industrial countries (AICs) have developed new areas of competitive advantage and disadvantage. Some formal linkages among countries (the European colonial empires and the Council for Mutual Economic Assistance, the CMEA or COMECON system of the former USSR) have weakened or disappeared, while new forms of regional and global integration, the European Union (EU) and the World Trade Organization (WTO), have emerged. In this environment of increasing interdependence and continuing dynamic change, opportunities for cooperation and collaboration, competition and conflict, among enterprises, industries, nations, and regions have multiplied. This book examines the ways in which these diverse economic actors have attempted to respond to these situations by developing mutually supportive agreements and understandings.

1.1 RULES OF THE GAME

We refer here to this evolving framework of agreements and under-standings as the "rules of the game" of international business or, more formally, as international policy regimes. Business and economic activities are often characterized in a game metaphor, with strategies, rules, wins, losses, and so forth; and this characterization is particularly appropriate in the international context. Young describes the institutions governing international affairs as "the rules of the game that define the character of social practices" (1994, p. 28). Sauvant and Aranda state that "the international framework for transnational corporations consists of conventional norms and customary rules" (1994, p. 85). Stopford and Strange introduce their analysis of contemporary state-firm relations by asserting that "structural change in the international political economy has altered *the nature of the game* ..." (1991, p. 4, emphasis added). We share this view and further note that changes in the "nature" of a game necessarily imply changes in the rules by which it is played. Both cooperation and rivalry are fundamental aspects of international economic affairs, and the ultimate choice of playing or not playing is generally available as well. A special feature of international economic games is that they involve a large, diverse, and changing group of players over an indefinite time period; hence, there are many possibilities for forming new coalitions and for shifting the balances among long- and short-term benefits and costs.

Every game is governed by a set of rules, which specify the acceptable range of strategic and tactical moves and countermoves, and their consequences. Such rules may arise from various origins, but in most games (and certainly in international economic games) they evolve over time in response to changing circumstances, which may well include changes in the objectives of the players themselves. During the late nineteenth and early twentieth centuries, two very different international economic games were played. One, which had very ancient origins, was the game of *colonialism*, in which more advanced nations gained control of less advanced peoples and territories, exploiting them primarily for home-country advantage. Enterprises and governments from an advanced country usually joined together as "partners" in this game, and they often developed secondary "partners" in the colonies as well. The other game, *free trade*, a nineteenth-century innovation, was based upon unrestricted market contact and competition among enterprises, regardless of national jurisdiction, with government involvement limited to the maintenance of law and order and a suitable framework of monetary exchange. The colonialism game was primarily governed by a *rule of capture* (although if third parties objected to any particular "capture," an "imperialist war" might ensue). The free trade game was governed by the *rule of competition*, meaning that low-price sellers and high-price buyers would complete transactions and other parties would be left out of the market.

Over the decades since World War II, new and different kinds of international economic games have emerged. For the most part, these new games are based on economic and political alliances involving both governments and businesses. They involve foreign investment, rather than colonialism, and trade that is to some extent "managed" rather than entirely "free." The rules of these games are typically established and altered by negotiations and agreements among the participating parties and are often quite complex (cf. Sauvant and Aranda, 1994).

Economic, political, technological, and sociocultural developments are all involved in the emergence of these new games and the evolution of their corresponding rules. Conventional firms and governments, more numerous and diverse than ever before, continue to be major players. In addition, new dimensions are introduced by the presence of giant multinational enterprises (MNEs), many of which operate at least partially beyond the control of individual national governments and which are, in addition, increasingly linked with each other through ownership and contractual agreements.

A major question about this new environment is the extent to which it has altered fundamental power relations among states at different levels of development and between states and enterprises, particularly the large multinationals. Initial postwar concern with the power of multinational enterprises vis-à-vis nation states was dramatized in Vernon's widely cited title, *Sovereignty at Bay* (1971), and reflected in proposals for a United Nations (UN) Code of Conduct on Transnational Corporations. In response to these concerns, the most actively developing host countries found ways to shape the activities of "guest" corporations to serve their own national purposes. (Safarian, 1993, provides an exhaustive review of these arrangements; see also Hillman and Keim, 1995; Lenway and Murtha, 1994.) Stopford and Strange point out that the *"positive* power" of states to influence business activity that is related to *world* markets, on either the supply or demand side, is seriously constrained; "they cannot direct; they can only bargain." On the other hand, as these authors note, national states "retain considerable *negative* power" to disrupt and distort efficient patterns of economic activity (1991, p. 14).

One way in which states can convert their negative power into positive power is by collaborating to create international regimes, *rules of the game*, that establish mutual understandings and norms of behavior among relevant players. Firms and industries also have strong interests in such arrangements because they tend to harmonize national government-business relationships and reduce uncertainty. Ostry emphasizes that international business involves not only "competition among firms" but also, increasingly, "competition among systems," and "[A] globalizing world has a low tolerance for system divergence" (1992, p. 13). Hence, the new structural environment gives rise to "demand" for new "rules of the game," i.e., new understandings among businesses and governments about the way in which global economic activity is to be conducted.

This study intends to make a strong statement about the nature and importance of the "rules" of the international economic game as they are evolving during the closing years of the twentieth century. In brief, we believe that the increasing scale and complexity of the global economy necessarily lead to the development of rules, norms, understandings, and procedures that facilitate, guide, and govern the activities of its major participants—in short, to the evolution of new and stronger international policy regimes.

The Brookings authors anticipate the development of "a world of clubs" in which international integration and national decentralization are combined in various ways to achieve specific objectives (Lawrence, Bressand, and Ito, 1996, p. 64 and passim). They share the view of Dunning (1995) and many other authorities, as well as ourselves, that such "clubs" or "regimes" are particularly important in the current international environment, where "hard law" is weak or absent and where dynamic changes frequently occur outside the bounds of preexisting formal organizational and decision-making structures. We believe that specific regime features may have distinct effects on international business relationships and activities and that a broader understanding of regimes (their sources, characteristics, and effects) can make a positive contribution to the management of international business enterprises and to the process of worldwide economic development.

1.2 LINKAGES AND INTERDEPENDENCE

The new global business environment is knit together by three principal types of transnational linkages, which are themselves strongly inter-related (figure 1-1). The basic elements, underlying all the others, are *trade and investment flows*, which, as we show in chapter 3, have grown more rapidly than world gross national product (GNP) since the end of World War II. The growth of worldwide foreign investment is of particular importance, since investment leads to ownership links that persist over time and generate additional interactions, both economic and political. A second type of linkage arises from the existence of *multinational enterprises* (MNEs), the managerial units created by foreign investment. The activities of these firms in multiple national jurisdictions give rise to economic and policy impacts that are beyond the purview of any individual government and hence are subject to control, or even to scrutiny, only through international means. These two major types of linkages give rise to a third, the *international policy regimes* that are the focus of this study. These regimes arise to facilitate and regulate the flows of trade and investment and the activities of enterprises, whether multinational or domestic, participating in or impacted by the growth of the global economy. It is particularly important to emphasize, along with Dunning (1995) and the Brookings authors (Lawrence, Bressand, and Ito, 1996, and other contributors to that series), that international policy regimes not only bring the *international* activities of various states, industries, and enterprises within a common framework but also penetrate *domestic* economies and policy structures as well. (The importance of political behavior, largely domestic, in international business strategy is stressed by Boddewyn and Brewer, 1994.)

Figure 1-1. Complex Linkages in the Global Economy

These three strong forms of international economic and policy linkage rest, of course, on underlying foundations of history, language, and culture, geographic proximity, economic complementarity, and so forth. In addition, these functional links are supported by a continuously expanding global web of communication and information that is itself a major source of increased international interdependence.[1]

All discussions of the evolution of the global economy refer to "increasing interdependence," but the specific meaning of this term is rarely specified. In fact, two distinct aspects of international interaction are involved. One has to do with the *magnitude* of crossborder contact, the *number* of linkages and interactions, and the *volume* of merchandise, funds, or whatever is moving among the various participants in the global economy. The other aspect of interdependence is the mutual *sensitivity* of the participants, "the extent to which consumption patterns, production structures, money and capital markets [in any one country] are influenced significantly by policies and developments outside its borders" (Panic, 1988, p. 5; see also Cooper, 1985, chapter 1).

Both types of interdependence have increased in recent decades. The functional links among nations, industries, and enterprises are now more numerous, more diverse, and more complex than ever before; and the volumes of goods, services, financing, and communications flowing through these links are also larger than ever, even relative to the overall growth of the world economy. The speed with which knowledge of events spreads throughout the world is unprecedented. The result is that price changes, interest rate movements, stock market developments, and government policy actions taking place anywhere in the global economy reverberate almost instantaneously throughout the entire system and produce simultaneous effects in widely separated locations.

Policy-makers and executives in both governments and enterprises have responded to these developments by creating new institutional arrangements and understandings that attempt to preserve and enlarge the benefits arising from these new global economic interconnections while reducing the associated costs and risks. As a result, structures and agreements facilitating and governing international business operations have become increasingly numerous and important. These policy systems are necessarily multinational. They thus involve common understandings and mutually consistent behaviors among actors representing and operating within numerous and diverse political jurisdictions and reflecting varied interests. Although some international business activities are still regulated bilaterally, activities of substantial size or continuity inevitably lead to consequences that require support, acceptance, or at least toleration by third parties or even the worldwide business and economic community. Moreover, in the contemporary era, no single hegemonic power or small group of like-minded actors can establish and enforce international economic arrangements inimical to the interests of other significant groups of participants. On the contrary, worldwide economic activity is increasingly governed by norms and behaviors established by the mutual consent of multiple and diverse entities (governments, enterprises, and other organizations) and therefore reflecting their different and changing interests and objectives.

The regulation of international business activity emerged as "a major new international economic problem" in the 1970s (Waldmann, 1980, p. 1). Toward the end of the 1980s, Bryant and Hodgkinson observed that "interdependence has become more intense and the need to cooperate more urgent. ... There has been an increase in both the number and the significance of the problems that can be solved only through international agreement" (in Cooper et al., 1989, p. 1). In the "world of clubs" envisioned by the Brookings authors, national and international interests will be balanced in "a world community of nations marked by openness, diversity and cohesion" (Lawrence, Bressand, and Ito, 1996, p. 105). Even analysts critical of some regime developments and proposals acknowledge their value in many areas: "Certainly not all international regulation is inimical to international business interests. ... The US government and American industry continue to support and contribute to the beneficial international regulatory regimes [in a variety of areas]" (Adelman, 1988, p. xvi).

Panic's penetrating analysis of increasing international economic interdependence summarizes the forces leading to the growth and strengthening of international regimes as follows:

> The only way to achieve a stable system of international relationships under these conditions [i.e., interdependence] is for individual countries ... either to agree formally on a mutually satisfactory code of behavior or to accept one tacitly. In other words, stability of the international economic system depends now critically on the ability and willingness of individual countries to pursue policies which are compatible with their national economic objectives *and* with the objectives and policies of other countries. ... This involves the acceptance of certain obligations and rules of behavior (Panic, 1988, p. 283).

1.3 ACTIVE ROLE OF GOVERNMENTS

The notion that governments and industries from different countries might collaborate to work out mutually satisfactory operating arrangements necessarily implies an active role for political institutions in international economic affairs. Economically active governments can, however, also play roles that work against the harmonization of international interests. In both advanced and developing countries, governments adopt broad development strategies and industrial policies that lead them to take on important partnership roles with private enterprises and even to assume primary initiative and operating responsibility in key industries. In spite of the recent and well-documented global wave of privatization, significant segments of many national economies (and not only postcommunist ones) remain state owned. Moreover, even in the absence of state ownership, national governments attempt to exercise broad policy guidance over enterprises operating within their borders. As Stopford and Strange emphasize, "states are now competing more for the means to create wealth within their territory than for power over more territory" (1991, p. 1).

We have noted above that the growth of international policy regimes inevitably creates linkages among domestic systems that are fundamentally different from each other in character. Firms operating within competitive domestic environments become linked with national monopolies in other countries; privately-owned enterprises from one jurisdiction engage in joint ventures with state-owned enterprises (SOEs) from another; market-based arrangements and administrative allocation mechanisms become subject to the same international policies and competitive pressures.

Although any classification of national policy regimes is likely to be simplistic, and changes in particular countries are always in progress, we believe that it is helpful to recognize a spectrum of domestic policy systems ranging from "free market" regimes at one extreme, through various degrees and forms of governmental direction, to extensive state control and planning. The principal elements of such a spectrum, with national examples as they appeared in the mid 1980s, are shown in figure 1-2. Within the broad category of market-oriented systems, we note two types of distinctions:

    1. The distinction among systems that are fundamentally "free" (e.g., Switzerland, Hong Kong) and those that are more heavily government influenced, either for regulatory control or developmental purposes;
    2. The distinction between systems where government ownership of enterprises is scattered and unsystematic (e.g., the US) and those in which a deliberate pattern of state ownership in basic industries and infrastructure (e.g., socialist Britain) could once be discerned. (The extreme of nearly universal state ownership is, of course, found in the nonmarket systems governed by formal state planning.)

Both socialist infrastructure and central planning regimes declined in importance during the 1990s because of worldwide movements toward privatization and marketization. China (PRC) is the chief remaining example of a central planning regime, and even there use of the market mechanism is increasing. Vestiges of planning regimes remain in many postcommunist and less developed countries (LDCs), and their retention or expansion appears on the agendas of some political groups.

Even within the most market-oriented economies, there is a powerful, and largely inevitable, policy debate underway between the advocates of "managed trade," a form of neomercantilism, and supporters of a liberal "free trade" regime based on neoclassical economic principles. Neomercantilists favor export promotion and domestic protection in various degrees and types. Neoclassical analysts predict and favor the evolution of an integrated world economy in which competitive advantage and innovation will produce benefits for all (Wolf, 1996a&b). There are many features of the international economic system that are not taken into account in neoclassical analysis. The question is whether the impact of these anomalies creates a compelling case for additional governmental intervention and what such intervention would actually achieve (Root, 1993).

	Market-Oriented Systems		Planning-Oriented Systems	
	"Free Market" Regimes	*Government Influence Regimes*	*Development Regimes*	*Central Planning Regimes*
Haphazard State Ownership				
Advanced Countries	Switzerland United States	Japan Germany		
Newly Industrialized Countries	Chile Hong Kong	Singapore		
Developing Countries	Kenya		Nigeria	
State Domination of Basic Industries and Infrastructure				
Advanced Countries	Canada Britain	France Austria		
Newly Industrialized Countries			India Mexico	
Developing Countries			Egypt	
Predominantly State Ownership				
Advanced Countries				
Newly Industrialized Countries				China
Developing Countries			Iraq	Cuba Mongolia

Figure 1-2. National Regimes Spectrum.

1.4 CONCLUSION

The overall growth of the world economy, the increasing number and variety of active participants (both nations and firms), and the widening scale and scope of the MNEs have greatly increased the extent and importance of global economic interdependence. The result is increased worldwide recognition of common concerns and interests, among both countries and enterprises, and hence an increasing effort to respond to these pressures and opportunities. These developments set the stage for worldwide multilateral policy discussions and the creation of formal and informal international mechanisms. In fact, a considerable network of international policy regimes is already in place, as the case studies in this volume clearly illustrate. By analyzing the sources and processes leading to the creation of these regimes and their effects on international business activity, we hope to illuminate the problems and potentials of their future evolution.

Notes

1. Our analysis does not include the much discussed topic of multilateral macroeconomic policy coordination, except insofar as it involves the international monetary system. For comprehensive overviews of this issue, see Cooper et al., 1989; McKibbin and Sachs, 1991; Bryant, 1995.

References

Adelman, Carol C., ed. 1988. *International Regulation: New Rules in a Changing World Order*. San Francisco, CA: Institute for Contemporary Studies.

Boddewyn, Jean J., and Thomas L. Brewer. 1994. "International-Business Political Behavior: New Theoretical Directions," *Academy of Management Review*, vol. 19, no. 1 (January), pp. 119–143.

Bryant, Ralph C. 1995. *International Coordination of National Stabilization Policies*. Washington, DC: Brookings Institution.

Bryant, Ralph C., and Edith Hodgkinson. 1989. "Problems of International Cooperation," in Cooper et al., eds., *Can Nations Agree? Issues in International Economic Cooperation*. Washington, DC: Brookings Institution, pp. 1–11.

Cooper, Richard N. 1985. *Economic Policy in an Interdependent World*. Cambridge, MA: MIT Press.

Cooper, Richard N., Barry Eichengreen, Gerard Holtham, Robert D. Putnam, and C. Randall Henning, eds. 1989. *Can Nations Agree? Issues in International Economic Cooperation*. Washington, DC: Brookings Institution.

Dunning, John H. 1995. "The Global Economy and Regimes of National and Supranational Governance," *Business and the Contemporary World*, vol. 7, no. 1, pp. 124–136.

Hillman, Amy, and Gerald Keim. 1995. "International Variation in the Business-Government Interface: Institutional and Organizational Considerations," *Academy of Management Review*, vol. 20, no. 1 (January), pp. 193–214.

Lawrence, Robert Z., Albert Bressand, and Takatoshi Ito. 1996. *A Vision for the World Economy: Openness, Diversity, and Cohesion*. Washington, DC: Brookings Institution.

Lenway, Stefanie A., and Thomas P. Murtha. 1994. "The State as Strategist in International Business Research," *Journal of International Business Studies*, vol. 25, no. 3 (September), pp. 513–535.

McKibbin, Warwick J., and Jeffrey D. Sachs. 1991. *Global Linkages: Macroeconomic Interdependence and Cooperation in the World Economy*. Washington, DC: Brookings Institution.

Ostry, Sylvia. 1992. "The Domestic Domain: The New International Policy Arena," *Transnational Corporations*, vol. 1, no. 1 (February), pp. 7–26.

Panic, M. 1988. *National Management of the International Economy*. New York: St. Martin's Press.

Root, Franklin. 1993. Review of David B. Yoffie, *Beyond Free Trade, Firms, Governments, and Global Competition*, Boston: Harvard Business School Press, 1993, in *Transnational Corporations*, vol. 2, no. 3 (December), pp. 171–174.

Safarian, A. E. 1993. *Multinational Enterprise and Public Policy: A Study of the Industrial Countries*. Brookfield, VT: Edward Elgar.

Sauvant, K.P., and V. Aranda. 1994. "The International Legal Framework for Transnational Corporations," *Transnational Corporations: The International Legal Framework*, vol. 20, pp. 83–115.

Stopford, John M., and Susan Strange. 1991. *Rival States, Rival Firms: Competition for World Market Shares*. Cambridge, England: Cambridge University Press.

Vernon, Raymond. 1971. *Sovereignty at Bay: The Multinational Spread of U.S. Enterprises*. New York: Basic Books.

Waldmann, Raymond J. 1980. *Regulating International Business through Codes of Conduct*. Washington, DC: American Enterprise Institute for Public Policy Research.

Wolf, Charles. 1996a. "The Coming of the Neo-Classical World," *Wall Street Journal*, February 23.

Wolf, Charles. 1996b. "Taking On the Global Gurus," *Wall Street Journal*, May 1.

Young, Oran R. 1994. *International Governance: Protecting the Environment in a Stateless Society*. Ithaca, NY: Cornell University Press.

2

THE NATURE OF
INTERNATIONAL POLICY REGIMES

The concept of international policy regimes has come into widespread use over the last couple of decades, but this usage has also involved significant controversy. Some analysts have challenged the validity of the regimes concept itself. Others have debated the origins of regimes and their connections with underlying forces such as economic and military power, national or group interests, and social values. And others have questioned the importance of regimes, raising the ultimate analytical question: Do regimes matter? In this chapter we review some of the issues raised in this literature, offer our own responses to them, and explain our intended (and we believe appropriate) use of the regimes concept to analyze major policy developments and institutions relevant to the conduct of international business.

2.1 DEFINITIONS AND CONTROVERSIES

The *international policy regimes* with which we are concerned in this study are arrangements and understandings among numerous and diverse actors involved in facilitating or influencing the conduct of international economic affairs and business activity. The international relations literature is filled with definitions, explications, and critiques of the "regime" concept, but the formal definition of such regimes developed by Krasner is generally accepted by leading international relations scholars:

A regime is composed of sets of explicit or implicit principles, norms, rules and decision-making procedures around which actor expectations converge in a given area of international relations (Krasner, ed., 1983, p. 2, emphasis added).

A critical feature of this definition, and of related formulations offered by others, is that "regimes" include not only 1) the formal *institutional arrangements* that embody and implement international agreements and understandings but also 2) the *principles* (such as dominance, sovereignty, fairness, cooperation or consistency of behavior) underlying and legitimizing such institutions and 3) the expected *behavior patterns* associated with them. Cooper notes, with particular reference to monetary and financial arrangements, that the term *regime* "seems preferable to system or order ... since it encompasses arrangements that are neither orderly nor systematic ... [and includes] internal consistency and technical proficiency" (Cooper, 1987, p. 2).

The term "regime" is sometimes used as a synonym for "government," but that meaning is not intended here. We view regimes as sets of functional relationships and behaviors among diverse entities, particularly among enterprises and other economic interests and the various governments and international organizations with which they come in contact. National policy regimes are those prevailing within individual countries; for example, there is a national regime for commercial banking within the US, with responsibilities and roles distributed among federal and state authorities, the Federal Reserve Board, and the banks themselves. International regimes, the subjects of this study, involve relationships among actors and interests operating within, and sometimes on behalf of, diverse national jurisdictions.

It is important to emphasize that a *regime* consists primarily of functional and behavioral relationships and that formal organizations and agreements are subsidiary or, occasionally, entirely absent. The international gold standard was a well-recognized and powerful regime that lacked any formal organizational base. (For an analysis of the gold standard as an international regime, see chapter 6.) Nor are all important international organizations key elements of significant regimes. The International Labour Organization (ILO) is a well-established agency, but there is no corresponding "regime" for international labor relations. The Organization for Economic Cooperation and Development (OECD) is an important forum for consultation and the exchange of information, but its influence on actual economic and business activity is at best indirect. Young emphasizes that, in analyzing regimes, "it is important not to conflate institutions and functions"; although the former may be essential, it is the functions themselves (or, more specifically, the "practices" and "behaviors" involved in accomplishing them) that constitute the regime (Young, 1989, chapter 1). He stresses the importance of differentiating between "effective institutions likely to generate predictable consequences ... and arrangements that are institutions in name only" (Young, 1994, p. 2). Soroos observes: "Regimes are identified in terms of 'problem areas'; one or more international organizations are integral parts of most regimes, and many international organizations are involved in more than one regime" (Soroos, 1987, pp. 17–18). Cooper stresses that "the role of international organizations [is] derivative from the task to be performed. ... The presence and the appropriate form of international organization depends on the regime actually selected" (Cooper, 1987, p. 33).

Kratochwil bases his analysis of regimes on "norms," which may be either explicit (i.e., embodied in formal rules), or implicit (i.e., evidenced only in behavior) (Kratochwil, 1989, p. 12). He views international regimes, which he terms "soft law," as a supplement to the conventional dichotomy between domestic "order" based on formal government power and the interjurisdictional "anarchy" that might be expected to prevail because of the absence of a formal international governmental system. He notes that international economic relations are not, in the main, anarchical, and observes: "Markets are probably *the* social institution most dependent on normative underpinnings" (1989, p. 47). Kratochwil's treatise probes the philosophical and legal bases for the regimes concept, which he considers poorly developed in the mainstream literature. In their 1989 volume *Rediscovering Institutions*, March and Olsen essentially equate "institution" and "regime," both terms referring to well-established and continuing social relationships involving "roles, procedures and arrangements" within society. Young takes a similar position, referring to "sets of rules of the game ... that serve to define social practices, assign roles to the participants in these practices, and guide the interactions among occupants of these roles" (Young, 1994, p. 3).

In any event, it is generally agreed that international policy regimes embody the normative as well as the institutional underpinnings for the conduct of economic and business activity among both governments and enterprises in an international setting. The central idea is that participants in regimes behave in accordance with a "rule of anticipated reactions" by others (Friedrich, 1963, chapter 11); so long as most participants behave in mutually anticipated ways (including ways for resolving disputes and modifying the regime itself), the regime continues in force. Contemporary international economic regimes rarely possess, or are willing to exercise, the power to compel appropriate behavior from their participants. Compliance with regime norms is obtained more on the basis of benefits received, in relation to costs, than on the threat of sanctions.

The strongest attack on the validity and usefulness of the regimes concept has come from Susan Strange. In an exchange in 1983 with Krasner, she criticizes the concept as faddish, imprecise, value biased, static, and overly state-centered (Strange, pp. 337–354, and response by Krasner, pp. 355–368, in Krasner, ed., 1983). In her own comprehensive 1988 study, she identifies a set of basic "structures of power" (national security, production, finance, and "knowledge") and shows how these basic structures lead to the development of "secondary structures" governing international transport, trade, energy, and "welfare" (e.g., foreign aid). Her discussion of "structures" tends to conflate underlying conditions, such as historical developments and resource endowments, with arrangements deliberately established in response to these conditions. However, she is right to stress the roles of nongovernmental actors, too frequently neglected in the mainstream regimes literature, which has primarily emphasized the roles of states and international organizations. In more recent work, Strange stresses that international competition now involves both states and industries and that to operate in this environment states must negotiate not merely among themselves but also with multinational firms, which have themselves become "more statesmanlike as they seek ... to enhance their combined capacities to compete with others for world market shares." These developments "have multiplied the number of possible policy options for governments and for firms, and thus have greatly complicated the problems for both of managing multiple agendas" (Stopford and Strange, 1991, p. 2). In both individual and collaborative work, Strange presents a rich analysis of the origins and impacts of contemporary regimes, in spite of her resistance to the use of the term itself.

Our own view is that some concept very similar to the generally accepted meaning of "international regimes" is useful, and probably unavoidable, for analyzing the contemporary policy environment of international business and economic affairs. The various major types of international economic contact (trade, investment, services, communications, etc.) are carried out according to "rules of the game" that arise from and operate through mutually reinforcing expectations and behaviors among the participants involved. Such "rules," some of which are quite elaborate, are often embodied in organizations or institutions, which then become additional and somewhat independent "actors" in the international business environment. It is, in fact, difficult even to talk about the kind of continuous coordination and harmonization that goes on in the international economy without reference, either explicit or implicit, to something like the "regimes" concept.

2.2 CONTEMPORARY INTERNATIONAL REGIMES AND ORGANIZATIONS

A preliminary list of the major international regimes and related organizations affecting international business is shown in figure 2-1. We include here a few organizations that lack regime status (e.g., OECD, APEC), and we note that some important regime elements (such as the global foreign-exchange markets) operate without any formal organizational structure. We refer to these regimes and organizations in various combinations and at various levels of detail in the course of our analysis. We acknowledge at the outset that any such list, or any selection of regimes for special study, is subject to critique; our selections and classifications are intended to be illustrative, not exhaustive. We believe, however, that the threefold classification of regimes shown here and reflected in our case studies is of particular significance:

Global and Comprehensive Regimes — Institutional and behavioral arrangements that are, at least in principle, unrestricted in both their geographic and functional scope. A genuine "world government" would, of course, constitute such a regime. The collection of regimes, both actual and proposed, evolving within the UN framework illustrates some features and problems of such a set of arrangements.

Regional or Associative Regimes — Arrangements involving groups of national states drawn together by location or other common characteristics and interests. These arrangements might take the form of economic union, common market, free trade area, or other specific multinational agreement of more limited scope.

Functional Regimes — Regimes limited in their coverage to specific industries, activities, or problems; within this category, we further distinguish "economic" and "environmental" regimes because of their substantial differences in structure and character.

2.3 REGIME ORIGINS AND IMPACTS

The two major substantive controversies about the regimes concept in the international relations literature involve 1) the *origins* of regimes, and 2) the *impacts* of regimes on actual processes and outcomes in international affairs.

International relations scholars have attempted to explain the origins, stability, growth, and decline of regimes in both structural and functional terms. The structural or "realist" thesis holds that regimes reflect the underlying power and interests of international actors, chiefly national states. Its strongest contention is that regimes are established by (and hence reflect the goals of) dominant hegemonic states or state coalitions; from this perspective, regimes are extensions of state-based power and

Global and Comprehensive Regimes and Organizations
United Nations regime system, including:
    World Court
    Convention on International Sale of Goods
    Restrictive Business Practices Code
    Codex Alimentarius (WHO and FAO)
    Technology Transfer Code (UNCTAD)
    Code of Conduct on Transnational Corporations (UNCTC—in preparation)
    UN-based Consumer Protection Codes (e.g., Infant Formula)
    UN-based Environmental Regimes (e.g., Moon Treaty)

Regional and Associative Regimes and Organizations
European Union (EU), including:
    European Economic Community (EEC)
    European Atomic Energy Agency (Euratom)
    European Coal and Steel Community (ECSC)
    European Monetary System (EMS)
North American Free Trade Agreement (NAFTA: US, Canada, Mexico)
Mercosur (Argentina, Brazil, Paraguay, Uruguay)
Organization for Economic Cooperation and Development (OECD)
Asia Pacific Economic Cooperation (APEC)

Functional Regimes: Economic
Air Transport
    International Air Transport Association (IATA)
    International Civil Aviation Organization (ICAO)
Ocean Shipping
    UNCTAD Liner Conference Code
    International Maritime Organization (IMO)
Telecommunications
    International Telecommunications Union (ITU)
    INTELSAT
Trade
    World Trade Organization (WTO), successor to General Agreement on
        Tariffs and Trade (GATT)
    Product and commodity agreements, WTO/GATT–related and other
Money, Exchange, and Payments
    International Monetary Fund (IMF)
Investment
    World Bank (IRBD)
    International Finance Corporation (IFC)
    Multilateral Investment Guarantee Agency (MIGA)
    Bilateral Tax Treaties

Functional Regimes: Environmental
Air Pollution Agreements: transboundary air pollution, sulfur, nitrogen
    oxides, chlorofluorocarbons (Vienna/Montreal Protocol), ozone layer
Law of the Sea Treaty
Moon Treaty
Antarctic Treaty

Figure 2-1. Major Policy Regimes and Organizations Affecting International Business. Although this list contains primarily the names of *organizations*, it is the *regimes*, and not the institutional forms, that are of primary interest.

should be expected to decline when and if the underlying power base erodes. By contrast, functional analysts (sometimes referred to as "neoliberals") argue that regimes come into being in order to achieve the common objectives of member-participants; they place a strong emphasis on the importance of information sharing, reducing transactions costs, and the general benefits arising from cooperative behavior. Krasner (ed., 1983) is generally cited as the leading advocate of the structural or "realist" perspective and Keohane (1984) as a persuasive proponent of functional or "neoliberal" views.

Our own view is that both types of explanations of the origins and evolution of regimes have some validity. International economic relations involve both conflict and cooperation; mixed strategy games are usually being played. Structural effects may be more important where hegemonic power is strong; functional considerations are probably more important in multipolar situations, and therefore, in general, for the international business environment of the future. The current consensus seems to be "that hegemony is neither necessary nor sufficient for the creation or the persistence of strong international institutions" (Kahler, 1995, pp. 6–7), and the Brookings authors note that even private companies and industries seek the type of institutional development that promotes "deeper integration ... [with] comparable rules and credible governance" (Lawrence, Bressand, and Ito, 1996, p. 27). The force of private-sector demand for international policy harmonization is also stressed by Gray (1995).

Like many other contributors to this literature, we adopt the term "complex interdependence" to refer to the multiple forces and relation-ships that contribute to the creation and evolution of regimes (cf. Cooper, 1985). We believe that the provision of information, reduction of uncertainty, and reduction of transaction costs are critical features. We also believe that many different arrangements might contribute to these broad goals; hence (and this is a significant point) no single *optimal*, and thus no unambiguously *predictable*, regime can be specified in any particular industry or area of international business. Kahler emphasizes that the connections between international regimes and domestic politics provide additional explanations for the presence or absence of regimes in various situations and account for some of the differences among them (Kahler, 1995, pp. 6–11).

The second controversy, concerning the substantive impact of regimes, raises more difficult questions. How, if at all, are the relationships among states, enterprises, and other entities different from what they would be otherwise because a particular regime is in place? In short: *Do regimes matter?* A negative response to this question rests on the view that, although any substantial area of international economic activity requires some set of operating arrangements and understandings, the specific features of any particular regime are of little significance. (Analogously, some standardized system of automobile traffic control is essential for efficiency and safety, but whether driving is on the left or the right, parking is parallel or diagonal, etc., is of little significance; the main concern is that there be general adherence to a common practice.) The mainstream view, by contrast, is that regime characteristics and changes therein have significant impacts on both processes and outcomes in the global economy. As March and Olsen put it: "Institutions affect the flow of history. ... [They] not only respond to their environments but create those environments at the same time" (1989, pp. 159–162).

We believe that our analysis supports the conclusion of the mainstream international relations literature: *Regimes do matter*. The many original research studies that we have surveyed and synthesized in the course of this research analyze in detail the impact of specific regimes and regime changes on the content and processes of international economic affairs. We must, of course, avoid the assumption that some "regime" must be present in every international activity or that institutional arrangements, where present, inevitably have significant (either intended or unintended) effects. In particular, we must avoid the "value bias" for which some of the mainstream literature has been justly criticized. Young, among others, cautions against the belief that the development of regimes is inherently desirable or that their effects are uniformly benign. He notes that the mere existence of a regime may lend an element of "orderliness" to some area of international affairs, but "there is no reason to assume that institutional arrangements will guide human activities toward well-defined substantive goals" (1989, p. 14). In particular, there is no guarantee that operating procedures developed within any specific regime will be fair or open or that the results achieved will be equitable or efficient. The most that can be said, in general, is that explicit attention to the development and functioning of regimes may increase the likelihood that problems of mutual concern will be recognized and addressed. Criteria that might be used to determine the specific effects of particular regimes are further discussed below.

2.4 PRINCIPLES INFLUENCING REGIME DEVELOPMENT

The literature suggests that a number of different and potentially conflicting *fundamental principles*, such as power, efficiency, and equity, have influenced the establishment and evolution of various regimes at various times. Such principles may influence the *processes* through which regimes are established and operated as well as their ultimate *substance* and *impact*. Some of the most important principles involved in the creation and evolution of regimes are discussed in the following paragraphs.

1. *Power and interests*. Hegemonic power has unquestionably been a critical element in the establishment of many regimes. But power alone is insufficient. As Kindleberger notes, the momentum of regime development "tends to run down pretty quickly unless it is sustained by a powerful commitment. ... There needs to be positive leadership, backed by resources and a readiness to make some sacrifice in the international interest" (1988, p. 137). Power in various forms may also be used in attempts to *prevent* certain types of regime evolution, but these attempts need not be successful, as recent developments in international telecommunications illustrate.

2. *Efficiency*. The efficiency aspects of international regimes may be two different types: 1) *technical efficiency*, lowering operating and transaction costs, reducing risks, for regime participants; and 2) *allocative efficiency*, in the strict economic sense that the most valuable of all viable transactions are accomplished. Technical efficiency can be a very important factor in regime success, since it can provide direct benefits to participants (e.g., reducing risk, lowering costs). Allocative efficiency (channeling activities toward least-cost sources or most valuable uses) determines a regime's contribution to global economic welfare.

3. *Equity or fairness*. Some acknowledgment of a principle of equal treatment, or at least equal opportunity to participate in some sphere of economic activity, has been a major element of many contemporary regime debates. Specifics often involve equal access to information and to natural resources (particularly new and unexploited ones). The notion that equal *outcomes* (i.e., equal welfare benefits) should be obtained by all regime participants, however, is not widely accepted.

4. *Sovereignty*. National sovereignty is an essential element of all regimes that require any kind of endorsement or support by governments, yet most regimes involve some reduction in sovereign authority as a means of obtaining other desirable benefits. That is, each participating government has to accept some restriction on its own freedom of action in order to obtain agreement to corresponding restrictions by others. The choice between freedom of separate national action on one side, and the attainment of mutually beneficial results on the other, is an inherent aspect of regime evolution.

5. *Economic development/protection*. Many contemporary regimes have as an explicit purpose the economic modernization of less developed countries (LDCs) and/or some modification of processes of change that are already underway. Although some critics argue that the LDCs are occasionally willing to sacrifice economic gains for status and control, it is unquestionably true that the liberal trade regimes of the postwar period have contributed greatly to the development and growth of the poorer

regions of the world. (Krasner, 1985, presents a detailed discussion of the role of LDCs in major international regimes; this role is also a major focus of Stopford and Strange, 1991).

These and other fundamental principles may be operative, in various combinations and relative strengths, in any particular regime. They may also be sources of intraregime or interregime conflict and/or compatibility and reinforcement. The role of these principles in the evolution of specific regimes will become obvious in the case studies presented in part II of this volume.

2.5 REGIME CHARACTERISTICS AND RESEARCH ISSUES

To guide our research on the evolution and impact of specific regimes, we adapt an analytical framework originally proposed by Haggard and Simmons (1987), modifying and supplementing their analysis with other ideas from the literature and from our own research. The resulting generalized set of regime characteristics, summarized in figure 2-2, is used throughout this research and particularly in our case studies. (A similar framework, with "domestic political linkage" included as an additional feature for consideration, is presented by Kahler, 1995, pp. 2–4.) The elements of our framework are explained in the following paragraphs.

Scope — Sphere of international economic/business activity covered by the regime specific aspects involved (e.g., market participation; access to resources; price; output).

Purpose — Specific objectives to be achieved by the regime (e.g., harmonization, coordination, or competition; stabilization, redistribution, development, etc.).

Organizational Form — Institutional structure of the regime; base in government or private organizational structures and collaborative agreements; membership requirements and restrictions.

Decision and Allocation Modes — Role of voting; distribution of costs and benefits in equal or weighted proportions; relative scope of market and administrative processes.

Strength — Extent to which members conform to the norms and guidelines of the regime; forces making for change.

Figure 2-2. Basic Regime Characteristics. This exhibit establishes the format to be used for descriptive summary exhibits in each of the case studies in part II.

Scope defines the range of business and economic activity over which the regime is intended to have influence. The intended range may be, at least in principle, unlimited as to both industries/functions and geographic reach, as in the case of the UN, which we describe as the source of a "global and comprehensive" system of regimes. Most regimes are limited geographically, as in the case of the European Union (EU) and other regional systems, and/or according to specific industries and functions. The concept of *scope* also includes the particular features or activities of relevant actors that the regime intends to influence, such as market access, price, output, or technology.

Purpose identifies the objectives of the regime, within the given scope. Among the broad purposes to be accomplished by regimes, we distinguish at least three critical differences:

1. *Harmonization* — Participants intend to behave *alike*, often because of technical or economic considerations (e.g., international transport).
2. *Coordination* — Participants intend to make mutually acceptable moves, which may be quite different from each other depending upon the situation (e.g., monetary adjustments).
3. *Competition* — Participants agree to abide by the rules of a competitive market game (e.g., the General Agreement on Tariffs and Trade/World Trade Organization, or GATT/WTO.)

These broad procedural purposes may, of course, be used to accomplish many different specific goals: stabilization, redistribution, economic development, etc.

Organizational form is the most conspicuous aspect of most regimes and the most convenient means of quick reference to many of them, but it must be reemphasized that it is the functional activity, not the formal structure, that constitutes the regime. Many functionally focused regimes arise within the context of preexisting organizations, rather than the other way around, as some of the regime proposals generated within the UN system clearly illustrate. Both regimes and their associated organizations change over time in response to both internal and external developments. Most regimes involve both *substantive* and *procedural* elements, in various combinations (Kahler, 1995, p. 4). Their organizational structures (rules enforcement mechanism versus negotiating body) will reflect those differences. Within a given organizational form, regime membership or participation may be limited (i.e., named entities only, with specific admissions criteria) or open and may be based on commonalities among participants (e.g., the regional regimes) or diversity among them. Both the "closed" colonial regimes (mother country plus colonies) and the "open" UN regime system are structured in ways that emphasize diversity among participants, for very different purposes.

Decision and allocation modes include both the one participant/one vote option (where the participants may be either governments or enterprises) and arrangements in which decision-influencing power is related to size, resource endowments, volume of regime activity, etc. Benefits and costs may also be distributed equally and/or by weighted formula. Young notes that the "rules" of decision and allocation within regimes include: 1) procedural rules governing regime operations and the handling of disputes; 2) use rules, which often limit access to regime resources; and 3) liability rules, which deal with the "locus and extent of responsibility" in the event of injuries or violations among regime participants (Young, 1989, pp. 16–17).

Strength is the ability of the regime to influence the behavior of the participants (and perhaps of others as well). However, it is important that regime strength not be tested solely by evidence of choice of less preferred over more preferred alternatives. Many regimes facilitate, and reduce the cost and riskiness of, *preferred* behaviors. People drive on the right side of the road in the US and on the left side in the UK because they *prefer* to avoid the oncoming traffic. The traffic regime is only superficially restraining; it enables drivers to achieve their fundamental objective: completion of a safe trip. The analysis of strength involves identification and impact of forces making for change, since these forces provide empirical evidence of the regime's strength or weakness.

2.6 DO REGIMES MATTER?

Once the existence and operations of a particular regime have been examined within this framework, we come to the ultimate analytical issue: Do regimes matter? Again building upon the work of Haggard and Simmons, we pose two more specific questions:

1. Have regimes altered the situations within which relevant actors function, so that collaboration (conflict) among them is more (less) likely than it would be otherwise?
2. Have regimes altered the preferences and interests of relevant actors, so that new strategies and actions emerge, with results that would not otherwise occur?

These questions, in many different specific forms and contexts, are repeatedly addressed in the course of our analysis. At this point, we simply repeat our overall conclusion, noted above, that *regimes do matter*. Indeed, the entire history of international economic relations involves an evolution from anarchy, based on the primitive rule of capture, to a system of regimes that both facilitates and constrains international economic contact.

Young (1994, chapter 6) considers the impact or effectiveness of regimes as "a multidimensional variable," with the following possible aspects:

problem solving — dealing with the problems that led to their initial creation.

goal attainment — achieving specific objectives (e.g., allocating shares of resources, markets, etc., among participants).

behavioral effectiveness — changing the way participants carry out their activities.

process effectiveness — coordinating policies and practices of institutions in various jurisdictions (e.g., central banks).

constitutive effectiveness — creating an entity, such as a consultative mechanism, that then becomes a significant regime element in itself.

evaluative effectiveness — yielding different performance results (e.g., reducing costs).

Many of these dimensions or forms of regime impact necessarily involve an increased role for governments, both collectively and individually, within the international economic system. However, as Panic strongly emphasizes, the "spontaneous integration" of the world economy through enterprise-level decisions and actions has often *preceded* rather than *followed* "institutional integration" through intergovernmental policies (Panic, 1988, pp. 6–7). Moreover, an expanded role for government *policy*, through international agreements and understandings, need not involve an increase in government *economic activity* or in the use of political rather than economic allocation mechanisms within the international economy. A commitment to adhere to basic free trade principles, rather than ad hoc protectionism, constitutes explicit government *policy*; such a commitment enlarges rather than constricts the scope of *market forces* in international trade. Lenway (1985) argues that the US policy commitment to the General Agreement on Tariffs and Trade (GATT) has had precisely this effect in a number of specific industries. Similarly, Haas concludes that "the Mediterranean Action Plan (Med Plan), a regime for marine pollution control, ... played a key role in ... the development of convergent state policies" (1989, p. 377).

References

Cooper, Richard N. 1985. *Economic Policy in an Interdependent World*. Cambridge, MA: MIT Press.

Cooper, Richard N. 1987. *The International Monetary System: Essays in World Economics*. Cambridge, MA: MIT Press.

Friedrich, Carl J. 1963. "Influence and the Rule of Anticipated Reactions," in *Man and His Government: An Empirical Theory of Politics*. New York: McGraw-Hill, pp. 199–215.

Gray, H. Peter. 1995. "The Modern Structure of International Economic Policies," *Transnational Corporations*, vol. 4, no. 3 (December), pp. 49–66.

Haas, Peter M. 1989. "Do Regimes Matter? Epistemic Communities and Mediterranean Pollution Control," *International Organization*, vol. 43, no. 3 (Summer), pp. 377–403.

Haggard, Stephan, and Beth A. Simmons. 1987. "Theories of International Regimes," *International Organization*, vol. 41, no. 3 (Summer), pp. 491–517.

Kahler, Miles. 1995. *International Institutions and the Political Economy of Integration.* Washington, DC: Brookings Institution.

Keohane, Robert O. 1984. *After Hegemony: Cooperation and Discord in the World Political Economy.* Princeton, NJ: Princeton University Press.

Kindleberger, Charles P. 1988. *The International Economic Order.* Cambridge, MA: MIT Press.

Krasner, Stephen D., ed. 1983. *International Regimes.* Ithaca, NY: Cornell University Press.

Krasner, Stephen D. 1985. *Structural Conflict: The Third World Against Global Liberalism.* Berkeley and Los Angeles, CA: University of California Press.

Kratochwil, Friedrich V. 1989. *Rules, Norms and Decisions: On the Conditions of Practical and Legal Reasoning in International Relations and Domestic Affairs.* New York: Cambridge University Press.

Lawrence, Robert Z., Albert Bressand, and Takatoshi Ito. 1996. *A Vision for the World Economy.* Washington, DC: Brookings Institution.

Lenway, Stefanie A. 1985. *The Politics of U.S. International Trade: Protection, Expansion and Escape.* Boston, MA: Pitman.

March, James G., and Johan P. Olsen. 1989. *Rediscovering Institutions: The Organizational Basis of Politics.* New York: Free Press.

Panic, M. 1988. *National Management of the International Economy.* New York: St. Martin's Press.

Soroos, Marvin S. 1987. *Beyond Sovereignty: The Challenge of Global Policy.* Columbia, SC: University of South Carolina Press.

Stopford, John M., and Susan Strange. 1991. *Rival States, Rival Firms: Competition for World Market Shares.* Cambridge, England: Cambridge University Press.

Strange, Susan. 1983. *"Cave! Hic Dragones*: A Critique of Regime Analysis," in Krasner, ed., *International Regimes.* Ithaca, NY: Cornell University Press, pp. 337–354.

Strange, Susan.. 1988. *States and Markets.* New York: Basil Blackwell.

Young, Oran R. 1989. *International Cooperation.* Ithaca, NY: Cornell University Press.

Young, Oran R. 1994. *International Governance: Protecting the Environment in a Stateless Society.* Ithaca, NY: Cornell University Press.

3

TRADE, INVESTMENT, AND
ENTERPRISE LINKAGES

This chapter examines the ways in which economic, financial, and enterprise linkages arising from conventional trade and investment activities are contributing to the creation of a truly global economy. The chapter is divided into four sections. The first briefly describes the basic structure of the global economy from contemporary data. The second section deals with *trade* linkages, the flows of exports and imports among countries. The third section deals with *investment* linkages, both in terms of annual flows (i.e., net *new* investment per time period) and the patterns of international ownership (i.e., aggregate investment *stocks*) that result from them. The *multinational enterprises* (MNEs) that account for a substantial portion of these international investment flows and stocks are analyzed briefly in the fourth section.

3.1 THE GLOBAL ECONOMY

During the half century since World War II, economic activity has increased tremendously in almost every part of the world, and international economic activity (trade, investment, and foreign ownership) has expanded in both volume and importance. These worldwide trends, expressed in current dollar values, are summarized in table 3-1. Part of the increase in all of these series over the period is, of course, due to worldwide inflation (estimated at 7.6% annually, using a gross national

Table 3-1. Growth in World Economic Activity, 1970-1994 (current US$)

Year	Gross Domestic Product (GDP)	Exports by Origin	Foreign Direct Investment (FDI Outflows) by Origin
	$ Billions	$ Billions	$ Billions
1970	3032.4	314.6	12.956
1975	5934.4	882.4	27.846
1980	11,790.2	2022.4	57.143
1985	13,640.3	1958.7	53.298
1990	22,339.7	3483.4	226.358
1994	25,677.0	4300.3	222.254
% increase 1970-1994	746.8%	1266.9%	1615.5%
Compound annual growth rate	16.48%	20.54%	22.51%

Sources: GDP taken from UN Conference on Trade and Development (UNCTAD), *Handbook of International Trade and Development Statistics* or *Supplement* (New York: UN), various years; 1994 from World Bank, *Global Economic Prospects and the Developing Countries* (New York: 1996).

Exports "free on board" (f.o.b.) taken from UNCTAD, *Handbook of International Trade and Development Statistics, 1994* (New York: UN, 1995); 1994 from International Monetary Fund (IMF), *International Financial Statistics* (Washington, DC: 1995). IMF export series differs only slightly from UNCTAD estimates.

FDI taken from IMF outflows data series (dated January 10, 1991) supplied by UN Centre for Transnational Corporations (UNCTC); 1994 from UNCTAD, Division on Transnational Corporations and Investment, *World Investment Report, 1995* (New York: UN, 1995), p. 397.

Notes: Source excluded Eastern Europe and USSR from GDP in 1985. The region's GDP was valued at $429.3 billion in 1970 (14.2% of world total), $719.6 billion in 1975 (12.1%), and $1698.7 billion in 1980 (14.4%). 1985 GDP has not been adjusted here.

product, GNP, deflator measure, for 1974–1990, according to the World Bank, 1996, p. 78). However, even in real terms, all of these series show remarkable growth, and the growth of investment and trade relative to gross domestic product (GDP) is particularly dramatic. The orders of magnitude involved in these important global economic flows are, of course, very different. The value of worldwide foreign direct investment (FDI) amounts to only about 5% of the value of total exports, which in turn is equal to about one sixth of global GDP.

Within this broad pattern of evolutionary growth, four major types of developments stand out:

- The trend toward increasing *interlinkage* among economically active nations and regions, both through trade and investment and through the operation of multinational enterprises.

- The continuous appearance of *new economic actors* (nations, regions, industries, and enterprises) in the international arena.

- Both of these developments contribute to a third, the growth of *global industries* that operate within and among many different countries, creating new networks of international supplier-customer relationships and giving rise to new kinds of collaborative-competitive interactions.

- The persistence, and even increase, of *inequality* and *stress* between ad-vanced and less developed countries and regions.

Although, as figure 3-1 shows, the greatest volume of international trade is still intraregional (that is, among the European countries, or within the Asia/Pacific region or the Western Hemisphere), extensive trade links also exist within the so-called "Triad," the advanced industrial countries (AICs) of North America (Canada and the US), the European Union (EU) and European Free Trade Area (EFTA) countries, and Japan, Australia, and New Zealand in the Pacific Rim (Ohmae, 1985). The Triad countries correspond closely to the membership of the Organization for Economic Cooperation and Development (OECD). The complex linkages among these economies have created the "borderless world" described by Ohmae (1990) and clearly evidenced by the almost instantaneous reverberation of major stock market movements, oil price changes, currency revaluations, etc., among these economies (cf. Panic, 1988, chapter 2).

Expanding linkages between the Triad and other countries illustrate the second trend: increases in the number of significant actors and forces involved in the global economy. The members of the Organization of Petroleum Exporting Countries (OPEC) took on new importance during the 1970s. In the 1980s, Japan (already an important participant in the global economy) became a major world economic power; at the same time, a number of newly industrialized countries (NICs), particularly the four "Asian Tigers" of the Pacific Rim (Hong Kong, Singapore, South Korea, and Taiwan), greatly increased their roles in the world economy. The most recent development is the opening up of Eastern Europe and the former Soviet Union to worldwide economic contact.

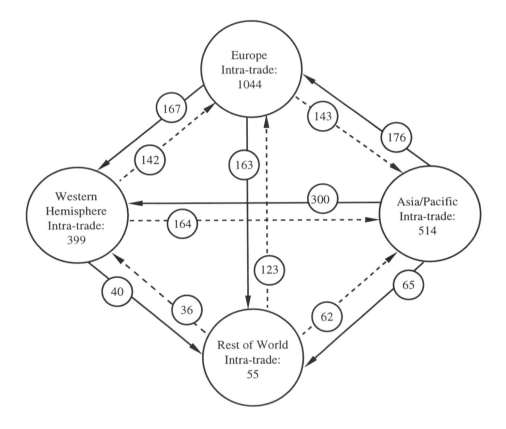

Figure 3-1. World Trade Flows, 1993 (current US$ in billions)

Source: Computed from UN Conference on Trade and Development (UNCTAD), *Handbook of International Trade and Development Statistics, 1994* (New York: UN, 1995), table A.1. Data rounded here.

Notes: Total trade of $3593 billion does not sum to UNCTAD world total of $3708 billion reported in source table. Exact trade balances cannot be computed from these approximate figures. "Europe" includes EU and EFTA. "Asia/Pacific" includes Japan, Australia, New Zealand, Oceania, and Developing East, Southeast, and South Asia. "Western Hemisphere" includes US, Canada, and Developing America. "Rest of World" includes Africa, West Asia (and thus the Arab members of OPEC), and Eastern Europe, including the former USSR.

Both AIC and NIC economies are involved, and increasingly integrated with each other, in the growth of global industries: automobiles, chemicals, electronics, pharmaceuticals, and petroleum and petrochemicals (Porter, ed., 1986). These developments lead to the growth of intra-industry trade, in which products within the same broad industrial class flow in both directions between two countries or regions and also intra-company trade among the operating units of the same multinational enterprise.

Finally, all three of these developments contribute to the fourth trend: the widening and increasingly conspicuous gap between incomes and living standards in the economies participating in these developments and the conditions that prevail in societies that remain, for whatever reasons, outside the scope of the worldwide economic development process. These poorer countries, many with large populations, constitute challenges and opportunities for the global economy, and their persistent poverty may threaten its continuing growth and prosperity.

All four of these globalization trends stimulate the development of international policy regimes. Interlinkage within the Triad, and between Triad countries and others, fosters the creation of institutionalized arrangements to facilitate and stabilize the increasing volume and variety of economic interactions. Increases in the number and diversity of significant actors, along with the growth of MNEs and global industries, stimulate the need for explicit agreements and structures that reflect diverse but mutually interdependent interests. And the plight of the poorer countries becomes increasingly conspicuous and pressing within this context, attracting worldwide policy attention.

3.1.1   Data Classification and Statistical Profile

The several official data collections describing various aspects of the global economy have been constructed for different purposes and possess different strengths and limitations. (See appendix for a more detailed discussion.) In particular, different data sources use different classification systems for nations and economic systems and assign countries to various categories according to somewhat different criteria. (The membership of various organized international economic groups, OECD, OPEC, EU, EFTA, etc., has also changed over time.) We rely here primarily on data published by the World Bank, the UN Conference on Trade and Development (UNCTAD), the International Monetary Fund (IMF), and the UN Centre on Transnational Corporations (UNCTC). All of these data sources have significant gaps, errors, and omissions; and all of the classification systems are problematic in one way or another. Fortunately, most of these discrepancies are not significant for our purposes, since our primary interest is in the *patterns* and *trends* in global economic relationships, and these are essentially the same in all major data sources.

International and comparative data on trade, investment, and enterprises, the focus of interest in this chapter, can be examined for geographic regions, for individual countries, or for countries grouped according to various criteria, such as income levels or types of economy. Our analysis relies primarily on the "type of economy" classification shown in table 3-2, which is based upon the system used by the UNCTAD. Other groupings will be indicated in the text or exhibits as appropriate.

As table 3-2 indicates, UNCTAD recognizes five types of economies:

1. Industrial (or developed) market economies, often termed the advanced industrial countries (AICs). We restrict this classification to the OECD or Triad countries, although UNCTAD adds a few other jurisdictions (South Africa, Faeroe Islands, Gibraltar, and Israel) to this group. We group countries appropriate to the data source and analysis purpose in each case and typically reassign the non-OECD countries to the "Other" category defined below.

2. Eastern European economies, including the successor states of the former USSR. These countries are now changing rapidly and in diverse ways. Their 6% share of world exports is probably the best single indicator of these countries' global economic importance. As much as 40% of Russia's GDP may occur in the black market or underground economy (Knight and Possehl, 1996, p. 39).

3. Asian "socialist" states, including the People's Republic of China (PRC). These countries are distinguished from those in the previous category by level of development as well as location. They are poor by any standard, having 23% of world population and just 2% of world GNP and 2% of world exports; however, they contain pockets of development, such as the Chinese Special Economic Zones, that are of global economic significance.

4. Members of OPEC. Some of these countries rise out of the "less developed" category because of their high per capita incomes; however, their economies are typically not "advanced" overall, and many of them are relatively poor in spite of their export earnings. Also, the reader should note that some important oil exporting countries (e.g., Bahrain, Brunei, etc.) are not OPEC members, hence OPEC is more a political than an economic classification.

5. "Other" countries, including both developing and stagnant economies as well as NICs and the four small industrial (i.e., developed) economies noted above, have in common only their exclusion from the foregoing categories.

Table 3-2. Basic Data by Type of Economy (current US$)

Type of Economy	Population (Millions)	% of World Population	$ GNP at Market Prices (Billions)	% of World GNP	$ GNP Per Capita (Computed)	$ Exports By Origin (Billions)	% of World Exports By Origin	1994 % of Foreign-Owned World Capital Stock By Origin
			1993					
World Total	5525	100	23,715	100	4293	4709	100	100.0
Industrial Market	813	15	18,549	78	22,821	3253	69	98.8
US	258	5	6276	26	24,344	648	14	42.8
EU and EFTA	381	7	7194	30	18,882	1976	42	46.0
Japan	124	2	4230	18	34,113	398	8	3.8
Other Industrial	50	1	849	4	16,980	231	5	6.2
CIS and Eastern Europe	415	8	766	3	1959	260	6	–
Russia	149	3	321	1	2154	124	3	–
Asian Socialist	1275	23	461	2	362	106	2	–
OPEC	462	8	631	3	1382	192	4	–
Other	2560	46	3308	14	1292	898	19	1.2
NIC7	354	6	1875	8	5297	545	12	–
India	898	16	247	1	275	29	1	–

Sources: World Bank, *World Data 1995 CD-ROM* (Washington, DC). Source reports 5523 million population for world; a few missing areas estimated for 1993 from *Statistical Abstract of the United States, 1995* (Washington, DC: US Government Printing Office, 1995). Capital stock from table 3-3 below. Taiwan data from other sources.

Notes: For definitions of the countries included in each type of economy, see appendix "Note on Data and Sources." Exports defined as goods and nonfactor services. All data rounded.

"Other" GNP and exports understated due to missing cases. A few 1992 estimates used. Libya (OPEC) and former Yugoslavia not in population in computing per capita GNP. Hong Kong exports used for GNP; no export data for North Korea.

"Other Industrial" is Canada, Australia, and New Zealand. "Asian Socialist" dominated by China (PRC), not reported separately. CIS (Commonwealth of Independent States) is former USSR. Eastern Europe includes Albania and former Yugoslavia.

The added category of newly industrialized countries (NICs), included by most official data sources within "Other" countries, has come to be widely used in analyses of global economic change, although the specific characteristics and identity of the NICs are subject to debate. In general, NIC designation implies both a certain level of development (they are sometimes described as "*nearly* industrialized countries") and an emphasis on global economic participation. Most references to NICs[1] include at least the NIC7 identified in table 3-2:

> East Asia: Hong Kong, Singapore, South Korea, Taiwan;
> Latin America: Argentina, Brazil, Mexico.

Some analysts also include in addition to South Africa:

> Israel: more than twice as rich per capita as South Korea and
>   comparable to Spain;
> Venezuela: comparable to South Korea;
> China and India: because of their aggregate size and the volume of their
>   industrial exports.

Even a cursory examination of aggregate data on the world economy, such as that summarized in table 3-2, reveals one overwhelming fact: the dominant economic size and role of a relatively small group of advanced countries, variously referred to as the Triad, First World, or Developed Market Economies. These economies include the US and Canada; most members of the European Union (the EU 12 or EU 15, depending on the year), although Greece and Portugal are closer to developing than developed economies in important respects, and even Ireland is relatively poor by West European standards; remaining members of the EFTA, which is rapidly merging with the EU; Japan; Australia and New Zealand. These nations, which contained in 1993 only 15% of the world's population, generated 78% of the world's GNP, provided 69% of world exports in the same year, and controlled nearly 99% of world foreign-owned capital stock (in 1994). The US alone generated 26% of world GNP and controlled nearly 43% of world foreign-owned capital stock.

3.2 TRADE LINKAGES IN THE GLOBAL ECONOMY

Our analysis of trade linkages in the global economy involves levels and trends in three dimensions:

- The volume of trade: the aggregate amount of trade taking place within the global system;
- The structure of trade: the pattern of imports and exports among trading countries;

- The content or composition of trade: the kinds and combinations of goods and services that are traded internationally.

Over the decades since World War II, the volume of world trade has increased enormously in absolute terms and also relative to national and world economic growth. This expansion has been a major force in the development of the contemporary global economy. World trade continues to be dominated by the Triad economies, which account for more than two thirds of the total; but their relative share has inevitably been declining over time due to the growth of the NICs and other factors. (This conclusion is true even if the distorting short-term effects of fluctuations in international oil prices are taken into account; the data presented here have been selected so as to bracket the effects of the OPEC-generated oil price increases during the 1970s.) The content of world trade has also changed somewhat over recent decades, particularly with respect to the growing importance of world trade in services and high technology products (Ostry and Nelson, 1995; Cooper and Bahree, 1996).

Between 1970 and 1990, the dollar value of world exports increased more than $3 trillion, or approximately 1300% as of 1994 (see table 3-1 above). These changes in dollar values reflect, of course, effects of inflation and fluctuations in exchange rates, but the data nevertheless reveal an unprecedented growth in real export/import activity throughout the world. This growth occurred primarily in the industrial market economies of the Triad (see appendix table A-1).

The industrial market economies not only account for the largest part of world trade, but they trade very largely with each other. The 1990 data (see appendix table A-2) show that roughly two thirds of world exports originated in, and a similar proportion was received by, the industrial market economies; and nearly three quarters of this volume consisted of trade among themselves. Other data in appendix table A-2 show that most of these structural relationships have been fairly stable over the past quarter century. Within the OECD group of countries, trade (and all other forms of economic activity) is dominated by five nations: France, Germany (with East and West united in 1991), Japan, the UK, and the US. The other two members of the Group of Seven (G7), Canada and Italy, are important international actors, but Canada is tied largely to the US and Italy to the EU. A few other individual countries (particularly the Benelux states, Sweden, and Switzerland) also play significant international roles.

The NICs and other developing countries also give rise to significant international trade, investment, and organizational activities, both among themselves and with more advanced countries. Longitudinal data (appendix table A-2) indicate a basic stability in the relative proportion of exports (about 19% in 1970 and 1990, albeit with fluctuations in between those years) going to the developing countries from the industrial market economies. The OECD countries are clearly dependent upon import of critical materials (especially oil, gas, minerals, and certain agricultural commodities) from the developing regions, which therefore cannot be viewed as "peripheral" elements of the international economic system. There is also some evidence to suggest that intra-Third World trade may be increasing (see appendix table A-2).

World exports and imports consist of both *services* and *merchandise*, the latter customarily subdivided into *manufactures* and *nonmanufactures*. Data at this level of detail are collected from a variety of sources; and, for a variety of reasons, the reported totals of exports and imports in these and other disaggregated categories (which should in principle be identical) do not coincide. Since our concern here, as elsewhere, is with broad patterns rather than with statistical detail, we follow common practice and focus on *export* data, with no attempt at reconciliation.

Manufacturing is of central importance in the process of economic development and particularly in the integration of new participants into the global economy. Hence, the level and growth of trade in manufactured goods is of particular interest. In 1992, according to UNCTAD export data (1995a, tables A.1 and A.13), manufactured goods ($2707 billion) were 73.4% of total exports ($3686 billion). (Appendix table A-3 shows the distribution of manufactured exports by origin and destination for 1970 and 1990.) The industrial market economies are even more important in manufactured exports than in total trade (79% in 1990 as opposed to 69% in table 3-1 above), although the trend has been downward since 1970 due to the rise of the NICs.[2] The change in world exports over the 1970-1990 period is analyzed in more detail in appendix table A-4, which makes the striking point that industrial market economy manufactured exports have increased at one third the rate of the developing economies (including OPEC and the NICs), although double the rate of Eastern Europe and socialist Asia. Such a difference might be expected for the oil exporting countries because of relative price changes; however, the comparable increase for other less industrialized countries is a major factor in the transformation of the global economy over recent decades. Also notable from these data is the fact that, although non-OPEC developing countries have increased the share of their manufactured exports going to industrial market economies (from 5% to 14%), a similar change has also occurred for trade in manufactured exports among non-OPEC developing countries (from 9% to 21%). Ostry and Nelson (1995) emphasize the increasing importance of high technology exports for the US, Japan, and the NICs (but not for European countries), and the growth of two-way intraindustry trade among the advanced countries.

3.3 INVESTMENT LINKAGES IN THE GLOBAL ECONOMY

International investment, according to many analysts, has become more important than trade as a source of integration and interdependence of the global economy. Julius comments:

> We are rapidly approaching a new level of economic integration through direct investment: a cascading of flows from more countries, into more sectors and involving more actors than ever before. Unlike trade, these FDI flows represent long-term commitments by companies to build viable businesses in one another's markets. They may be slowed, but they will not easily be reversed, by economic downturns or shifts in exchange rates (1990, p. 6).

Lash notes that FDI, although "feared in the 1960s and 1970s by developing states, has now become in many sectors the engine for globalism and development," and cites evidence from a McKinsey Global Institute study of the US, Japan, and Europe that FDI improves domestic productivity, puts competitive pressure on other domestic producers, and transfers knowledge of best practices to other domestic producers through natural personnel mobility among enterprises (Lash, 1996, p. 7, citing Lewis, 1993).

Trade and investment are, of course, intimately linked. At times, they appear to be alternatives: a producer in one country might choose to export product to another or might establish a production facility there to serve the local market. In fact, however, through the dynamics of economic development, trade stimulates investment and investment correspondingly stimulates trade. The long-term relationships established through FDI are, however, as Julius emphasizes, quite different from those arising out of arm's-length trade transactions alone.

Analysis of the role of international investment in the global economy involves two distinct concepts. One is the current *flow* of new investment among countries during any time period; data reflecting this flow are exactly comparable to trade data, although the magnitudes are quite different and the errors involved are more difficult to identify. The other is the accumulated *stock* of investment that enterprises and nationals from one country hold in another at any time period. Net investment flows from country A to country B during any time period add to the total stock of country A ownership in country B. Note, however, that even if no current *flow* takes place, the current *stock* of country A investment holdings in country B, built up by investment flows during previous time periods, may still remain large.

The holding of investment stocks generates a third type of relationship, the flow of *earnings* from country B to investors located in country A. These earnings may be repatriated in the form of trade (exports from country B into country A), or as reverse capital flows (i.e., country B investors make investments in country A). They may also be reinvested in country B, further expanding country A investors' ownership interests there. An additional complication is that investment, both stocks and flows, can take a variety of forms: "real" investment (facilities, equipment, etc.), financial investment (securities), and cash holdings.

For all of these reasons, appropriate conceptualization and measurement of investment linkages among countries is extremely difficult, and there are significant differences between the reported values of conceptually identical magnitudes (country A's outbound investment in country B, and country B's record of inflows from country A). These differences, like differences in disaggregated import and export data, arise because the two sets of raw data are collected independently and from different sources. Outward stocks, outward investment flows, and inward earnings flows are reported by "home" countries (country A, in this example); inward stocks, inward investment flows, and outward earnings flows are reported by "host" countries. Differences between reported figures for conceptually identical magnitudes may arise due to incomplete reporting, differences in definitions and in source/destination information among countries, fluctuations in exchange rates, and even differences in the timing of transaction records and data collection activities. In any event, differences in inward and outward estimates of conceptually identical magnitudes may be quite substantial, as the data tables in this section reveal.

Fortunately, just as with the trade data, in spite of these deficiencies the general *pattern* of international investment relationships revealed by all data sources appears to be about the same and is, in fact, very similar to the pattern of the corresponding trade flows. The OECD countries dominate global foreign investment, and intra-OECD investment is by far the most important element in the global total. According to the data shown in table 3-3, more than 85% of all foreign-owned investment (whether measured in terms of annual flows or aggregate stocks) arises in the industrial market economies; these countries are also the "hosts" of three quarters of all foreign investment stocks. The US accounts for a fifth to a quarter and Europe for about half of global FDI. The emergence of Japan as a major international investor was one of the most important developments in the global economy during the 1980s. The UK plays a considerably more important role in world investment than in trade, partially because its historic role in trade led to the accumulation of substantial foreign investments (*The Economist*, 1990). The valuation of capital stock, even within a single economy, involves many complexities,

Table 3-3. Foreign Direct Investment Flows and Stocks by Origin and Destination, Various Years (current US$ in billions)

	1983-88		1994		1980		1994	
	Annual Average	% of World	Dollar Estimate	% of World	Actual Dollar	% of World	Dollar Estimate	% of World
By Origin	*FDI Outflows*				*FDI Outward Stocks*			
World Total	93.71	100.00	222.25	100.00	514.22	100.00	2378.03	100.00
Industrial Market	88.28	94.21	189.28	85.17	508.03	98.80	2229.81	93.77
US	14.20	15.15	45.64	20.54	220.18	42.82	610.06	25.65
Western Europe	51.86	55.34	113.92	51.26	236.59	46.01	1183.88	49.78
France	5.86	6.25	22.86	10.29	23.60	4.59	183.41	7.71
Germany	7.90	8.43	20.56	9.25	43.13	8.39	205.61	8.65
UK	18.76	20.02	25.14	11.31	80.43	15.64	281.17	11.82
Japan	14.04	14.98	17.94	8.07	19.61	3.81	277.73	11.68
Other	8.18	8.73	11.78	5.30	31.65	6.15	158.14	6.65
Developing	5.42	5.78	32.91	14.81	6.12	1.19	147.77	6.21
Asia	3.86	4.12	30.31	13.64	2.69	0.52	124.87	5.25
Americas	0.42	0.45	1.90	0.85	2.91	0.57	19.21	0.81
Mexico	0.10	0.11	0.18	0.08	0.14	0.03	1.22	0.05
CIS and Eastern Europe	0.01	0.01	0.07	0.03	0.08	0.02	0.44	0.02
Addendum: Oil Exporters	2.08	2.22	3.30	1.48	1.53	0.30	18.50	0.78
Addendum: Group of 5	60.76	64.84	132.14	59.46	386.95	75.25	1557.98	65.52

By Destination	FDI Inflows				FDI Inward Stocks			
World Total	91.55	100.00	225.69	100.00	480.61	100.00	2319.29	100.00
Industrial Market	71.78	78.41	134.98	59.81	372.25	77.45	1715.48	73.97
US	34.39	37.56	49.45	21.91	83.05	17.28	504.40	21.75
Western Europe	28.90	31.57	73.66	32.64	198.99	41.40	964.13	41.57
France	3.93	4.29	16.93	7.50	22.62	4.71	142.09	6.13
Germany	1.52	1.66	4.41	1.95	36.63	7.62	132.41	5.71
UK	9.34	10.20	10.23	4.53	63.01	13.11	214.23	9.24
Japan	0.33	0.36	0.89	0.39	3.27	0.68	17.77	0.77
Other	8.16	8.92	10.99	4.87	86.95	18.09	229.18	9.88
Developing	19.76	21.58	84.27	37.34	108.27	22.53	583.56	25.16
Asia	10.04	10.97	60.66	26.88	37.96	7.90	339.59	14.64
China	1.82	1.99	33.80	14.98	0.00	0.00	90.97	3.92
Americas	7.44	8.13	20.25	8.97	48.03	9.99	186.22	8.03
Mexico	2.27	2.48	4.40	1.95	8.99	1.87	46.34	2.00
CIS and Eastern Europe	0.02	0.02	6.44	2.85	0.09	0.02	20.75	0.89
Addendum: Oil Exporters	7.05	7.70	15.82	7.01	41.90	8.72	200.85	8.66
Addendum: Group of 5	49.51	54.08	81.91	36.29	208.58	43.40	1010.90	43.59

Source: UN Conference on Trade and Development (UNCTAD), *World Investment Report, 1995* (New York: UN, 1995), annex.

Notes: 1994 FDI inflow for Mexico as reported in this table revised during UNCTAD publication process by International Monetary Fund (IMF) to $8 billion (nearly double). This adjustment affects Americas, Developing, and World Total. "Group of 5" (G5) is France, Germany, Japan, UK, US. "Other" industrial market is Australia, Canada, Israel, New Zealand, and South Africa. Difference between "Developing" and its components is Africa, Pacific, and Developing Europe. "Developing" includes all NICs. Source data adjusted so that certain Asian countries are included in Commonwealth of Independent States (CIS), the former USSR. For definition of UNCTAD oil exporters, see appendix "Note on Data and Sources."

and comparisons and accumulations among different economies over different time periods introduce further complications. Particular problems include estimation of depreciation rates, variations in inflation rates among countries, and variations in currency exchange rates over time. According to the data summarized in table 3-3, the total value of foreign-owned capital stock, whether measured from origin or destination sources, increased more than fourfold between 1980 and 1994. A rough accounting for inflation effects would cut this figure less than in half, but even a doubling of capital stock within such a short period is extraordinary. (Investment into and out of the US in 1994 is reported in appendix table A-5.)

3.4 MULTINATIONAL ENTERPRISES

The international trade and investment linkages that have evolved since World War II have been importantly influenced by, and have in turn greatly influenced, the growth of multinational enterprises (MNEs). We use the term *enterprise* rather than any more restrictive term, such as *corporation*, to refer to organizations engaged in business activities such as production, service, and sales, regardless of their legal form or type of ownership. In particular, both investor- and state-owned entities are included, along with various hybrid combinations. The appearance and growth of hybrids (both private-government partnerships and multinational joint ventures and strategic alliances) is a particularly significant feature of the contemporary international business environment. We follow Dunning in defining a *multinational* enterprise as one that "owns and controls income-generating assets in more than one country" (Dunning, ed., 1974, p. 13), or more recently "a coordinator of value added in two or more countries" (Dunning, 1991, p. 3; see also Dunning, 1979). More elaborate terminological distinctions among such enterprises, such as those suggested by Porter (1986, 1990), Bartlett and Ghoshal (1989), and others (Hoogvelt, 1987, provides a comprehensive compilation), are useful for some purposes and are introduced as relevant below.

It is important to emphasize that international economic linkages can and do arise without the involvement of MNEs. Trade can take place among enterprises in different jurisdictions, each of which is purely domestic in its own operations; and international capital movements can occur without any integration of management and policy among the capital-sending and capital-receiving organizations. In fact, however, the management and operations of most MNEs are significantly integrated across countries; and substantial and increasing proportions of total world trade and investment take place within the MNE framework. Hence, over the past half century, MNEs have been intimately involved in both the growth of international trade and investment, and the process of economic development and integration, throughout the world. In some instances, initial trade and investment flows stimulated by independent economic forces lead to the formation and growth of MNEs. On other occasions, MNEs are created when successful domestic firms move into new markets or production locations. In either case, once established, MNEs in turn generate (or impede) new trade and investment flows and create (or prevent) new forms of international coordination, always in the context of their own organizational structures and objectives.

The growth and evolution of MNEs is closely related to the development of international policy regimes. MNEs form important links within the global economy that go beyond, and sometimes supersede, the relationships established by governments. They create new structures of international economic integration; and the flows of managerial and technical knowledge and control that occur within MNE structures are significantly different from product and capital flows that occur through market channels. MNE structures and activities may be either welcomed or resisted by various national governments and other economic and political actors, and a major concern in both advanced and developing countries over the postwar decades has been the harmonization of MNE operations with national economic and social goals. Many international policy regimes include enterprises (both domestic firms and MNEs) and representatives of industry groups as active participants for purposes of policy-making and/or implementation.

MNEs for their own part are steadily evolving new types of collaborative relationships in response to the opportunities and problems arising in the global economy. The opportunities lie in the product-market and geographic diversification and expansion possibilities arising from the globalization process. The problems lie both in interfirm relationships and in the difficulties caused by tremendous variations in national operating conditions and national policy treatment of foreign-owned enterprises. One stimulus for international regime development is the need to shape a more stable and less risky global environment for MNEs.

This section first examines the nature of the multinational enterprise, a topic which is the subject of a very large literature (cf. Slomanson's extensive bibliography, 1989). We then present a schematic framework for analyzing the various types of enterprises participating in the global economy on the basis of their ownership-control structures and geographic bases. Finally, we examine the patterns of international linkage that have evolved as a result of growth in the numbers, size, and importance of MNEs in the global economy. Throughout this discussion the increasingly important roles of global industries and MNE networks are emphasized.

3.4.1 The Nature of the Multinational Enterprise

The increasing number and size of MNEs over the postwar decades, and their increasing importance within the global economy, have attracted considerable attention to the theory of the MNE and the evolution of global business structures. The contemporary literature has focused on several interrelated issues: Why do MNEs emerge? In what ways are they different from purely domestic enterprises? How does their appearance and growth affect the development of individual industries, national economies, and the global system?[3]

Porter (1986, 1990) points out that international industries can be configured in either "multidomestic" or "global" patterns, with many mixed structures possible between these extremes. In a multidomestic industry, competition takes place within national or regional markets that are essentially independent of each other; the industry is "international" only in the sense that it exists in parallel form in many different countries. Some multidomestic industries are the exclusive province of purely domestic firms within each national environment; in other cases, MNEs from various countries may also be active, along with local competitors. In any event, in a multidomestic industry, competitive interaction takes place on a national/regional basis, and products and operating practices may be quite different from country to country.

By contrast, in a global industry, the competitive environment itself is defined in international terms. The key feature, according to Porter, is that "a firm's competitive position in one nation significantly affects (and is affected by) its position in other nations"; the competitive enterprises in such an industry, which are necessarily MNEs, interact "on a truly worldwide basis, drawing on competitive advantages that grow out of their entire network of worldwide activities" (Porter, 1990, p. 53).

The post–World War II expansion of MNEs can be seen as an essentially "natural" extension of products and technologies, including management technology, already in existence (initially) in the US and (subsequently) in Western Europe and Japan. However, evolution from earlier colonialist and international trade models is also still important. Current worldwide growth of MNEs, including those emerging in the newly industrialized countries (NICs) and the less developed countries (LDCs) as well as state-owned/supported enterprises, has a rationale and dynamic of its own, which is not necessarily consistent with conventional notions of comparative advantage and protectionism.

Explanations for the evolution of MNEs include a number of factors: exploitation of scale and scope advantages; relative ease of *intra*organizational (as compared to *inter*organizational or "market") transfers of management skills, technology, and capital across borders; "early mover" advantages in extending domestic innovations into new markets; and so forth (Buckley, 1990). The scale-economy argument holds that larger markets create cost and market power advantages; the scope-economy argument explains diversification of products and services along related lines (Teece, 1986). Reduction of transaction costs through improvements in transportation and communication technologies have been instrumental in generating the opportunities to exploit such scale and scope economies (Williamson, 1975, 1985).

The distinctive characteristics of MNEs include their need to operate within diverse national cultures and their complex governance structures, which are strongly affected by differences among national policies and by international policy developments. While MNE expansion may arise in economic rent seeking and transaction cost reductions, organizational structure and culture are stressed by multinational operations. "Managers of today's multinationals are not so much economic decision makers as they are governors of a social and political strategic management process" (Bower and Doz, in Schendel and Hofer, eds., 1979, p. 165). The governance of enterprises involves both 1) formal legal arrangements (ownership and internal control), and 2) external relationships, both transactional and stakeholder. National governments are inevitably stakeholders in major enterprises operating within their jurisdictions, and this stakeholder relationship is strengthened and formalized by policy attention, regulation, and (in the most extreme case) partial or total government ownership. The MNE is inevitably a sociopolitical institution, and MNE management involves greater problems of governance than those of the typical purely domestic enterprise. Combining local autonomy and conformity to domestic conditions with global strategic integration presents both internal and external governance problems.

The impact of MNEs on the growth and development of individual economies, particularly in the LDCs, has been a matter of considerable debate, and differences of opinion about this matter have been highly significant in the evolution of international policy regimes during the postwar decades (Committee for Economic Development, 1981). According to Boddewyn, "Political behavior by MNEs has usually been ignored, downplayed or passively treated in dominant economic models of the multinational enterprise" (1988, p. 341). In fact, however, there are important political dimensions to the ownership, activity internalization, and geographic location advantages associated with MNEs, and their social and political role may be as important as their economic impact. The nonmarket environment of the MNE, including its political dimensions, interacts with the market environment and with the character of the enterprise itself to yield complex results for which no single element is responsible; and political expertise may be as important as managerial and technological skill in accounting for MNE success or failure.[4]

3.4.2 Types of Multinational Enterprise

Many different types of firms, both domestic and MNE, are active participants in the global economy, and the differences in their structure and ownership have significant impact on their status and treatment under national and international policies. Figure 3-2 presents a classification system for enterprise types designed to highlight these important features, with illustrative examples. The vertical dimension of the figure differentiates enterprises by type of ownership, investor-owned, state-owned, or mixed.[5] The horizontal dimension of the figure differentiates enterprises according to their national/international status, including the (presently only theoretical) possibility of "stateless" global corporations.

Before turning to the various MNE forms suggested by this framework, the variety of domestic enterprises depicted is worth brief attention. It is particularly notable that enterprises of various ownership types may exist within the same national economic setting and indeed may be engaged in active competition with each other. For example, in Australia two principal domestic airlines compete: Trans Australian Airline (TAA) is state-owned; Ansett Australian National Airways (Ansett ANA) is owned by private investors. (Qantas, a national-base, state-owned enterprise, competes with foreign firms in the overseas travel market.) A similar situation is found in the Canadian railroad industry, where Canadian National (state-owned) and Canadian Pacific (investor-owned) are competitors in transcontinental service. In the US, Conrail was originally a government corporation, formed out of preexisting private firms, for intercity rail freight transport, that was subsequently reprivatized. Amtrak is a government corporation offering intercity rail passenger service. None of these domestic enterprises has any significant international role, but their existence illustrates the fact that, even in highly market-oriented countries, various combinations of investor- and state-owned firms are engaged in providing goods and services in the marketplace. Varied ownership-control patterns within the same industry are very common in socialist states, where nationally- and provincially-controlled enterprises (both state-owned) may interact with foreign MNEs in joint ventures or other forms of cooperation. Privatization efforts in various countries are transferring many economic activities out of formal state ownership, but important private-government links remain in place.

Multinational Enterprises

	Purely Domestic Enterprises	National-Base Enterprises	Joint Ventures, Strategic Alliances, Enterprise Networks	Stateless Global Enterprises
Investor-Owned Enterprises	Ansett Australian National Airways (Ansett ANA) Canadian Pacific	Nestle (Switzerland) Union Carbide (US)	Caltex (US) Auto	BCCI (seized by bank regulators) Companies
Jointly-Controlled Enterprises and Private-Government Combinations	Conrail (US)	British Petroleum (BP)	Union Carbide India, Ltd. (UCIL) SAS (Sweden, Norway, Denmark)	
Stated-Owned Enterprises	Trans Australian Airlines (TAA) Amtrak (US) Canadian National	Qantas (Australia)	Renault (France), now being privatized	

Figure 3-2. Classification of Enterprises.

Among MNEs, the national-base enterprise operating through foreign subsidiaries or affiliates is by far the most common type. These enterprises are chartered and headquartered in a particular country, which is also the primary source of their managerial staff; hence, they tend to reflect that country's culture, standards, and values. Nestle (Switzerland) and Union Carbide (US) are national-base, investor-owned MNEs that

have gained recent and unfavorable notice in connection with their operations in LDCs. (Nestle's involvement in the international infant formula
controversy of the 1980s is discussed in chapter 4.) British Petroleum
(BP) originated as a private-government combination; BP supplied oil to
the Royal Navy and government representatives on the BP board pos-
sessed veto power. Renault (France) is a state-owned enterprise, a di-
versified conglomerate making and selling a variety of products (including, of course, automobiles) throughout the world; it is in the process
of being privatized.

Between such national-base enterprises and the "stateless" corporations
that may appear in the future, there are many different hybrid combinations.[6] These may take the form of informal cooperation, consortia,
strategic alliances, contractual agreements, equity joint ventures, mergers
and acquisitions of various types, and so forth. Participants may be
investor-owned, state-owned, or both. According to Reich (1991), MNEs
are increasingly operating through "global nets" in which more or less
formal relationships among specific organizations are maintained on a
relatively permanent basis. He argues that national products, technologies, and enterprises are disappearing; what will matter in the twenty-
first century will be national origin of the major shares of *value added* in
global products or services sold through global nets. These hybrid arrangements are alternatives to both arm's-length market transactions and
the establishment of wholly-owned foreign subsidiaries. Joint ventures
typically involve equity participation, and thus represent a form of FDI.
Contractual relationships such as licensing, management contracts,
franchising, turnkey operations, subcontracting, and so forth "are more
akin to sales transactions than to investment, since they usually do not
involve a long-term ownership interest by one entity in another"
(UNCTC, 1983, p. 40).

Caltex, headquartered in Dallas, Texas, and jointly owned by Standard Oil
of California and Texaco, is a good example of an equity joint venture
between two investor-owned MNEs; the firm markets petroleum products
in LDCs. In 1987, Corning Glass Works participated in at least 20
strategic alliances in other countries, including Australia, China, France,
Germany, and the UK; these activities contributed half of its net income
(Kanter, 1989, p. 192). General Electric had over 100 cooperative
ventures with other enterprises in 1986 (Kanter, 1989, p. 183).

The special situations that may arise as a result of combined investor and
state ownership are well illustrated by the case of Union Carbide India Ltd.
(UCIL), owner of the Bhopal chemical plant that caused death and injury
to hundreds of people in 1984. Union Carbide (US) held a majority
interest (51%) in UCIL, and Indian investors, including a state government, held the remainder. Under government pressure, UCIL had turned

all plant operations over to Indian nationals, although the parent company retained primary operating responsibility. After the disaster, both the locus of responsibility for the accident and the jurisdiction (India or the US) in which the matter was to be adjudicated became subjects of widespread international debate (Steiner and Steiner, 1985, pp. 180–195, presents a concise summary).

The Scandinavian Airlines System (SAS) is a classic example of a private-government joint venture involving multiple countries. Denmark, Norway, and Sweden each have domestic airlines owned half by private investors and half by the national government. SAS is a combination of these three airlines to serve the international travel market. It also operates various other enterprises and once owned a substantial share of Continental Airlines in the US. In spite of this diversity, however, SAS is not likely to become a "stateless" enterprise because of its strong focus on Scandinavia.

The auto industry, however, may be moving toward a truly "stateless" character, as a result of joint ventures and strategic alliances among US, Japanese, and European firms. General Motors has had a US joint venture with Toyota, plus ownership positions in Suzuki and Isuzu in Japan, and Saab in Europe. Ford has had complex links with three European and two Japanese companies, and Chrysler has been primarily linked with Mitsubishi. Ford has purchased Jaguar (UK) and Mazda (Japan). Isuzu, Fuji Heavy Industries, and Nissan (all of Japan) have been interlinked, and both Nissan and Toyota have been linked with Volkswagen, which was in turn linked with Ford (Weidenbaum and Jensen, 1990).

In the (as yet) theoretical case of a "stateless" or "international" corporation, an MNE would no longer be tied to a particular national base. Such an enterprise might be a kind of organizational chameleon, taking on local camouflage as appropriate in each jurisdiction. For example, its headquarters (staffed on a multinational basis) might be located in Liechtenstein or the Caribbean. Its national affiliates or subsidiaries, scattered around the world to optimize costs and market access, might be staffed entirely with local personnel. Its ownership might be dispersed among individuals, other corporations, and governments throughout the globe. Although such an entity is beyond the range of current experience, proposals for the establishment of pan-European enterprises ("European Corporations"), and even for "United Nations Corporations," may be harbingers of things to come (Schelpe, 1991).

The international legal and financial problems arising in connection with the operations of the Bank of Credit and Commerce International (BCCI), officially controlled by BCCI Holdings (Luxembourg) S.A. but operating throughout the world, illustrate the difficulty in regulatory and legal oversight of global MNE operations in the absence of any kind of comprehensive international system. It has been alleged that BCCI units engaged in laundering criminal funds and in supporting terrorist activities around the world; and, in July 1991, in a move headed by the Bank of England, the assets of BCCI were seized by bank regulators of several countries (Truell and Bray, 1991).

3.4.3 Enterprise Linkages

Worldwide, some 35,000 MNEs operate through 170,000 foreign subsidiaries; the 100 largest MNEs control an estimated 16% of the world's productive assets, and the 300 largest 25% (Lash, 1996, p. 8, citing UN estimates and *The Economist*, 1993). Since, as demonstrated above, international economic activity is dominated by relatively few advanced industrial countries that are increasingly linked with each other through trade, investment, and policy coordination, it is no surprise that these countries also are the home bases for the great majority of the world's largest enterprises (see table 3-4).[7]

Available data on MNEs are subject to a number of limitations with respect to both coverage and classification procedures. In the first place, not every one of the giant enterprises enumerated in table 3-4 may be an MNE in the strictest sense; however, most of them clearly are and no more selective compilation of data is currently available. In addition, some large and internationally important entities, particularly state-owned enterprises and alliance/network arrangements, may escape coverage in these compilations. In spite of these discrepancies, there is little doubt that the industrial market economies are home to well over 90% of all large MNEs and the US alone to about one third of them. Gradual decline in the relative role of the US, which accounted for well over half of all MNEs during the early postwar decades, has been due to the postwar recovery of Europe and, more recently, to the rapid growth of MNEs based in Japan and, to a much lesser extent, in NICs and other less advanced countries.

A 1986 UNCTC study of 600 large industrial and agricultural MNEs with $1 billion or more in sales (the "billion dollar club") reported that US-based MNEs accounted for 51% of the total sales of this group of enterprises; Japan-based firms for 14%; and firms from other industrial market economies for 32%. These figures left only 3% of giant MNE sales to be accounted for by enterprises based in the NICs and elsewhere (UNCTC, 1986, p. 36).

These data, which focus on the largest MNEs in the world, may give an incomplete indication of the important and growing role played by smaller MNEs from the less advanced countries. The *Business Week*

Table 3-4. National Base of the World's Largest Enterprises, Selected Years

	Fortune Industrial 1980 (Composite "Global 500")		Fortune Industrial 1995 (Reported "Global 500")		Business Week 1995 ("Global 1000" and "Top 100")		Forbes 1995 ("500 Largest Foreign Companies")	
	Number	%	Number	%	Number	%	Number	%
Total	500	100.0	500	100.0	1106	100.0	506	100.0
Industrial Market	477	95.4	476	95.2	978	88.4	473	93.5
US	219	43.8	153	30.6	422	38.2	–	–
EU4	125	25.0	128	25.6	193	17.5	162	32.0
Other Europe	41	8.2	44	8.8	93	8.4	75	14.8
Japan	71	14.2	141	28.2	227	20.5	207	40.9
Other	21	4.2	10	2.0	43	3.9	29	5.7
Other	23	4.6	24	4.8	128	11.6	33	6.5
NICs	18	3.6	21	4.2	96	8.7	33	6.5
OPEC	2	0.4	1	0.2	–	–	–	–
LDCs	3	0.6	2	0.4	32	2.9	–	–

Sources: *Fortune* "Global 500" (August 6, 1996); *Business Week* "Global 1000" (July 8, 1996); *Forbes* "The 500 Largest Foreign Companies" (July 15, 1996). Jointly-owned firms (all European) allocated to both countries.

Notes: "Other Industrial Market": Australia, Canada, New Zealand. NICs: Argentina, Brazil, Chile, Hong Kong, India, Mexico, Pakistan, Singapore, South Korea, Taiwan, and Turkey. Other ASEAN members in LDC category.

and *Forbes* "global" surveys are conducted on a broader scale than the *Fortune* industrial or UNCTC industrial/agricultural surveys. *Business Week* and *Forbes* include all industries, and the 1000-enterprise coverage of the former better captures the effects of increasing enterprise size in the NICs. The most notable change over the 1980-1990 period, according to the *Business Week* data, is the dramatic decline in the relative importance of LDC-based enterprises, which category includes OPEC and the increasing number of MNEs based in South Korea and other NICs. (The importance of "nonconventional" MNEs, whether smaller or LDC-based, is also emphasized in a 1990 UNCTC report on this topic and in Kahn, ed., 1986.)

The emergence of global industries (that is, industries operating in many parts of the world and often dominated by MNEs that operate in many countries and markets) is a major feature of worldwide economic evolution during the past half century (Porter, 1990). The "global" status of particular industries can be gauged to some extent from the activities of the world's largest industrial firms, summarized for the 1995 *Fortune* "Global 500" in appendix table A-6. The three largest industries, each accounting for more than 10% of total "Global 500" sales (trading, insurance, banks and savings), together comprised about one third of total sales but only about 13% of total employees. Petroleum refining, motor vehicles and parts, and electronics and electrical equipment (which dominated the 1990 "Global 500" reported in the 1992 edition of this book) brought the share of total sales of the top six industries to nearly 60% and of employees to nearly 38%. No other industry accounted for more than 4.5% of total sales of the group. Other changes in industry composition of the "Global 500" since 1990 are also evident.

3.4.4 MNE Networks

The structure and function of individual MNE networks (OECD, 1987) is difficult to grasp from aggregate data. In fact, several different kinds of network linkages are involved. At any point in time, an MNE is a *structure* of business units located in various national jurisdictions and linked by ownership patterns and control arrangements. Such a structure can be described in static terms, e.g., assets, employment, and sales at each location, or production and marketing links among them. However, the activities of MNEs must also be described in terms of the *flows*, both those that take place *within* the structure and those that take place *between* it and the outside world. Some of these flows, such as investment flows, initially create and then expand the structure itself; others simply utilize the existing structure in order to perform MNE functions.

To analyze the functional character of MNEs, Gupta and Govindarajan (1991) identify three types of flows: 1) capital and revenue flows, including investment, sales (both interaffiliate and external), and repatriation of profits; 2) product-service flows (again, both interaffiliate and external); and 3) communication flows, both managerial and technological. Attempts to "map" these flows within an individual MNE generally produce diagrams that look much like a ball of string, with overlapping lines running in all directions. Nevertheless, these flows are the true essence of MNE operations.

Aggregate trade data may improperly convey a mistaken impression that foreign trade is largely a matter of arm's-length transactions between unrelated buyers and sellers in different countries (Helleiner and Lavergne, 1979). In fact, internal transactions *among* the affiliated units of single enterprises comprise a large and growing segment of all international commerce. The accuracy of present methods for calculating international trade balances between countries was criticized by a panel of economists appointed by the US National Academy of Sciences. The panel concluded that US trade statistics do not incorporate intraenterprise sales, that is, exports from a US parent enterprise to its own foreign affiliates. Such sales account for more than 25% of US exports. Measured on this revised basis, the 1987 US trade deficit was $64 billion rather than the $148 billion officially reported (*Time*, February 10, 1992, p. 49).

Reliable data on intraenterprise trade is available only for the US, where the Department of Commerce (Bureau of Economic Analysis) collects such information as part of its periodic surveys of MNE activities. In 1993, US nonbank parent enterprises shipped $130.7 billion in exports to their foreign affiliates (10% or more ownership or control) and received $122.2 billion in imports from those affiliates for a slight positive trade balance on this basis. US affiliates of nonbank foreign MNEs (10% or more interest and assets, sales, or net income of $10 million or more) shipped $105 billion in merchandise exports and received $198.5 billion in merchandise imports for a strongly negative trade balance on this basis (US Department of Commerce, *Survey of Current Business*, May 1995). US MNE-associated merchandise exports constituted 58% of all US merchandise exports in 1993; intra-MNE exports constituted 24% of merchandise exports, or half of the US MNE-associated value. (Hipple, 1990, analyzes 1977, 1982, and 1988 data). About 40% of US merchandise imports were US MNE-associated, and 18% were intra-MNE imports (US Department of Commerce, *Survey of Current Business*, June 1995).

Only very limited aggregate data are available concerning the structure of worldwide MNE affiliate networks. The relative importance of foreign affiliate operations in total MNE activity certainly varies from firm to firm, and even among groups of MNEs based in various countries. Some indication of this variation is suggested by UNCTC data covering the operations of the world's largest industrial MNEs during the period 1971–1980 (UNCTC, 1983, p. 48). Foreign operations accounted for 40% of the aggregate sales of all included enterprises in 1980 and 53% of their aggregate net earnings; both of these figures are increases from 1971 levels. By country, the foreign share of sales was above 50% for MNEs based in France and Germany and above 40% for Japan and the UK. The share of foreign affiliate sales for US-based MNEs (31%) was then by far the lowest in the group. All of these figures reflected substantial increases over the preceding decade.

In 1983, foreign affiliates accounted for 27% of the worldwide sales of US MNEs; this proportion had risen to 31% in 1993 (see table 3-5). Worldwide employment for US MNEs declined some 369,000 over the decade, while foreign affiliate employment rose by 348,000 (the loss in US parent employment was thus some 717,000). Affiliate sales were very important in wholesale trade, petroleum, and services and less than 20% in finance and other industries. The foreign activities of US-based MNEs occur primarily through majority-owned affiliates. In 1993, majority-owned affiliates accounted for 81% of all US affiliate sales, and for the majority of sales in all industries and in most host countries except for Japan. Shares for minority-owned affiliates were relatively high in Mexico, the Pacific Rim in general, and developing countries outside the Western Hemisphere.

The 1993 data, which include only nonbank entities, reported in table 3-5 also show that MNEs based in industrial market economies account for 90% or more of all foreign MNE affiliate assets, sales, and employees in the US; affiliates of US-based MNEs are rather less concentrated in those same economies (79% of assets and sales, 66% of employees).[8]

Historical data on the affiliates of all types of US-based MNEs are available for selected years 1950-1980 (UNCTC, 1973, 1983, cited in 1992 edition, p. 68). The tremendous growth in the number of affiliates, from 7417 to 33,647 (more than fourfold over three decades), is striking evidence of the expansion of MNE networks. Affiliates located in industrial market economies dominated throughout the entire period (about 65%); however, the continuing importance of Latin American affiliates and the growth of Asian contacts were evident. In 1993, of 18,698 nonbank foreign affiliates of US parents enterprises, 88% were majority-owned and 79% wholly-owned (appendix table A-7). About half were located in Europe (where employment was somewhat below this share), a quarter in the Western Hemisphere (where employment exceeded this share), and a fifth in the Pacific Rim. Ownership shares were low in Mexico and Japan and high in Europe, Canada, and Singapore.

Table 3-5. MNE Affiliate Activities by Country and Industry, 1993 (current US$)

	Foreign Affiliates of US Parents				US Affiliates of Foreign Parents		
	Assets in $ Billions	Sales in $ Billions	Majority-Owned Affiliates	Thousands of Employees	Assets in $ Billions	Sales in $ Billions	Thousands of Employees
Parents	8138	5068		24,413.4			
Affiliates	2053	1573		6731.1	2049	1302	4722.3
% of Affiliates	% of Assets	% of Sales	% of Sales	% of Employees	% of Assets	% of Sales	% of Employees
Total by country	100	100	81	100	100	100	100
Europe	55	51	88	41	52	52	61
Western Hemisphere	22	22	86	34	15	13	17
Canada	10	12	95	13	13	10	14
Mexico	3	3	61	10	0	0	1
Other	9	7	82	11	2	3	2
Asia/Pacific	20	24	63	23	28	32	20
Japan	11	11	47	6	24	27	15
Australia/New Zealand	3	4	*	6	2	2	0
Other and Unassigned	3	3	–	3	5	3	2
Addendum: OECD	79	79	–	66	91	91	90
Affiliates Only	% of Assets	% of Sales	% of Sales	% of Employees	% of Assets	% of Sales	% of Employees
Total by industry	100	100	81	100	100	100	100
Petroleum	12	18	77	3	5	9	2
Manufacturing	30	48	82	60	25	35	47
Wholesale Trade	7	17	93	8	10	29	9
Finance	41	5	91	2	48	10	5
Services	4	4	83	9	6	4	11
Other	6	7	53	18	7	12	25

Source: US Department of Commerce, *Survey of Current Business* (June 1995).

Notes: "Finance" excludes banking, includes insurance and real estate. "Other" industry includes retail trade.
"Other" country includes US for US affiliates of foreign parents (proportion unknown, since data suppressed).
*Australia/New Zealand included in Asia/Pacific (not reported separately).

The UNCTC (1988) has published some limited information on the affiliates of 243 service-industry MNEs (business services and finance accounted for 69%) for 1987. Only large companies were included in the study, and all parent companies included were headquartered in the industrial market economies. Over 60% of the service-MNE affiliates in this study were located in industrial market economies; only Japan-based MNEs had fewer than half of their affiliates in these economies.

Foreign acquisitions are an important means of creating and enlarging MNE networks, and the 1980s witnessed a boom in international mergers and acquisitions by both US and foreign firms. According to a study by Smith and Walter (1991), the dominant flow of transnational acquisitions was *into* the US. During the period 1985-1989, US firms completed an estimated 305 crossborder transactions (defined as mergers, tender offers, purchases of stakes, divestitures, recapitalizations, exchange offers, and leveraged buyouts) with an aggregate disclosed value of $38.8 billion. During the same period, there were 941 foreign transactions involving US companies, for a total disclosed value of $178 billion. (As a basis for comparison, there were 6195 comparable domestic transactions within the US, valued at just over $1 trillion, during the same period.) Outside the US, there were a total of 3098 domestic and crossborder transactions, valued at $328.8 billion.

3.5 CONCLUSION

The world economy has expanded rapidly during the last three decades through the growth of trade and investment, both of which have increased much more rapidly than world production. This pattern of growth has greatly increased the scope and variety of international linkages, which in turn are creating a complex economic system that is truly "global" in character. At the present time, these linkages are dominated by and occur largely within the Triad economies and heavily involve the activities of multinational enterprises. The greatest structural changes in the world economy in recent years have been the relative growth in the size and importance of Japan and the appearance and impact of certain smaller countries commonly described as NICs. The rise and decline of oil prices over the past two decades produced distorting effects, both in the real economy and in its statistical descriptors, but little substantial long-term change in the relative importance of oil exporting countries. Increasing economic integration within Europe, and probably between Europe and North America, will probably reinforce the domination of global trade and investment linkages by industrial market economies, although continued rapid growth in some peripheral economies can also be expected. And, in spite of periodic announcements that the great age of the multinationals has ended, their current role in the global economy seems certain to continue, although in evolving forms, for the foreseeable future.

Notes

1. We refer to NIC7 (Hong Kong, Singapore, South Korea, and Taiwan in East Asia; Argentina, Brazil, and Mexico in Latin America—together accounting for about 12% of world exports) as appropriate in connection with specific data. Reference to NICs in other than a statistical context connotes all such economies at an intermediate stage of development and significantly engaged in international economic.

2. In 1992, the US accounted for 11.8% of world manufactures, Germany 14%, Japan 11.8%, the other G7 countries (Canada, France, Italy, and the UK) 21% jointly, and the four East Asian NICs (Hong Kong, Singapore, South Korea, and Taiwan) 8.1% (versus 2.8% in 1970–1974). These nations accounted for 65.4% of exports in 1970–1974 and 66.7% in 1992 (US Department of Commerce, 1995, table 1255).

3. For a comprehensive historical perspective on these issues, see Teichova, Levy-Leboyer, and Nussbaum, eds., 1986, particularly the paper by Fieldhouse. Other major references include Casson, ed., 1983; Caves, 1982; Clegg, 1987; Dunning, 1992; Hymer, 1976; Rugman, ed., 1982; Taylor and Thrift, eds., 1986. Some of the classic contributions to this literature are collected in Casson, ed., 1990.

4. Key references include Boddewyn, 1988; Behrman and Grosse, 1990; Mahini, 1988; Poynter, 1985; Safarian, 1983.

5. The following are classic sources on the international activities of state-owned enterprises (SOEs): Anastassopoulos, Blanc, and Dussauge, 1987; Lewin, ed., 1981; Mazzolini, 1983; Walters and Monsen, 1979.

6. Important references include: Auster, ed., 1987; Badaracco, 1991; Fennema, 1982; Gerlach, in Carroll and Vogel, eds., 1987; Ghemawat, Porter, and Rawlinson, 1986; Harrigan, 1987; Kanter, 1989; Morris and Hergert, 1987; Ohmae, 1989; Porter and Fuller, 1986.

7. UNCTAD (using a variety of latest available years between 1978 and 1994 with various, most likely developing, countries missing) reports 34,353 parent corporations in the developed countries, 3788 in the developing economies, and 400 in Eastern Europe (1995b, table 1.2). It reports 93,311 foreign affiliates located in the developed countries, 101,139 in developing economies, and 55,000 in Eastern Europe.

8. In 1991, 48,247 foreign-controlled US corporations (50% or more foreign ownership or control) filed federal income tax returns; these enterprises accounted for about 10% of the assets and receipts of all corporations in the US (US Department of Commerce, 1995, table 893).

References

Anastassopoulos, Jean-Pierre, Georges Blanc, and Pierre Dussauge. 1987. *State-Owned Multinationals*. Chichester, England: Wiley.

Auster, Ellen R., ed. 1987. "International Corporate Linkages: Dynamic Forms in Changing Environments," *Columbia Journal of World Business*, vol. 22, no. 2 (Summer).

Badaracco, Joseph L. 1991. *The Knowledge Link: How Firms Compete Through Strategic Alliances*. Boston, MA: Harvard Business School Press.

Bartlett, Christopher A., and Sumantra Ghoshal. 1989. *Managing Across Borders: The Transnational Solution*. Boston, MA: Harvard Business School Press.

Behrman, Jack N., and Robert E. Grosse. 1990. *International Business and Governments*. Columbia, SC: University of South Carolina Press.

Boddewyn, Jean J. 1988. "Political Aspects of MNE Theory," *Journal of International Business Studies*, vol. 19, no. 3 (Fall), pp. 341–363.

Bower, Joseph, and Yves Doz. 1979. "Strategy Formulation: A Social and Political Process," in Dan E. Schendel and Charles W. Hofer, eds., *Strategic Management*. Boston, MA: Little, Brown, pp. 152–179.

Buckley, Peter J. 1990. "Problems and Developments in the Core Theory of International Business," *Journal of International Business Studies*, vol. 21, no. 4 (Winter), pp. 657–665.

Casson, Michael, ed. 1983. *The Growth of International Business*. London: George Allen & Unwin.

Casson, Michael, ed. 1990. *Multinational Corporations*. Brookfield, VT: Gower.

Caves, Richard E. 1982. *Multinational Enterprise and Economic Analysis*. Cambridge, England: Cambridge University Press.

Clegg, Jeremy. 1987. *Multinational Enterprise and World Competition*. London: Macmillan Press.

Committee for Economic Development (CED). 1981. *Transnational Corporations and Developing Countries*. New York: CED.

Cooper, Helene, and Bhushan Bahree. 1996. "Nations Agree to Drop Computer Tariffs," *Wall Street Journal*, December 13.

Dunning, John H., ed. 1974. *Economic Analysis and the Multinational Enterprise*. London: George Allen & Unwin.

Dunning, John H. 1979. "Explaining Changing Patterns of International Production: In Defence of the Eclectic Theory," *Oxford Bulletin of Economics and Statistics*, vol. 41, no. 4 (November), pp. 269–295.

Dunning, John H. 1991. "Governments—Markets—Firms: Towards a New Balance," *The CTC Reporter*, no. 31 (Spring), pp. 2–7.

Dunning, John H. 1992. *Multinational Enterprises and the Global Economy*. Reading, MA: Addison-Wesley.

The Economist. 1990. "A Rentier Economy in Reverse," September 22, pp. 63–64.

The Economist. 1993. "Multinationals, Back in Fashion," March 27, p. 5.

Fennema, M. 1982. *International Networks of Banks and Industry*. The Hague, The Netherlands: Martinus Nijhoff.

Fieldhouse, D.K. 1986. "The Multinational: A Critique of a Concept," in Teichova, Levy-Leboyer, and Nussbaum, eds., *Multinational Enterprise in Historical Perspective*. New York: Cambridge University Press, pp. 9–29.

Gerlach, Michael. 1987. "Business Alliances and the Strategy of the Japanese Firm," in Glenn Carroll and David Vogel, eds., *Organizational Approaches to Strategy*. Cambridge, MA: Ballinger, pp. 127–143.

Ghemawat, Pankaj, Michael E. Porter, and Richard A. Rawlinson. 1986. "Patterns of International Coalition Activity," in Porter, ed., *Competition in Global Industries*. Boston, MA: Harvard Business School Press, pp. 345–365.

Gupta, A.K., and V. Govindarajan. 1991. "Alternative Value-Chain Configurations for Foreign Subsidiaries," working paper, College of Business and Management, University of Maryland, College Park, MD.

Harrigan, Kathryn R. 1987. "Strategic Alliances: Their New Role in Global Competition," *Columbia Journal of World Business*, vol. 22, no. 2 (Summer), pp. 67–70.

Helleiner, G.K., and Real Lavergne. 1979. "Intra-Firm Trade and Industrial Exports to the United States," *Oxford Bulletin of Economics and Statistics*, vol. 41, no. 4 (November), pp. 297–311.

Hipple, F. Steb. 1990. "Multinational Companies and International Trade: The Impact of Intrafirm Shipments on U.S. Foreign Trade, 1977-1982," *Journal of International Business Studies*, vol. 21, no. 3 (Fall), pp. 495–504.

Hoogvelt, Ankie. 1987. *Multinational Enterprise: An Encyclopedic Dictionary of Concepts and Terms*. New York: Macmillan.

Hymer, Stephen E. 1976. *The International Operations of National Firms: A Study of Direct Investment*. Cambridge, MA: MIT Press.

Julius, DeAnne. 1990. *Global Companies and Public Policy: The Growing Challenge of Foreign Direct Investment*. New York: Council on Foreign Relations Press for The Royal Institute of International Affairs.

Kahn, Khushi M., ed. 1986. *Multinationals of the South: New Actors in the International Economy*. New York: St. Martin's Press.

Kanter, Rosabeth M. 1989. "Becoming PALs: Pooling, Allying, and Linking Across Companies," *The Academy of Management Executive*, vol. 3, no. 3 (August), pp. 183–193.

Knight, Robin, and Suzanne Possehl. 1996. "Calling Eliot Ness," *U.S. News and World Report*, August 12, pp. 38–39.

Lash, William H. 1996. *The Exaggerated Demise of the Nation State*. Center for the Study of American Business, Washington University, St. Louis, MO.

Lewin, Arie Y., ed. 1981. "Research on State-Owned Enterprises," *Management Science*, vol. 27, no. 11 (November), pp. 1324–1347.

Lewis, William. 1993. "The Secret to Competitiveness," *Wall Street Journal*, October 27.

Mahini, Amir. 1988. *Making Decisions in Multinational Corporations: Managing Relations with Sovereign Governments*. New York: Wiley.

Mazzolini, Renato. 1983. "The International Strategies of Government-Controlled Enterprises," in Robert Lamb, ed., *Advances in Strategic Management*, vol. 1, pp. 183–201. Greenwich, CT: JAI Press.

Morris, Deigan, and Michael Hergert. 1987. "Trends in International Collaborative Agreements," *Columbia Journal of World Business*, vol. 22, no. 2 (Summer), pp. 15–22.

Ohmae, Kenichi. 1985. *Triad Power: The Coming Shape of Global Competition*. New York: Free Press.

Ohmae, Kenichi. 1989. "The Global Logic of Strategic Alliances," *Harvard Business Review*, vol. 67, no. 2 (March-April), pp. 143–154.

Ohmae, Kenichi. 1990. *The Borderless World: Power and Strategy in an Interlinked Economy*. New York: Harper Business.

Organization for Economic Cooperation and Development (OECD). 1987. *Structure and Organization of Multinational Enterprises*. Paris: OECD.

Ostry, Sylvia, and Robert R. Nelson. 1995. *Techno-Nationalism and Techno-Globalism*. Washington, DC: Brookings Institution.

Panic, M. 1988. *National Management of the International Economy*. New York: St. Martin's Press.

Porter, Michael E., ed. 1986. *Competition in Global Industries*. Boston, MA: Harvard Business School Press.

Porter, Michael E. 1990. *The Competitive Advantage of Nations*. New York: Free Press.

Porter, Michael E., and Mark Fuller. 1986. "Coalitions in Global Strategy," in Porter, ed., *Competition in Global Industries*. Boston, MA: Harvard Business School Press, pp. 315–343.

Poynter, Thomas A. 1985. *Multinational Enterprises and Government Intervention*. New York: St. Martin's Press.

Reich, Robert B. 1991. *The Work of Nations*. New York: Knopf.

Rugman, A.M., ed. 1982. *New Theories of the Multinational Enterprise*. London: Croom Helm.

Safarian, A.E. 1983. *Governments and Multinationals: Policies in the Developed Countries*. Washington, DC: British-North American Committee.

Schelpe, Dirk. 1991. "A Statute for a European Company," *The CTC Reporter*, no. 31 (Spring), pp. 17–19.

Slomanson, W.R. 1989. *International Business Bibliography*. Buffalo, NY: William S. Hein.

Smith, Roy C., and Ingo Walter. 1991. *The First European Merger Boom Has Begun*. Center for the Study of American Business, Washington University, St. Louis, MO.

Steiner, G.A., and J.F. Steiner. 1985. *Business, Government and Society*. New York: McGraw-Hill, sixth edition.

Taylor, Michael, and Nigel Thrift, eds. 1986. *Multinationals and the Restructuring of the World Economy*. London: Croom Helm.

Teece, David. 1986. "Transactions Cost Economics and the Multinational Enterprise: An Assessment," *Journal of Economic Behavior and Organization*, vol. 7, no. 1 (March), pp. 21–46.

Teichova, Alice, Maurice Levy-Leboyer, and Helga Nussbaum, eds. 1986. *Multinational Enterprise in Historical Perspective*. New York: Cambridge University Press.

Truell, Peter, and Nicholas Bray. 1991. "Loss Estimates from BBCI Closure Rise and Are Said to Total at Least $5 Billion," *Wall Street Journal*, July 10.

UN Centre for Transnational Corporations (UNCTC). 1973. 1983. 1986. 1988. *Transnational Corporations in World Development: Trends and Prospects*. New York: UNCTC.

UN Centre for Transnational Corporations (UNCTC). 1990. "Non-Conventional TNCs," *The CTC Reporter*, no. 30 (Autumn), pp. 37–45.

UN Conference on Trade and Development (UNCTAD). 1995a. *Handbook of International Trade and Development Statistics*. New York: UN.

UN Conference on Trade and Development (UNCTAD). 1995b. *World Investment Report, 1995*. New York: UN.

US Department of Commerce. 1995. *Statistical Abstract of the United States, 1995*. Washington, DC: US Government Printing Office.

Walters, Kenneth D., and Joseph Monsen. 1979. "State-Owned Business Abroad: New Competitive Threat," *Harvard Business Review*, vol. 57, no. 2 (March-April), pp. 160–170.

Weidenbaum, Murray, and Mark Jensen. 1990. *Threats and Opportunities in the International Economy*. Center for the Study of American Business, Washington University, St. Louis, MO.

Williamson, Oliver E. 1975. *Markets and Hierarchies*. New York: Free Press.

Williamson, Oliver E. 1985. *The Economic Institutions of Capitalism: Firms, Markets, Relational Contracting*. New York: Free Press.

World Bank. 1996. *Global Economic Prospects and the Developing Countries*. Washington, DC: World Bank.

II INTERNATIONAL REGIMES: CASE STUDIES

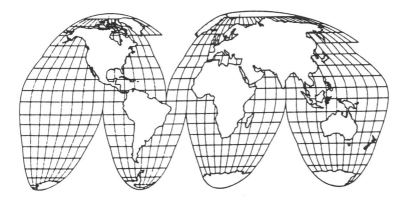

4

GLOBAL AND COMPREHENSIVE REGIMES: THE UN SYSTEM

The scope of multinational economic policy regimes must be defined in at least two different dimensions: 1) *geographic* or *political scope*, referring to spatial and/or other jurisdictional dimensions of the regime; and 2) *functional scope*, referring to the kinds of activities over which the regime is intended to have some influence. The geographic/political scope of the European Union (EU), for example, is limited to certain countries in Europe that have opted and been accepted for membership. The functional scope of most multinational regimes is also typically limited; they deal only with the specific set of concerns (e.g., trade, air travel, environmental issues) agreed upon among their participants. A regime that is (at least in principle) open to all participants that might have an interest in its activities, or that takes actions intended to affect all parts of the world, may be termed *global*. A regime that may (again, at least in principle) address any and all concerns that might arise among its participants, without regard to specific prior agreement as to the appropriateness of the inquiry, may be termed *comprehensive*. (National political regimes, i.e., governments, are functionally comprehensive within their individual borders.)

The United Nations is the only contemporary source of regime initiatives that, taken together, are both global and comprehensive. The UN is clearly *global*, since it involves nations and interests from all parts of the world, and it takes actions intended to have worldwide effects, even among nonmember countries and in international waters and extra-terrestrial space. It is also, at least in principle, *comprehensive* with respect to functional coverage. Its original charter and its broad concern with issues of peace and human welfare throughout the world permit the UN and its various agencies to direct attention to any aspect of international life that may be of interest to a significant number of its members. The so-called "General Debate" with which each UN General Assembly session opens is precisely that; speakers from various countries raise an incredible range of issues, none of which can be arbitrarily declared "off limits." (The only significant basis for declaring a topic "off limits" for UN consideration is the claim that it involves only the "internal affairs" of a member country, but even this distinction is often hotly debated.) Most individual UN initiatives are, of course, functionally limited, and a number of UN-related activities of narrower scope are discussed in subsequent chapters. This chapter stresses the overall scope, *global* and *comprehensive*, of the UN regime system and discusses some significant issues that have arisen within that setting which have general implications for regime development. The final section of the chapter examines some UN-based regime initiatives specifically concerned with the worldwide status and activities of business enterprises.

4.1 KEY ELEMENTS OF THE UN SYSTEM

The United Nations was formed in 1945 as an organization of governments devoted to world peace and to economic and social development. The structure and activities of the UN have been strongly influenced by prior experience with the League of Nations, which was created by the Treaty of Versailles (1919) and dissolved in 1946. Membership in the UN has expanded from the original fifty-one founding states to a 1994 level of 185. The central organ of the UN is the General Assembly, in which all participating states are represented. The Security Council, consisting of five permanent members with veto power (US, UK, China, France, and the Russian Federation, successor to the former USSR) plus ten rotating members elected by the General Assembly, has a limited range of func-tions, primarily involving international peace and security.

The UN inherited from the League of Nations, and subsequently created on its own, a group of agencies and organizations with diverse scopes and functions. Some of these, such as the Economic Commissions for various regions of the world and the UN Conference on Trade and Development (UNCTAD), are subunits of the UN itself; the UN Economic and Social Council (UNECOSOC), embraces many subsidiary units, including the UN Commission on Transnational Corporations (UNCTC). Others are affiliated organizations with somewhat independent status, such as the International Court of Justice (World Court), International Labour Organization (ILO), World Health Organization (WHO), Food and

Agriculture Organization (FAO), UN Children's Emergency Fund (UNICEF) and so forth. The broad range of UN concerns, both procedural and substantive, is evident from these titles alone.

4.1.1 The UN and International Business Activity

The conduct of business activity was not a major concern of the League of Nations, and there was little indication in 1945 that the UN would develop a major role in this area. However, as UN activities have expanded in both scale and scope, its potential impact on international business has inevitably increased. (For a broad overview of these developments as observed from within the UN structure, see Dell, 1990.) Like the broad scope of certain clauses of the US Constitution that have provided the basis for pervasive federal government policies and programs, the general framework of the UN creates a setting for consideration of any international issue that may be of concern to a substantial number of members. As Weidenbaum accurately, if rather critically, states: "Few areas of private business decision making escape the attention of one or another UN agency" (1985, p. 350).

The UN's expansion into business-related areas is welcomed by some and opposed by others. Weidenbaum, for example, notes a shift of emphasis from "a desire to improve business performance" to "redistribution of economic power, and especially of income and wealth"; he believes that the UN is becoming "an economic body involved in radically changing the performance and character of private economies throughout the world" (1985, pp. 349, 362). Others, however, stress the limited power and influence of the UN and other international organizations and believe that their impact is derived from "moral" rather than "legal" considerations (Frederick, 1991). Development of a broad multinational policy regime for international economic and business activity was conceived as the initial task of the proposed International Trade Organization (ITO), as described in the Havana Charter of 1948. This broad initiative was abandoned in 1950, but some of its elements have survived in the General Agreement on Tariffs and Trade (GATT) and its successor, the World Trade Organization (WTO) (see further discussion in chapter 6).

The broadest attempt to convert the UN into an agency of worldwide economic reorganization occurred during the mid 1970s when a Group of 77, the organized body of less developed countries (LDCs) sometimes termed the "proletariat ... within the world political system," demanded the establishment of a "New International Economic Order" (Luard, 1977, p. 4; see also Ghosh, ed., 1984; de Rivero, 1980). The NIEO proposal, formalized by UN resolution in 1974, was based on a perception by many Third World countries that neither they nor their predecessor constituencies had played significant roles in the establishment of the present system of international ownership, finance, and trade (including the framework of "international law" intended to govern this system) and that the resulting arrangements were therefore seriously biased against their interests. They proposed a wholesale overhaul of international economic arrangements, including much wider use of commodity agreements, increased aid from rich to poor countries, debt relief, and other measures which, taken together, came to be known as NIEO. These proposals produced considerable discussion but very little action and are no longer prominent on the international agenda. Indeed, the most important UN policy initiatives concerning business specifically assume the continuation of existing international economic arrangements and work toward modification of business and government behavior within the established framework. The NIEO proposal itself, however, suggests the potential *scope* of a truly global and comprehensive policy regime; and some of the issues raised in the NIEO discussions remain significant for the future. (Some analysts believe that the NIEO proposal also represented a frontal attack on the entire liberal international economic order that had grown up during the postwar decades; for a detailed analysis, including the impact of LDC demands on some of the most important international business and economic regimes, see Krasner, 1985.)

4.2 CRITICAL ISSUES IN REGIME EVOLUTION

Before turning to a discussion of some examples of important UN policy initiatives affecting international business, it is appropriate to examine some conceptual issues that have arisen in the context of UN debates. These issues, in various forms, arise in many other contexts and have pervasive implications for the evolution of multinational regimes of both broad and narrow scope and under various organizational auspices. (A useful compendium of views on these issues is Horn, ed., 1980; see also the valuable collection of papers assembled by Fatouros, ed., 1994.)

4.2.1 International vs. Supranational: The Power Issue

As noted above, both the general concept of the UN and some of its most important characteristics and functions can properly be regarded as vestiges of the League of Nations. In particular, the UN shares one of the League's critical characteristics: lack of sufficient power, either military or economic, to compel compliance with its decisions. The UN and its various constituent and affiliated agencies are thus *international* organizations but not *supranational* organizations. (By contrast, the European Union is, in principle, a *supranational* organization, with authority to override national policy decisions, at least to a limited extent.) Lacking the power to compel compliance with its authority, the

UN, like the League before it, cannot be described as a "government." However, as Luard emphasizes, compulsion actually plays a limited role in government, even at the national level:

> The citizen in a national state does not obey his government mainly because he is afraid of the buffets of the policeman's truncheon or the threat of imprisonment. He obeys because he is usually aware, if only unconsciously, that the effective functioning of his society would be impossible without some co-operation among its citizens; because he wishes, through such co-operation, to enjoy its benefits; above all because he is *conditioned* to conform with those behavior patterns widely expected within his community (Luard, 1977, p. 1).

Compliance with authority is inevitably a product of complex forces, but the "power" issue may be least significant with respect to the UN's influence on economic and business activities. The most effective power that any international business and economic regime possesses derives from an ability to exclude nonconformists from the regime's activities and benefits. And, since acceptance by actors in other jurisdictions is a critical necessity for most international business operations, the ability to deny access is uniquely important in this area. Moreover, as Kratochwil emphasizes, since every possible eventuality cannot be covered by law or contract, "markets are probably *the* social institution ... most dependent on normative underpinnings" (1989, p. 47).

4.2.2 Temporal Orientation: Ex Post vs. Ex Ante

Two of the League's surviving entities, the World Court and the International Labour Organization (ILO), both of which reflect broadly shared goals and concerns among diverse constituencies, constitute foundation elements of the UN system. Neither of these institutions forms the core of a distinct policy regime, but the characteristics of these two institutions, including the differences between them, reflect many of the current features and controversies about international policy development. There is, for example, an important difference between 1) dealing with problems on an *ex post* basis, attempting to redress grievances and rectify objectionable situations after they arise, as opposed to 2) anticipating problems and developing guidelines and standards on an *ex ante* basis (in advance).

The World Court, located at The Hague, The Netherlands, was founded as the Permanent Court of World Justice in 1921 and reestablished under UN auspices in 1946 as the International Court of Justice. By the nature of its mandate, the World Court takes an *ex post* approach to policy problems. Problematic situations arise and are subsequently brought be-

fore the Court for resolution. In this instance, formal complaints are
brought by national governments, either on their own or on behalf of
some of their constituents. All but the most basic principles governing
the Court's activities are determined by the accumulation of precedents
in individual case decisions.

The ILO was founded as an autonomous agency of the League in 1919
and converted to a UN agency in 1946; its 150 member countries are
represented in an annual conference by teams of government, labor, and
employer delegates (ILO, 1986). ILO operations illustrate an *ex ante*
approach to policy-making. Its principal policy actions take the form of
conventions and *recommendations* that become operational only when,
and to the extent that, they are subsequently ratified by individual
member countries. The ILO develops standards and principles which
become multinational through a process of nation-by-nation ratification.
In effect, the ILO and similar organizations aim to establish norms and
standards governing broad sets of activities that will take place in the
future; past experience is relevant for diagnosis of problems and design of
responses, but the basic orientation is anticipatory and aimed at problem
avoidance rather than at subsequent corrective action.

The choice of one or the other of these alternative approaches to policy
formation is a major step in the evolution of all policy regimes. Regimes
taking an *ex post* approach tend to focus on the development of
reporting systems and procedures for dispute resolution; those
emphasizing an *ex ante* approach tend to stress the development of
substantive rules and formal guidelines. Although these two types of
activities necessarily overlap and interact in actual practice, the two
fundamental orientations are quite different. (This distinction between *ex
post* and *ex ante* regulation, with specific reference to multinational
enterprises, is particularly stressed by Tharp, 1976.)

4.2.3 International Law vs. Obligations

A major issue underlying both the past and future development of
international policy regimes has been identified in the UN debates as a
conflict between the concepts of *international law* and *international
obligations*. (This issue is comprehensively developed in Robinson,
1986, and Vagts, 1986; see also Dell, 1990, pp. 87–90.) In the context
of this debate, *international law* refers not only to formal agreements
and treaties among nations which take on the authority of law within
their respective borders but also to customary doctrines that have
evolved over past decades (largely at the initiative of the advanced
industrial countries) with respect to the responsibilities of nation-states
for the persons and property of aliens, including the local subsidiaries of
foreign-owned multinational enterprises (MNEs). Oversimplifying some-

what, the "international law" perspective holds that alien entities are entitled to all of the rights/protections of domestic entities and, moreover, are protected by an "international" standard, which may be more demanding. According to this view, for example, although the confiscation of domestically-owned property without compensation is entirely an internal matter, foreign owners of confiscated property are entitled to restitution or compensation according to "customary international procedures." Thus, such persons should have legitimate recourse, through their governments, to international tribunals and negotiations (all avenues unavailable to domestic parties in comparable circumstances) in order to obtain satisfaction. The existence and activities of the World Court embody the concept that relations among countries and their nationals are regulated by "international law" in this procedural sense.

The contrasting concept, identified as *international obligations* by some parties to this debate, holds that only obligations specifically accepted by a national government can be legitimately enforced upon it. The notion that foreign interests are somehow protected by a "higher" international standard is specifically rejected; indeed, it is argued that the whole concept of "customary" standards and practices is largely illusory. One version of this idea is the "Calvo Doctrine," named for Argentine lawyer and diplomat Carlos Calvo (1824-1906), which holds that each sovereign state is entitled to freedom from outside economic interference, whether by diplomacy or force; that foreign interests are entitled to the same, but no better, treatment as domestic ones; and that dispute redress can be obtained only within national courts (cf. Sauvant and Aranda, 1994, p. 85 and n. 8). Some variant of this position is typically put forward by most socialist states as well as by many LDCs and is reflected in many UN documents and statements. Both the emergence of new states and the evolution of new concepts of sovereignty within preexisting ones has favored the idea that prior arrangements, particularly control by foreigners over natural resources, may be altered without any recourse to "customary" principles, whatever they might be, toward which current governments feel little commitment or sympathy (cf. Dell, 1990, chapter 2 and passim).

4.2.4 Binding vs. Voluntary Standards

A closely related issue at the heart of international policy development is whether agreements and understandings reached through multilateral negotiations are or should be legally binding on the parties (as they would if they were considered elements of *international law*) or whether they are merely statements of intention which become binding only upon those individual jurisdictions that specifically ratify and attempt to enforce them. The latter is clearly the case, for example, with respect to

ILO conventions and recommendations.

The tension between binding and voluntary standards is clearly illustrated by Organization for Economic Cooperation and Development (OECD) policy initiatives with respect to foreign direct investment (FDI). In the early 1960s, OECD members agreed to a "Code of Liberalization of Capital Movements" specifically intended to encourage FDI, both among the members and between member and nonmember countries. In the mid 1970s, this policy base was expanded with a formal "Declaration on International Investment and Multinational Enterprises," which included explicit endorsement of "national treatment" (directed at governments) and a set of voluntary "Guidelines for Multinational Enterprises," together with recommendations on dispute resolution and investment incentives and disincentives. The principal purpose of these instruments was to discourage developing countries from placing restrictions on OECD-based MNEs operating within their jurisdictions. The recommendations themselves were primarily addressed to MNEs and non-member governments and hence were necessarily voluntary (Horn, ed., 1980). However, by 1995 conclusion of the Uruguay Round of GATT negotiations and a substantial increase in the number and importance of bilateral investment agreements had substantially changed the international investment environment, and OECD policy-makers perceived the need for "a comprehensive framework of *binding* investment rules. ... Such a Multilateral Agreement on Investment (MAI) would set standards for equal competitive opportunities and provide stable and consistent treatment of FDI across all sectors" (Witherell, 1995, p. 5, emphasis added). The current proposal is for an MAI that would stand as an independent multilateral treaty, open to signature by both OECD and non-OECD countries, and binding among all signatories.

As this experience indicates, in spite of some evidence that voluntary approaches are not without effect, pressures for development of binding agreements remain strong. Labor representatives strongly urged that the initial OECD "Guidelines for Multinational Enterprises" be presented in binding form, and the OECD Business and Industry Advisory Committee (BIAC) has recently supported binding agreements as a contribution to investor confidence.

Other experience, such as the international infant formula controversy (discussed below), suggests that voluntary standards and guidelines also have some validity. It is certainly true that voluntary and recommendatory codes and arrangements are much easier to develop, and tend to gain acceptance much more readily, than mandatory regulations. The UN Commission on International Trade Law (UNCITRAL)'s proposed Model Law on International Commercial Arbitration presents a broad scheme for an international regime based on voluntary and largely procedural, rather than binding and primarily substantive, norms and standards (Fleischhauer, 1986). In any event, the ultimate impact of any policy guidelines depends upon their acceptability among the parties involved and their eventual integration into the routine norms and behaviors of enterprises and governments.

4.2.5 National Treatment

The issue of *national treatment* has become a central substantive concern in the UN, OECD, ILO, and elsewhere. The national treatment principle requires that individual countries make no policy distinctions between domestically owned firms and the subsidiaries of foreign MNEs operating within their borders. The complex network of international ownership and control that has evolved during the post–World War II decades creates significant difficulties for determining the "nationality" of particular enterprises. When more and more operating units are owned through increasingly complex and frequently changing networks of international finance and investment, the task of distinguishing between domestic and foreign entities becomes insuperable, and national treatment becomes the only practical policy.

In spite of these realities, both nations and enterprises display mixed motivations with respect to the national treatment issue. Governments may well wish to offer selective incentives (loans or tax relief) either to domestic enterprises, to encourage their competitiveness, or to foreign subsidiaries, in order to attract them for purposes of economic development. They may also wish to place significant burdens (domestic content or export requirements) on foreign MNE subsidiaries in order to assure that specific development objectives are accomplished. And MNE subsidiaries may seek domestic status (i.e., national treatment) with respect to national subsidy or procurement programs, access to state-controlled resources, etc., and at the same time seek "guest" privileges with respect to disclosure of information or other responsibilities. At the present time, most governments and enterprises give lip service to the national treatment principle, but the exceptions in practice are very numerous.

4.3. UN REGIME INITIATIVES RELATING TO BUSINESS

The broad scope of its concerns and the diverse agencies through which the UN operates naturally leads to its involvement in numerous and varied international regimes, as reference to UN activities in the following chapters will illustrate. In this section we examine a group of business-related UN initiatives that are significant examples of the UN's global and comprehensive orientation but that are not related to other major functional regimes (see figure 4-1). One group of developments is center-

	I. Consumer Protection Initiatives		I. Business Practices		III. Code of Conduct on Transnational Corporations
	A. General Guidelines	*B. Infant Formula Code*	*A. Restrictive Business Practices Code*	*B. Convention on International Sale of Goods*	*Broad statement of guidelines for both MNEs and governments*
Description					
Purpose and Scope	Identify broad goals for consumer protection throughout the world, including product quality and safety; promotion and distribution; redress of consumer grievances; specific attention to water, food, and pharmaceutical products.	Intended to reduce abuses in marketing infant food products in LDCs; specific attention to communications and advertising.	Identifies a list of specific business practices considered unacceptable in international competition; based on US antitrust tradition; applies to state-owned as well as private enterprises.	Intended to standardize terms used in international contracts and transactions and to provide a basis for negotiation and settlement of disputes.	Intended to reduce ability of MNEs to take advantage of differences in national standards and practices, also to reduce discrepancies among national policies and protect MNEs from national discrimination; heavy emphasis on cooperation and disclosure of information.

Organizational Form	Stated as "principles" for implementation by individual governments.	Recommendatory guidelines for adoption and implementation by individual states.	Adopted as a *binding* agreement among participants; can be enforced through national courts or World Court.	Guidelines for adoption/ implementation by individual states, and for reference in settlement of international disputes.	Addressed as guidelines to both MNEs and governments.
Status	Adopted by General Assembly in 1985.	Adopted by World Health Assembly in 1981; fewer than 50 countries have formally adopted or implemented.	Adopted by General Assembly in 1982.	Adopted by General Assembly in 1980.	Under development since 1974; still awaiting General Assembly action in 1996.

Figure 4-1. UN Regime Initiatives for International Business. UN-related functional regimes are listed and discussed in other chapters.

ed around consumer protection issues, including specific concern with problems arising in the international marketing of infant food products. A second focus has involved business practices, particularly emphasizing restrictive arrangements, but including a variety of other matters as well. Consideration of these specific topics has also become intertwined with very general concerns with the impact of multinational enterprises (MNEs) on both national and international economic and political activity. Varied approaches to the regulation of MNE activity, and the draft UN Code of Conduct on Transnational Corporations, are reviewed in the last section of the chapter.

4.3.1 Consumer Protection

UN concerns about consumer protection arise from the perception of some member countries that collective arrangements for the regulation of certain problematic MNE activities may be required to reinforce, and perhaps also to standardize, individual national policies. This approach is illustrated by the WHO infant formula code, discussed in the first subsection below. That experience led UNECOSOC to prepare a more general set of guidelines for consumer protection, discussed in the second subsection.

4.3.1.1 Infant Formula

The story of the infant formula controversy is well documented and familiar. (Sethi, 1994, presents the most recent and comprehensive analysis.) It is usually and accurately presented as an extreme example of the clash between First World consumption patterns and marketing practices and Third World poverty and ignorance. It is also, however, a striking example of the evolution of an international policy regime. Environmental, institutional, and behavioral factors were combined, *first*, to create a situation that appeared to require international policy attention and *then* to produce an interactive response from both governments and private enterprises.

A brief summary of the situation is as follows. Powdered food/chemical products which, when mixed with water, could be used as a breast-milk substitute for infant feeding began to be produced and marketed in the US and Europe in the mid nineteenth century. Over the years, the product became a widely used supplement, and in many cases the food of choice, in infant nutrition throughout the world. In the post–World War II era, infant formula use expanded rapidly among the middle- and upper-income classes in many LDCs. Intensive marketing efforts by major international formula producers accompanied and increased this growth in demand. By the mid 1960s, health workers in various countries came to believe that mothers unable to afford sufficient supplies of formula, and lacking the clean water, sterilization, and refrigeration facilities necessary for its proper use, were using formula products in ways that harmed rather than helped their children. Indeed, misuse of infant formula was thought to be responsible for some infant deaths. Aggressive marketing by international producers (and specifically by Nestle, the largest international producer and marketer) was believed to be an important contributing factor in this process.

Extensive publicity about this situation, and extensive controversy concerning its extent and causes, developed throughout the 1970s. The issue was addressed more than once by the World Health Assembly, and at length, in October 1979, WHO and UNICEF jointly sponsored an International Meeting on Infant and Young Child Feeding to address a broad set of issues relating to infant nutrition in the Third World, with infant formula marketing and use as the central concern. Participants in this gathering reached a limited consensus on a number of issues, including the idea that an international code of marketing practices supported by both importing and exporting countries should be developed. A WHO/UNICEF drafting group was constituted for this purpose; an industry coalition also prepared a draft code for consideration by this group.

Apart from the specific content of the code, a principal issue facing the drafting group was whether the code would be proposed as a WHO *regulation*, directly binding upon all member states (unless a government gives formal notice to the contrary), or as a WHO *recommendation* for modification and adoption by the member countries in the light of their own specific circumstances. Eventually the latter alternative was chosen, and the WHO International Code of Marketing of Breast-Milk Substitutes was adopted by a vote of 118 countries in favor, three abstaining, and one (US) opposed, in May 1981 (WHO, 1981).

Implementation of the code clearly depended upon vigorous activity at the national level, particularly among importing countries, and also upon voluntary compliance by enterprises. Over the following decade, fewer than 50 countries have taken steps toward implementation, and not all of these have been completed. However, Nestle S.A. (Switzerland), the leading infant formula marketing company in the world and the principal target of international criticism, formally adopted the code as company policy and, in a significant innovation, appointed an independent Audit Committee of distinguished experts to monitor its own record of code compliance. (The Audit Committee disbanded in 1991.)

Experience with the infant formula controversy reflects many of the characteristics and problems associated with broad international policy initiatives. One is the difficulty of specifying exactly what the scope and content of the desired regime is to be. The WHO Code covers not only powdered formula mixtures but also other "milk products, foods and beverages" that might be marketed as breast-milk substitutes, and related feeding equipment (bottles). It contains specific provisions governing advertising, consumer contact, sampling, and other marketing and communications practices. In spite of (and perhaps, in part, because of) these details, the precise implications of the code remain subject to interpretation and controversy. A second problem is the issue of adoption and enforcement, whether in various jurisdictions (as intended in this case) or through an international mechanism.

A third aspect of particular significance is the role of the WHO Code as a precedent for UN or other international regime development. Concern with consumer welfare was not part of the League of Nations tradition, and expansion of the UN into this area (primarily through the activities of WHO, FAO, and UNICEF) has been surrounded by controversy. A principal reason for criticism of many of the initial infant formula proposals, and ultimate opposition to the code by some countries and enterprises, was the fear that this model (although perhaps appropriate on its own merits) might provide the basis for new initiatives in other areas: alcohol, pesticides, pharmaceuticals, tobacco, etc.

4.3.1.2 General Consumer Guidelines

In July 1981, almost simultaneously with the adoption of the Infant Formula Code, UNECOSOC initiated consultations on the preparation of a general set of guidelines for consumer protection. This process eventually produced a draft document that was unanimously adopted by the General Assembly in April 1985. The guidelines deal with a number of topics: product safety and quality, promotion, distribution, education and information, and redress of grievances. They also deal with a few specific types of products: food, water, and pharmaceuticals. The food section endorses worldwide use of FAO standards and the WHO Codex Alimentarius. The guidelines are presented as "principles" to be considered and implemented by individual governments within the context of their own economic and social circumstances; they also strongly recommend international exchange of information, consultation, and cooperation on consumer issues (Harland, 1987; Merciai, 1986).

During this same period, the WHO explored the possibilities for developing a worldwide code for the marketing and use of drugs, particularly in LDCs. This activity, initiated in 1978, culminated in the Nairobi Conference on the Rational Use of Drugs in 1985, which involved representatives of governments, the pharmaceutical industry, and medical-consumer organizations. According to the summary report of this conference, participants reached broad consensus on the responsibilities of both governments and the industry. It was also agreed that implementation would rest with individual governments, and with enterprises and user groups. Thus, these deliberations established a framework for a "voluntary" regime, with heavy reliance on compatible behavior among participants (WHO, 1987 and 1988).

4.3.2 Business Practices

Unlike the League of Nations, the UN has at least since the mid 1960s maintained an active interest in the business practices of MNEs (Dell, 1990; Fisher and Turner, 1983; Keohane and Ooms, 1975; Sanders, 1982). As in the case of consumer protection, the UN member countries apparently believe that collective arrangements will be more effective than uncoordinated national action. Reflections of this belief include the UNCTAD Restrictive Business Practices Code and the UN Convention on Contracts for the International Sale of Goods, along with some other initiatives that are discussed briefly below.

4.3.2.1 Restrictive Business Practices

Both the WHO infant formula code and the broader UN Consumer Protection Guidelines reflect, among other things, a concern that aggressive competition among enterprises might lead to undesirable results. The possibility that the absence of competition due to monopolization, cartelization, and other forms of market control might yield undesirable outcomes, not only for consumers but also for the modernization and growth of less developed areas, has also been a concern of the UN from its beginnings. The special concern of LDCs with this issue was reflected in the initial establishment of UNCTAD (1964), which eventually produced a set of principles dealing with restrictive business practices (referred to here as the "RBP Code") for General Assembly adoption in 1980.

The content of the RBP Code reflects primarily the US antitrust tradition and is aimed at situations involving "acquisition and abuse of a dominant position of market power" on the part of enterprises, whether domestic or multinational. Notably, the US is the only nation whose national procompetition policies are specifically applicable to foreign as well as domestic commerce. The "global" and "comprehensive" character of the RBP Code is specifically stated in the text: "[The Code] shall be universally applicable to all countries and enterprises regardless of the parties involved in the transactions, acts or behavior" (Section B, (i), 4). Inclusion of state-owned enterprises (SOEs) within the scope of the RBP Code was explicitly accepted by the former USSR and its satellites before more recent reform trends appeared. Intergovernmental agreements, however, are excepted from the code; and the status of subsidiary units within MNEs, although much discussed during code negotiations, is not specifically addressed. LDC negotiators argued that intra-MNE arrangements should be specifically identified as possible sources of code violations, while MNE representatives argued that they should be specifically exempt; in the end, the matter was left open for case-by-case consideration. The RBP Code is "voluntary"; it contains no provision for sanctions and lacks formal status as an element of "international law." It does, however, present a set of norms mutually agreed upon among many nations with diverse domestic economic systems. These code provisions, therefore, constitute standards for internationally consistent domestic legislation, which may be particularly useful to the developing countries. (For an appraisal of the RBP Code, see Dell, 1990, chapter 2.)

4.3.2.2 International Sale of Goods

During the same time period that the RBP Code was under consideration, a separate UN initiative resulted in development of a comprehensive set of regulations and norms governing the international sale of goods (*UN Conference on Contracts*, 1981). The resulting *convention*, eventually adopted by the General Assembly in 1982, includes a standard set of definitions of terms describing sales contracts and conditions, including provisions for remedies and damages, applicable to both buyers and sellers engaged in international trade. The significant point about this *convention* is not its contents, which are fairly standard among active trading countries, but the fact that it was adopted as a *binding* agreement among the participating parties, which included the USSR and its satellites as well as most LDCs. This status means that its provisions can be enforced in national courts or, if necessary, through the World Court.

4.3.2.3 Other Concerns

Many other aspects of international business activity have attracted attention within UN debates and agencies. The most notable of these is probably the international transfer of technology. One of the most obvious advantages of advanced countries is their accumulated technological base; also, advanced countries are much more active in generating new technology, particularly through government sponsorship of research and development. LDCs are naturally eager to obtain access to both base technologies and new developments, but they are not equally willing to accept and enforce concepts of property rights in technology (e.g., patent protection). Even among advanced countries, there are wide variations in standards and provisions for the provision of intellectual property. Efforts to develop a UN code for technology transfer originated within UNCTAD during the 1970s and continued for some years, but no final resolution of the conflicting objectives and implementation techniques has been achieved. Transactions involving intellectual property rights have also been considered in recent GATT discussions.

Other UN concerns with business practices include accounting standards, reflected in the establishment of the Working Group of Experts on International Standards of Accounting and Reporting in 1982; illicit payments and other inappropriate interactions among businesses, governments, and other political interests; and the responsibility of MNEs for disclosure of information, both to national governments and to international authorities. These concerns are reflected in various ways in the more general draft UNCTC Code of Conduct on Transnational Corporations, discussed below.

4.3.3 Regulating Multinational Enterprises

The growth of multinational enterprises has stimulated policy initiatives, both national and international, specifically focused on this type of enterprise. The size, growth, prominence, and apparent flexibility of MNEs have inevitably given rise to concern by governments, both home and host. Moreover, the MNEs themselves, both individually and collectively, have been active participants in the policy arena, since many of their activities require authorization or cooperation from governments.

Two distinct views of the relative strength of MNEs vis-à-vis national and international policies and institutions are found in the contemporary literature. One view, succinctly captured in the title of Vernon's classic study *Sovereignty at Bay* (1971) and reflected in many other well-known publications (e.g., Barnet and Muller, *Global Reach*, 1974), holds that large MNEs are more powerful than the governments of the various jurisdictions within which they operate. By playing one interest against another and by optimizing their operations in relation to national and international policies as well as in relation to resources, costs, and markets, they may select and control their environments in their own interest. The opposite view, associated with Wallace (1982, 1990) and Weidenbaum and Jensen (1990) and dramatized by reference to such celebrated international business incidents as the Dresser Industries case (Sethi, 1982) and Barcelona Traction (Wallace, 1982, pp. 281–292), holds that MNEs are victims rather than masters of national and international policies, and are more likely to suffer than benefit from differences in national policies and objectives. In addition, the growth of state-owned and state-sponsored/protected MNEs from both Third World and postcommunist countries in recent years adds to the ranks of enterprises which are more controlled by, rather than in control of, their own policy environments.

4.3.3.1 International Regimes for MNEs

National governments in both home and host country roles have responded to MNE growth and activity with a wide variety of policy initiatives (Safarian, 1993), but it is not surprising that a number of attempts have been made to establish a broader multinational framework of norms and understandings about the activities and responsibilities of MNEs. Wallace emphasizes that national and international policy developments are not mutually exclusive; instead, both elements are involved in the actual process of "international control," which "is not necessarily synonymous with a single international regulatory system or agency ..." (1982, p. 23). None of the proposals for comprehensive international surveillance or control of MNEs has achieved the status of a formal regime; and in fact the UN Code of Conduct on Transnational Corporations, the most comprehensive of these efforts, has never been formally adopted by its intended sponsors. (An historical overview of these developments is presented by Sauvant and Aranda, 1994.)

4.3.3.2 International Chamber of Commerce

It is of some significance that the first attempt to set forth a group of international policy standards specifically focused on MNEs arose from the business community rather than from governments. In the late 1940s, the International Chamber of Commerce (ICC), an organization composed of large, privately-owned MNEs, issued an "International Code of Fair Treatment for Foreign Investments," a document addressed entirely to the practices of host governments. Proposals for a parallel set of principles addressed to investing enterprises (i.e., MNEs) were discussed off and on thereafter and eventually, in 1972, the "ICC Guidelines for International Investment" were adopted, with recommendations directed toward both foreign investors (i.e., enterprises operating outside their home jurisdictions) and home and host governments. The ICC has over the years issued several sets of guidelines on specific topics: marketing practices, environmental protection, bribery, etc. A distinctive feature of all of this ICC activity is its emphasis on parallel and mutually reinforcing policies and practices on the part of both enterprises and governments. All of the recommendations, of course, involve only "voluntary" actions by all parties.

4.3.3.3 The UN Code of Conduct on Transnational Corporations

Worldwide interest in the implications of the growth of MNEs for domestic economies, and particularly for developing economies, increased continuously throughout the postwar decades. By the mid 1970s, both the OECD (as discussed above) and the ILO (*Tripartite Declaration of Principles Concerning Multinational Enterprises and*

Social Policy, 1977) had attempted to develop broad policy guidelines in this area. In 1972, the UN General Assembly focused attention on this issue in response to a formal protest by the Chilean representative to the alleged interference of ITT, a US-based MNE, in Chile's internal political affairs. The resulting UN resolution initiating general concern with MNE operations (UNESCO Resolution 1721) was therefore cast in a critical tone. The idea (apparently originating within the UN Staff) that the UN's response to these concerns would take the form of a "Code of Conduct" was adopted in 1974. (The entire code development experience is reviewed in Kline, 1985; see also Minta, 1988, and Asante, 1994.)

The UN Code was initially intended to harmonize the activities of MNEs (and, through them, those of advanced country governments) with Third World demands for the "New International Economic Order" (NIEO), previously discussed. Over the intervening years, however, the environment in which the Code was evolving changed in three important ways:

1. Increasing two-way investment and trade among both advanced industry countries (AICs) and newly industrialized countries (NICs), so that home and host perspectives are equally relevant to nearly all major international econmic participants.
2. Increasing numbers and diversity of active MNEs; the UNCTC "Billion Dollar Club" (enterprises with sales of $1 billion or more) now contains 600 members, with increasing numbers originating in NICs and LDCs.
3. Increasing ability of LDCs to strengthen desired impacts and reduce undesired impacts from foreign investment, along with increasing understanding of the benefits of foreign trade and investment, and hence of MNE activity, in the development process.

These changed circumstances, along with global experience with MNEs during the 1980s, have resulted in a negotiated draft document that details responsibilities and standards for both governments and enterprises and in terms that few appear to find offensive. Disclosure of information, an essential element of any enforcement activity as well as an end in itself, remains a central focus. Special topics include: ownership and control, employment and industrial relations, balance of payments and financing, transfer pricing, taxation, competition, technology transfer, consumer protection, and environmental protection. A key objective of the code, building on OECD and ILO experience, is to achieve "transparency" in the affairs of both governments and enterprises; that is, actual policies and practices should be made clear, and exceptions should be overtly identified and subject to challenge. The draft code is now conceived as a purely recommendatory document, requiring implementation by national governments and intergovernmental agreements.

(The current draft version of the Code appears in UNCTC, *The New Code Environment*, Series A, no. 16, April 1990.)

4.4 CONCLUSION

The UN has played a critical role in the evolution of international policy regimes over the postwar decades but not primarily by establishing new regulatory institutions under its own auspices. Instead, the UN has served as a forum for the identification of major international concerns, both substantive and procedural, and has provided a base for functionally specific agencies that have, in turn, become major elements of more narrowly focused regimes. The broad business-related regimes that have come from the UN itself, particularly the Restrictive Business Practices Code and the draft Code of Conduct on Transnational Enterprises, establish standards for implementation by individual governments and enterprise, but do not constitute elements of international law or formal regimes in their own right.

References

Asante, S.K.B. 1994. "The Concept of the Good Corporate Citizen in International Business," *Transnational Corporations: The International Legal Framework*, vol. 20, pp. 169–211.

Barnet, Richard J., and Ronald E. Muller. 1974. *Global Reach: The Power of the Multinational Corporations*. New York: Simon and Schuster.

Dell, Sidney. 1990. *The United Nations and International Business*. Durham, NC: Duke University Press.

de Rivero, Oswaldo. 1980. *New Economic Order and International Development Law*. New York: Pergamon Press.

Fatouros, Arghyrios A., ed. 1994. *Transnational Corporations: The International Legal Framework*. New York: Routledge.

Fisher, Bart S., and Jeff Turner. 1983. *Regulating the Multinational Enterprise: National and International Challenges*. New York: Praeger.

Fleischhauer, C.-A. 1986. "UNCITRAL Model Law on International Commercial Arbitration," *The Arbitration Journal*, vol. 41, no. 1, pp. 17–22.

Frederick, William C. 1991. "The Moral Authority of Transnational Corporate Codes," *Journal of Business Ethics*, vol. 10, no. 2 (February), pp. 165–177.

Ghosh, Pradip K., ed. 1984. *The New International Economic Order: A Third World Perspective*. Westport, CT: Greenwood Press.

Harland, David. 1987. "The United Nations Guidelines for Consumer Protection," *Journal of Consumer Policy*, vol. 10, no. 2, pp. 245–266. See also comments by Weidenbaum, pp. 425–432, and Peterson, pp. 433–439, vol. 10, no. 3, 1987; and subsequent response by Harland, vol. 11, no. 1, 1988, pp. 111–115.

Horn, Norbert, ed. 1980. *Legal Problems of Codes of Conduct for Multinational Enterprises*. Deventer, The Netherlands: Kluwer Academic Publishers.

International Labour Organization (ILO). 1977. *Tripartite Declaration of Principles Concerning Multinational Enterprises and Social Policy*. Geneva: ILO.

International Labour Organization (ILO). 1986. *Facts for Americans*. Washington, DC: ILO.

Keohane, Robert O., and Van Doorn Ooms. 1975. "The Multinational Firm and International Regulation," *International Organization*, vol. 29, no. 2 (Winter), pp. 169–209.

Kline, John M. 1985. *International Codes and Multinational Business*. Westport, CT: Quorum.

Krasner, Stephen D. 1985. *Structural Conflict: The Third World Against Global Liberalism*. Berkeley and Los Angeles, CA: University of California Press.

Kratochwil, Friedrich V. 1989. *Rules, Norms and Decisions: On the Conditions of Practical and Legal Reasoning in International Relations and Domestic Affairs*. Cambridge, England: Cambridge University Press.

Luard, Evan. 1977. *International Agencies: The Emerging Framework of Interdependence*. Dobbs Ferry, NY: Oceana Publications.

Merciai, Patrizio. 1986. "Consumer Protection and the United Nations," *Journal of World Trade Law*, vol. 20, no. 2, pp. 206–231.

Minta, I.K. 1988. "The Code of Conduct on TNCs: In the Twilight Zone of International Law," *The CTC Reporter*, no. 25 (Spring), pp. 29–33, 37.

Robinson, Patrick. 1986. *The Question of a Reference to International Law in the United Nations Code of Conduct on Transnational Corporations*. UNCTC Current Studies, Series A, no. 1. New York: UN Centre on Transnational Corporations.

Safarian, A.E. 1993. *Multinational Enterprise and Public Policy*. Aldershot, England: Edward Elgar.

Sanders, Pieter. 1982. "Implementing International Codes of Conduct for Multinational Enterprises," *The American Journal of Comparative Law*, vol. 30, no. 2, pp. 241–254.

Sauvant, K.P., and V. Aranda. 1994. "The International Legal Framework for Transnational Corporations," *Transnational Corporations: The International Legal Framework*, vol. 20, pp. 83–115.

Sethi, S. Prakash. 1982. "Dresser Industries, Inc.," in *Up Against the Corporate Wall: Modern Corporations and Social Issues of the Eighties*. Englewood Cliffs, NJ: Prentice-Hall, pp. 3-28.

Sethi, S. Prakash. 1994. *Multinational Corporations and the Impact of Public Advocacy on Corporate Strategy: Nestle and the Infant Formula Controversy*. Dordrecht, The Netherlands: Kluwer Academic Publishers.

Tharp, Paul A., Jr. 1976. "Transnational Enterprises and International Regulation: A Survey of Various Approaches to International Organizations," *International Organization*, vol. 30, no. 1 (Winter), pp. 47–73.

United Nations Conference on Contracts for the International Sale of Goods. 1981. New York: UN.

Vagts, Detlev. 1986. *The Question of a Reference to International Obligations in the United Nations Code of Conduct on Transnational Corporations: A Different View*. UNCTC Current Studies, Series A, no. 2. New York: UN Centre on Transnational Corporations.

Vernon, Raymond. 1971. *Sovereignty at Bay: The Multinational Spread of U.S. Enterprises*. New York: Basic Books.

Wallace, Cynthia Day. 1982. *Legal Control of the Multinational Enterprise*. The Hague, The Netherlands: Martinus Nijhoff.

Wallace, Cynthia Day, ed. 1990. *Foreign Direct Investment in the 1990s*. Dordrecht, The Netherlands: Martinus Nijhoff.

Weidenbaum, Murray L. 1985. "The UN as a Regulator of Private Enterprise," *Notre Dame Journal of Law, Ethics and Public Policy*, vol. 1, no. 3, pp. 349–365.

Weidenbaum, Murray, and Mark Jensen. 1990. *Threats and Opportunities in the International Economy*. Center for the Study of American Business, Washington University, St. Louis, MO.

Witherell, William H. 1995. "The OECD Multilateral Agreement on Investment," *Transnational Corporations*, vol. 4, no. 2, pp. 1–14.

World Health Organization (WHO). 1981. *International Code of Marketing of Breast-Milk Substitutes*. Geneva: WHO.

World Health Organization (WHO). 1987. *The Rational Use of Drugs*. Report of the Conference of Experts, Nairobi, 25-29 November 1985. Geneva: WHO.

World Health Organization (WHO). 1988. *Ethical Criteria for Medicinal Drug Promotion*. Geneva: WHO.

5

REGIONAL AND ASSOCIATIVE REGIMES

The contemporary integration trend within the world economy involves significant regional arrangements and other plurilateral (but subglobal) associations among nations. These coexist and interact with global initiatives, both within and outside the UN framework, and sectoral (i.e., industry-level) developments (Machlup, ed., 1976). This chapter examines regional and other subglobal associative arrangements in order to highlight the role of regional economic integration in the contemporary international business environment and to explore some of their distinctive features and impacts.

Not all regional and associative arrangements, including some examined in this chapter, constitute fully functioning *regimes*. Some, such as the Organization for Economic Cooperation and Development (OECD) and the Group of Seven (G7), are primarily frameworks for consultation, and others are even looser arrangements with limited structure and impact. The important point is that these kinds of arrangements (whether already well developed or tentative and nascent) appear certain to become increasingly important sources of opportunity and constraint for international business.

Regional and associative agreements among nations both reinforce and counter the broad global trend toward economic integration (Lawrence, 1996, chapter 1). They reinforce integration by facilitating international economic activity and promoting multilateral consultation; in particular, in the case of regional free trade areas, they enlarge the scale of markets and thereby promote both competition and efficiency. At the same time, regional arrangements may counteract globalization by creating the potential for economic conflict among regional blocs because of external barriers and discriminatory practices. The threat of trade war between the US and the European Union (EU) or Japan, for instance, has been frequently invoked as a negotiating tool. Hufbauer and Schott (1994, p. 161) conclude, however, that neither the 1994 North American Free Trade Area (NAFTA) nor a broader Western Hemisphere Free Trade Area (WHFTA) would separate the globe into three trading blocs (the Americas, Europe, Japan). Kobrin agrees that, in the long run, "regionalization ... will not affect the emergence of an integrated global economy." It will, however, affect "the distribution of benefits and costs, ... the 'competitive' position of individual economies and the welfare of individual countries" (Kobrin, 1995, p. 32). Haggard (1995) fears that regional regimes centered on advanced countries (EU and NAFTA) may well exacerbate rather than relieve economic conflicts between developed and developing countries and that integrating more and less developed countries into a single regime (as in NAFTA) is highly problematic.

In 1994, the International Monetary Fund (IMF) compiled a list of 68 regional economic agreements of various kinds, running alphabetically from the Andes to West Africa (cited in Lawrence, 1996, p. 1). Some of these involve nations with strong similarities, including geographic location and level of economic development. The European Economic Community (EEC 6), initially organized in 1957 by Belgium, France, Italy, Luxembourg, the Netherlands, and West Germany, was of this character. There are also a number of regional economic initiatives involving groups of less developed countries (LDCs): at least three in Asia and the Arab Middle East, five in Latin America, and ten or more in Africa (Robson, 1987, pp. 8–10). However, this pattern of economic cooperation among similar countries is hardly universal. By 1986, the European Community (EC 12) included countries such as Greece, Ireland, Portugal, Spain, and Turkey (associate membership) that did not possess the same level of economic development as the other members. The European Free Trade Area (EFTA), which except for Switzerland agreed in October 1991 (Liechtenstein at a later date) to join with the EC to form the European Economic Area (EEA), was comprised of small but otherwise economically dissimilar countries, geographically removed from one another. (EFTA, reduced to just four members, is now an arrangement of purely historical interest; the same is true of the Council for Mutual Economic Assistance, the CMEA or COMECON system involving the former USSR and its satellites.) The OECD includes only advanced industrial countries (AICs) but spans the globe: Europe, North America, East Asia, and the South Pacific.

5.1 MULTINATIONAL ARRANGEMENTS: TYPES AND EXAMPLES

Six general types of intercountry arrangements are included within the broad concept of regional or associative economic groupings. Listed in order of the degree of integration involved among their participants, these are as follows: loose association, free trade area, customs union, common market, economic integration, and political integration. By way of illustration, the major regional groupings created since World War II, not all of which may be formally termed *regimes*, are listed according to these categories in figure 5-1. Military and diplomatic arrangements such as the North Atlantic Treaty Organization (NATO), which may in fact have some significant economic aspects, are not included in this list. Some of these arrangements have significant political dimensions, while others do not. The European Union aims at further political integration in future years; by contrast, the Canada-US and NAFTA pacts carry no such intention or implication.

Most of the intercountry groupings listed in figure 5-1 are literally "regional"; the countries involved are geographically proximate and frequently similar to each other in level and type of economic, social, and political development as well. However, there are clearly important exceptions. The three geographic clusters of the OECD (North America, Europe, and the Pacific Rim) are widely separated from each other, as are Israel and the US. The EU and NAFTA include countries of considerably different levels of development. And, indeed, a number of arrangements involving proximate and similar countries, such as the Andean Pact (ANCOM) and the Central American Common Market (CACM/MCCA), have encountered difficulties because of their common domestic economic and political conditions and problems. Some arrangements have been specifically designed to take advantage of intercountry differences and complementarities rather than similarities. The now defunct USSR-dominated Council for Mutual Economic Assistance (CMEA or COMECON) is a striking example, but NAFTA and other US initiatives in Latin America also fit this description, as do scattered vestiges of former colonial empires such as the European dependencies in the Caribbean.

A *loose association,* as we use the term here, is a consultative and cooperative arrangement, through which member countries agree in principle to work together for mutual benefit on a (usually limited) group of concerns. Loose associations do not necessarily result in harmonization, much less integration, of policies and activities among their members. They are primarily consultative arrangements aimed at providing an organized forum for discussion of issues; the parties may agree on common practices in one instance and decide to follow different paths in another. The United Nations Conference on Trade and Development

Type	Title and Membership	Founding and Ending Years
1. *Loose Association*:	(1) Organization for Economic Cooperation and Development (OECD) 27 members (May 1996): EU 15, EFTA 3 (Liechtenstein is not an OECD member), NAFTA 3, Australia, Czech Republic, Hungary, Japan, New Zealand, Turkey; EU (special member). Poland, Russia, Slovakia, South Korea have applied	1961
	(2) Organization of Petroleum Exporting Countries (OPEC) showing date joined Iran, Iraq, Kuwait, Saudi Arabia, Venezuela (1960), Qatar (1961), Libya, Indonesia (1962), Algeria (1969), Nigeria (1971), Ecuador (1973–93), UAE (1974, Abu Dhabi, 1964–74), Gabon (1975)	1960
	(3) Asia Pacific Economic Cooperation (APEC) 18 members: ASEAN 6, NAFTA 3, Australia, China, Chile, Hong Kong, Japan, New Zealand, Papua New Guinea, South Korea, Taiwan	1989
2. *Free Trade Area*:	no internal tariffs; independent national external barriers	
a. *Bilateral*	(1) Australia–New Zealand FTA	1965
	Australia–New Zealand Closer Economic Relations Trade Agreement	1983
	(2) Ireland–UK FTA	1965
	(3) Israel–US FTA	1985
	(4) Canada–US FTA	1988
b. *Multilateral*	(1) European Free Trade Association (EFTA) Austria (joined EU 1995), Finland (joined EU 1995), Iceland, Liechtenstein (1991 on), Norway, Sweden (joined EU 1995), Switzerland; Denmark, Ireland, UK (joined EU 1973)	1960
	(2) North American Free Trade Area (NAFTA) Canada, Mexico, US	1994
	(3) Latin American Free Trade Area (LAFTA/ALALC) Argentina, Bolivia (1966 on), Brazil, Chile, Mexico, Paraguay, Uruguay, Venezuela (1967 on) Replaced 1980 by LAIA/ALADI (described below)	1960–80
	(4) Caribbean Free Trade Agreement (CARIFTA) Replaced 1973 by CARICOM (described below)	1967–73
	(5) Andean Group (ANCOM) Bolivia, Chile (1969–76), Colombia, Ecuador, Peru, Venezuela (1973 on)	1969

Type	Title and Membership	Founding and Ending Years
	(6) Association of South East Asian Nations (ASEAN) Preferential Trading Arrangement Brunei (1986 on), Indonesia, Malaysia, Philippines, Singapore, Thailand	1977
	(7) Latin American Integration Association (LAIA/ALADI) Argentina, Bolivia, Brazil, Chile, Colombia, Ecuador, Mexico, Paraguay, Peru, Uruguay, Venezuela	1980
3. *Customs Union*:	no internal tariffs; common external tariff (CET)	
a. *Bilateral*	(1) Switzerland-Liechtenstein customs and currency unions	1923–96
	(2) France-Italy Customs Union	1949
b. *Multilateral*	(1) BENELUX Customs Union (see below) Belgium, Luxembourg, Netherlands	1948
	(2) European Economic Community (EEC 6) BENELUX, France, Italy, West Germany	1957
	(3) Caribbean Community and Common Market (CARICOM) Antigua and Barbuda, Bahamas, Barbados, Belize, Dominica, Grenada, Guyana, Jamaica, Montserrat, St. Kitts and Nevis, St. Lucia, St. Vincent and the Grenadines, Trinidad and Tobago	1973
	(4) Central American Common Market (CACM/MCCA) Costa Rica (1962 on), El Salvador, Guatemala, Honduras, Nicaragua	1960
	(5) Common Market of the South (Mercosur) Argentina, Brazil, Paraguay, Uruguay, Chile (1996 on)	1995
4. *Common Market*:	customs union plus free movement of capital, goods, people, services	
	European Community (EC 12) EEC 6 described above (1957 on); Denmark, Ireland, UK (1973 on); Greece (1981 on); Portugal, Spain (1986 on); plus Turkey (associate member)	1986
5. *Economic Union*:	common market plus common or harmonized fiscal and monetary policies	
a. *Bilateral*	Belgium-Luxembourg Economic Union (BLEU)	1921
b. *Multilateral*	(1) BENELUX Economic Union (see above)	1958
	(2) European Union (EU 92) EC 12 described above joined by Austria, Finland, Sweden (1995)	1993

Figure 5-1. Important Contemporary Regional and Associative Groupings.

(UNCTAD) is a forum for multilateral discussion among advanced and developing countries.

The Organization for Economic Cooperation and Development (OECD), headquartered in Paris, is the most important current example of such multilateral economic cooperation. It comprised, as of May 7, 1996, with Hungary's entry, twenty-seven member countries. OECD includes virtually all of the industrial market economies of the "Triad" (North America, Europe, and the Pacific Rim) and is now embracing some of the more advanced economies of Eastern Europe. The OECD is a loose grouping of industrial democracies for discussion of a fairly wide variety of economic and monetary topics, including promotion of economic growth and financial stability in member countries, liberalization of international trade and capital movements, the activities of multinational enterprises (MNEs), economic relations with developing regions including coordination of economic aid (through the Development Assistance Council, or DAC, discussed below), and (until very recently) economic relations with the Soviet Union and its satellites. OECD is a purely consultative forum, operating under a rule of unanimity and funded by national contributions based on relative economic size, for information exchange and policy harmonization through moral suasion. OECD *decisions* are legally binding, while OECD *recommendations* are expressions of political will. An OECD Council, consisting of permanent representatives, typically ambassadors, from the member countries, and chaired by a secretary-general, directs the work of some 200 committees and working groups as well as an OECD secretariat of some 2,000 staff. OECD maintains official contacts with the EU, IMF, and the World Trade Organization (WTO) among other international bodies.[1]

An important subset of OECD governments, the Group of Seven (G7), consults periodically to coordinate fiscal and monetary policies: Canada, France, Germany, Italy, Japan, the UK, and the US. The goal of this activity is not only harmonization among the participants but overall management of the integrated world economy (Dobson, 1991). The G7 process is said to be deteriorating in the wake of continuing trade imbalances and recurrent currency crises, such as the Mexican crisis of late 1994–early 1995. However, Bergsten and Henning (1996) criticize this conclusion and recommend various measures for improving G7 and IMF capacity to anticipate and handle such events. At its July 1994 Naples summit, the G7 undertook to reexamine the institutional framework (IMF, World Bank, WTO) for managing the world economy in the twenty-first century (Kenen, ed., 1994).

A *free trade area* (FTA) eliminates trade barriers at the borders of two or more countries but permits each country to maintain its own restrictions against nonparticipants. Purely domestic activities of the members (such as taxation, regulation, and so on) need not be harmonized in any way. The 1985 Israel–US and 1988 Canada–US free trade agreements are recent bilateral examples. The six-member Association of South East Asian Nations (ASEAN) is often described as a free trade area and is so listed in figure 5-1. However, ASEAN is not scheduled to begin functioning as a true free trade area (AFTA) for at least a decade and is better understood as a preferential trading arrangement of six geographically proximate countries with similar political objectives (Hufbauer and Schott, 1994, p. 169). All ASEAN members also participate in Asia Pacific Economic Cooperation (APEC), but their economic objectives, circumstances, and trade and investment activities are significantly dissimilar. (For example, Indonesia is a member of the Organization of Petroleum Exporting Countries; Brunei, another oil exporter, is not.)

A *customs union* is, technically speaking, a free trade area whose members agree to maintain common trade policies with respect to nonmembers, especially a common external tariff (CET). The European Economic Community (EEC 6), as originally organized in 1957, was a customs union rather than a common market. Free trade areas and customs unions involve only trade in goods, while the concept of a common market connotes a fuller economic integration, as is explained below.

A *common market* includes a customs union but also provides for free movement among member countries of people, capital, and services as well as goods. Mercosur and the Central American Common Market (CACM/MCCA) in Latin America are officially termed common markets, but they fall somewhere between a customs union and a true common market because some intercountry restrictions are retained. The European Community (EC 12) became a full common market, at least in principle, only after 1992 (pursuant to the Single European Act of 1987); and the broader term European Union (EU), implying further integration among the members, came into use immediately thereafter. A common market, however, need not involve complete economic integration. For example, although a common monetary arrangement like the European Monetary System (EMS) is undoubtedly desirable for the proper economic functioning of a common market, the presence of such a system is not a necessary feature. Since the EU is working toward the development of supranational institutions and processes for economic (and ultimately political) integration, it is now evolving beyond the usual limits of a common market.

The leading example of a successful *economic union*, representing even further economic integration beyond a common market, is BENELUX, composed of Belgium, Luxembourg, and the Netherlands. This union evolved from an initial Belgium-Luxembourg Economic Union (BLEU), established in 1921, which joined in a customs union with Holland in 1948. BENELUX itself was created in 1950, and by 1970 all border controls among the three countries were abolished. BENELUX was the first regional grouping to permit free movement of capital, labor, and services as well as goods; it also provided for standardized postal and transport rates and coordinated welfare policies.

A *political union* is an economic union with the addition of a central government structure, which may have broad or narrow functions. Political unions of previously independent jurisdictions often encounter difficult problems, as illustrated by the forces of dissolution that tore apart the USSR in 1991, Yugoslavia in 1992, and Czechoslovakia in 1993. Bitter conflicts continue within the United Kingdom of Great Britain and Northern Ireland (UK), originally formed in 1801 (the present country of Ireland seceded in 1921). Imperial Germany (1871–1918) was a successful political union but was clearly dominated by a single participating state (Prussia). Some EU member countries apparently support full political integration with enthusiasm, although the resistance of some (e.g., the UK) and the possible expansion of the EU to include former EFTA and CMEA countries may delay this development.

The *degree of integration* involved in these various types of intercountry economic arrangements depends upon both the *scope* of activities included and the *goals* to be achieved. *Scope* may be either limited (and functional) or comprehensive; *goals* may include coordination, harmonization, or integration and may vary among functional areas. *Coordination* simply involves mutual understanding and adaptation among the parties involved; their actual behavior need not be similar or even mutually supporting. *Harmonization* is generally associated with a functionally limited activity, such as taxation, that can be managed in such a way that it does not matter whether the activity occurs in one member's jurisdiction or another (Andic, 1984, in Nunez del Arco, Margain, and Cherol, eds.; Shoup, ed., 1967). Under a tax harmonization arrangement between two countries, an MNE with a specific level of net earnings would be subjected to the same level of taxation in either. The US harmonizes its taxation system for MNEs through bilateral tax treaties with other countries. *Integration* necessarily involves both more comprehensive scope and more ambitious goals; integrated regimes operate through a common set of institutions, norms, and behaviors involving multiple functional activities.

5.2 THE EUROPEAN UNION

The world's largest and most important regional economic bloc is the fifteen-member European Union (EU), which evolved from the earlier European Community (EC 12) pursuant to the Treaty of European Union (Maastricht Treaty, signed December 1991, effective November 1993). The EU members have agreed in principle to form, first, an economic union and ultimately a European political union.[2]

The present EU 15 evolved in stages from the original EEC 6 of 1957: Belgium, France, Germany (unified in 1991), Italy, Luxembourg, and the Netherlands. The EC 12 emerged in 1986, with the addition of the UK (1973), Greece (1981), Denmark, Ireland, Portugal, and Spain. Three members of EFTA (Austria, Finland, and Sweden) joined in 1995. Turkey (an associate member), Cyprus, and Malta are joined with the EU through customs unions. The EU maintains some 100 such bilateral and multilateral trading arrangements. In March 1996, negotiations began in Turin, Italy, to examine how the EU institutions could absorb additional countries from Eastern Europe.

The European Economic Area (EEA), which went into effect on January 1, 1994, pursuant to an October 1991 agreement between the EU and the EFTA, appears to be simply a stage on the road to full economic integration in Western Europe. The EEA created a common market with free movement of labor, services, most goods, and capital (with some exceptions on investments). The agreement also provided for EFTA acceptance of EU regulations concerning company law, education, environmental protection, mergers, and social policy.

The degree of economic integration that will actually be achieved by the EU is problematic, and political integration is even more uncertain. The Maastricht Treaty of 1991 was barely ratified in Britain and France; it was accepted in Denmark only on a second referendum held after that country received certain exemptions. The UK and certain other countries did not commit to the monetary policies of the Maastricht agreement (see section 5.2.2 below). Although the EC 12, except for the UK, agreed to a "social chapter" stipulating greater EC authority over labor policies, there is considerable concern about the "social dumping" of welfare and labor problems across borders. The UK also did not accept the 1989 Charter of Fundamental Workers' Social Rights (Balandi, 1996). In foreign policy, the EC 12 rejected France's proposal for majority voting in favor of the UK's insistence on unanimous polling (Smolowe, 1991).

The original EEC 6 countries had much in common; but the EU 15 are very diverse in size and economic condition as well as in culture and sociopolitical character. (See data in table 5-1.) Per capita gross domestic

Table 5-1. Basic Statistical and Trade Data for the European Economic Area, 1993 Except Population (current US$)

	GDP ($ Billions)	% Share of OECD or Group	1995 Population (Millions)	% Share of OECD or Group	GDP Per Capita	World Trade Balance ($ Billions)	Exports ($ Billions)	Exports To EC 12
EU 15	6899.9	36.0	373.3	37.2	n.a.	94.2	1844.8	n.a.
EU 4	5095.3	73.8	256.0	68.6	n.a.	55.6	1165.8	n.a.
Germany	1910.8	27.7	81.3	21.8	23,631	5.6	412.5	47.9
France	1251.7	18.1	58.1	15.6	21,766	27.3	282.8	60.0
Italy	991.4	14.4	58.3	15.6	17,354	35.1	232.2	53.3
UK	941.4	13.6	58.3	15.6	16,253	-12.4	238.3	48.5
Other EU	1804.6	26.2	117.3	31.4	n.a.	38.6	679.0	n.a.
Benelux	532.3	7.7	26.0	7.0	20,691	27.1	312.0	72.0
Spain	478.6	6.9	39.4	10.6	12,112	-3.1	92.6	68.6
Sweden	185.3	2.7	8.8	2.4	21,312	6.8	60.8	53.3
Austria	182.1	2.6	8.0	2.1	23,155	2.1	69.1	63.4
EFTA 3	341.7	1.8	11.9	1.2	n.a.	18.9	131.4	n.a.
Switzerland	232.2	68.0	7.3	61.3	32,903	11.6	84.6	56.7
Turkey	174.2	0.9	63.4	6.3	2923	-10.6	23.1	n.a.
EEA	7183.6	37.5	441.3	44.0	n.a.	90.9	1914.7	n.a.
OECD 27	19,174.9	100.0	1,002.7	100.0	n.a.	103.6	3279.4	n.a.

Sources: Gross national product (GDP) data from UN Conference on Trade and Development (UNCTAD), *Handbook of International Trade and Development Statistics, 1994* (New York: UN, 1995), table 6.1. Trade data from World Bank, *World Data 1995 CD-ROM* (Washington, DC). Population data from *Statistical Abstract of the United States, 1995* (Washington, DC: US Department of Commerce, 1995). Liechtenstein (EFTA 4, but not a member of OECD) not reported in these sources.

Notes: OECD 27 includes NAFTA (see table 5-2); Japan, Australia, and New Zealand (see table 5-3); Czech Republic and Hungary (these two are the residual amounts after combining OECD countries from tables 5-1, 5-2, and 5-3). EEA comprises EU 15, EFTA 4 (except Switzerland), and Turkey. Group memberships for EEA, EFTA, EU, and OECD detailed in appendix, "Note on Data and Sources." 1993 imports may be computed from world trade balance and exports for each country or grouping.

GDP per capita: Luxembourg 31,654, Denmark 26,331, Norway 24,056, Iceland 23,103, Belgium 20,961, Netherlands 20,231, Finland 16,567, Ireland 13,529, Portugal 8708, Greece 7052, Hungary 3732, Czech Republic 3070.

product (GDP) of the richest countries (Luxembourg, Denmark, Germany) is between three and five times that of the poorest (Portugal, Greece), and even Ireland and Spain can be considered only "middle income" countries in a worldwide analysis. Differences in size among the countries are also substantial, and there is understandable concern among the smaller EU countries about the role of the four largest countries (France, Germany, Italy, and the UK) that jointly account for some 69% of EU population, 74% of aggregate GDP, and 63% of exports. Unified Germany alone accounts for about one fifth of EU population and one fourth of aggregate GDP. There are also significant differences in foreign trade patterns.

5.2.1 EU Organizational Structure

The EU, like the EC before it, legally consists of three overlapping "communities" with the same membership and common governing institutions: the European Coal and Steel Community (ECSC), established on April 18, 1951 (Treaty of Paris); the European Economic Community (EEC) and the European Atomic Energy Community (EURATOM), both established on March 25, 1957 (Treaties of Rome). A convention also signed at Rome on the latter date joined the European Assembly (the European Parliament after 1962), the Court of Justice of the European Communities, and the Economic and Social Committee (ECOSOC), entities created by the various treaties, into a common political structure; a subsequent treaty (April 18, 1965) created a single Council and Commission to govern the EC. The Single European Act of 1987 and the 1991 Treaty of European Union (Maastricht Treaty) have modified the original institutions and procedures. As the policy framework has evolved and membership has expanded, new member countries have been given considerable time to adjust their tariffs and other regulations to common standards. (Spain and Portugal, which joined in 1986, were allowed seven years.)

The EU has a complex four-institution legislative structure. The *European Council*, or "European Summit," consisting of heads of governments of the member states and the president of the European Commission (see below), meets at least biannually and deals only with broad political and strategic issues. The *Council of Ministers*, with a rotating six-month presidency, changes ministry composition depending upon the subject matter under consideration (e.g., taxation, transport, health); foreign ministers are present for major policy decisions. The Council of Ministers (commonly referred to as the Council) acts legislatively, as does the Parliament, only on proposals put forward by the European Commission, the secretariat of the EU. The original approach of the EC legislative process was that the Commission proposed, the Parliament advised, the Council decided, and the Court interpreted. The

Treaty of European Union increased the Parliament's role through consultation, cooperation, and codecision procedures. Most issues (e.g., agriculture, fisheries, internal market, environment, transport) are handled through qualified majority voting.[3] Other issues (e.g., taxation, industry, culture, development funds, research and technology development) require unanimity, as do common foreign and security policy issues and cooperation in justice and home affairs. In practice, a strong emphasis is placed on solidarity and trust, so that most decisions arise from unanimity. EU law, whether issued by the Council alone or by Council and Parliament in codecision, takes different four forms: 1) *regulations* (direct application); 2) *directives* (binding objectives with implementation delegated to member states); 3) *decisions* (binding on those to whom addressed); or 4) *recommendations* and *opinions* (non-binding statements). (The two councils are referred to collectively as the *Council of the European Union*.)

The *European Commission*, which meets weekly in Brussels, is specifically charged to ensure that all treaty objectives and provisions are carried out properly. The 20 Commissioners are former parliament members in their respective states or the European Parliament or former senior ministerial officers; each larger state has two commissioners, and each smaller state one. Each Commission holds office for a five-year term (currently 1995–2000). The ethos of the Commission requires the commissioners and their 15,000-person staff to serve EU and not national interests. The Commission provides an annual report and budget report to the Parliament, has a treaty right to speak before the Parliament, and can be dismissed only as a whole and only by a motion of censure in the Parliament (which has never occurred). The Commission polices EU laws and member country commitments to the single market; it can sue member countries in the Court of Justice and fine individuals, firms, and organizations. It also manages agricultural and regional development policies, development cooperation with other countries, and research and technology development programs. The Commission negotiates trade and cooperation agreements with non-EU countries and international organizations.

The *European Parliament*, directly elected every five years since 1979 by universal suffrage in each country, was initially a consultative body with no legislative role but with certain specific powers, including power to dismiss (but not to appoint) the Commission.[4] The Treaty of European Union strengthened its role in legislation, budget power, and supervision of the EU executive. Consultation requires a parliamentary opinion before the Council can adopt legislative proposals from the Commission; cooperation allows Parliament to amend proposed legislation; codecision results in joint Council and Parliament action. Codecision provides for a conciliation committee consisting of equal numbers of members from Parliament and Council, with the Commission also present, to reach compromises on proposed legislation, with Parliament reserving the right to reject proposals on which agreement cannot be reached. These various procedures are applied to certain kinds of issues and not to others. The European Parliament has the formal power to sue both the Council of Ministers and the Commission before the European Court of Justice for failure to take actions that are required under the treaty; it has the right to "question" the Commission and plays an important role in the budget reconciliation process, including its right to reject the proposed EU budget as a whole.

The *Economic and Social Committee* (ECOSOC) consisted most recently of 222 members ("counselors") appointed for four-year terms by unanimous consent of the Council of Ministers and apportioned among countries according to size and economic importance.[5] ECOSOC, meeting monthly in Brussels, represents economic and social interest groups: employers, employees, and other interests in roughly equal numbers. ECOSOC's role arises from the treaty requirement that it be "consulted" through published "opinions" on certain specific issues, such as freedom of establishment and worker mobility, and in all cases where harmonization of national laws, regulations, or administrative actions requires amendment of national legislation. ECOSOC represents about 250 EU-wide sectoral interest groups, which function largely as confederations of national groups. Biannually, it conducts a single market forum.

There are also four other EU institutions: the European Court of Justice, the European Court of Auditors, the European Investment Bank (EIB), and the Committee of Regions. The last named, with the same number of members distributed on the same country basis as ECOSOC, is a consultative body created under the Treaty on European Union to defend the principle of subsidiarity (i.e., dealing with matters at the lowest possible government level, as opposed to greater EU centralization). The nonprofit EIB uses loans and loan guarantees (funded by both member country contributions and capital market borrowings) to facilitate both regionally balanced and common development within the EU.

5.2.2   Critical Issues in European Integration

The 1987 Single European Act modified all of the previous EC treaties to establish qualified majority voting on a number of matters deemed vital to single market integration. No single country can veto a majority decision on any of these important steps toward a common market. A unanimous vote is still required, however, on some issues, such as harmonization of direct and indirect taxation among the member states.

Although the EU has been highly successful in reducing trade barriers against nonmembers, harmonization of domestic policies and practices remains a major issue; and there are still strong pressures for trade protectionism, investment controls, and continuation of domestic agricultural subsidies. Inflation rates in 1993–1994 varied from 1%–3% in several countries to 14% in Greece and 106% in Turkey. Unemployment rates also varied widely (US Department of Commerce, 1995, tables 1385 and 1387).

Variations in tax structures among countries give rise to particular problems. In 1992, the proportion of GDP collected as tax revenue ranged from 33% in Portugal to 50% in Sweden (US Department of Commerce, 1995, tables 1382 and 1383). There is also substantial variation in the mode of tax collection. The UK collects a relatively low proportion of revenue from social security taxes and is heavily dependent on consumption taxes and other sources, such as the local property tax. Corporate tax revenues are relatively low in France and Germany; individual income tax revenues are relatively low in France; and taxes in Turkey are relatively low overall. Compared to the EU as a whole, Australia, the US, Japan, and Switzerland are relatively low tax countries; Canada collects somewhat more taxes than the UK.

Money, credit, and capital are extremely sensitive to national economic policies, and capital movements among the EU countries have been much smaller than movements of goods. Full economic integration will require integration of money and capital movements and probably freedom of establishment and operation of financial services such as banks, insurance companies, and brokerage and securities firms (European Documentation, 1982). Separate stock markets can be operated in various locations, as in the US. In 1979, some EC members (together with Austria, whose currency is linked to that of Germany) established an exchange rate mechanism (ERM) within a European Monetary System (EMS) permitting currency exchange-rate fluctuation only within a narrow margin (labeled the "snake"); Greece, Portugal, Spain, and the UK did not immediately join. The EMS was operated through the European Monetary Cooperation Fund (EMCF), founded in 1973. The European Monetary Union (EMU), established in the Maastricht treaty of 1991, should result eventually in a single European central bank and a single European currency. (The Eurocurrency, valued in terms of weighted amounts of all member currencies, presently functions only as a common reserve currency analogous to the Special Drawing Rights, SDRs, created by the IMF and described in chapter 6 below. It is an instrument for settling central bank balances resulting from joint market-intervention activities.) A European Monetary Institute (to become the European central bank eventually) began coordinating EU monetary policy on January 1, 1994.

The Maastricht treaty stipulated certain macroeconomic and fiscal "convergence requirements" to be met by all participants in the EMS by 1997. These convergence requirements include an inflation rate within 2.5% of the three lowest in the EU, long-term interest rates within 2% of the three lowest, government deficit below 3% of GDP, and public sector debt of less than 60% of GDP. (The UK did not immediately commit to those arrangements.)

By treaty, there will be a European currency when at least seven member states meet those specified criteria, or on January 1, 1999, in any case, for qualifying countries. At the time of the treaty, only three countries met those criteria (Smolowe, 1991, p. 29). In December 1995, only Luxembourg and Germany qualified under those rules (*Wall Street Journal*, December 5, 1995). Although inflation was curbed in 1995 to 5.3% in Italy and 4.7% in Spain (US Department of Commerce, 1995, table 1385), it is predicted that only seven to nine countries will meet the criteria for the EMU in 1999 because of debt conditions (Kamm and Kline, 1995). The UN Economic Commission for Europe (in Geneva) has warned the EU that the effort to achieve convergence may choke off economic recovery and increase unemployment (*Wall Street Journal*, December 5, 1995). There have been discussions in Europe that the 1991 criteria may have to be relaxed (Gumbel and Kamm, 1995; *Wall Street Journal*, January 29, 1996a). Germany announced in June 1996 that its public debt will rise somewhat in 1997 and will exceed the 60% ceiling through the year 2000 (Marshall, 1996).

In spite of these major policy problems, the business response to European unification has been strongly positive. The 1993 common market opening was expected to increase EC 12 aggregate gross national product (GNP) by about 5% in addition to normal growth (European Documentation, 1989, pp. 12-13), and presumably this projection applies to the overall EEA as well. In addition, pan-European strategic alliances and mergers have become common, and after passage of the Single European Act there was a merger and acquisition boom within the EU. This boom followed on the heels of a similar merger wave in the US. Between 1985 and 1989, the US experienced more than 6000 such transactions, with a total value of more than $1 trillion. While there had been earlier restructuring movements in the US and the UK in the 1960s, neither Europe nor Japan had experienced such activity. In 1990, however, US merger transactions were expected to be less than half of the total value of global merger transactions, due to increasing European activity. During 1985–1989, about 60% of non-US transactions were intra-European (with a total value of $196 billion); an additional $156 billion represented Europe/non-Europe transactions, mainly in the US (Smith and Walter, 1991).

The growth of pan-European business organizations, anticipated to increase rapidly after 1992, led to the development of a new "European company statute" that offers MNEs the option of registration under a single body of law applicable throughout the EU rather than under individual national codes (Schelpe, 1991).

5.3 US AGREEMENTS: BILATERAL AND MULTILATERAL

Global competition placed tremendous pressure on the US economy and politics in the 1980s and 1990s. The US share of world imports rose from 12.9% in 1970 to 17.5% in 1986, while its share of world exports fell from 13.8% to 10.3% (US Office of Technology Assessment, 1991, p. 1, based on UN sources). The US merchandise trade balance was negative after 1975 and exceeded 3% of GNP in the mid 1980s. By contrast, Japan imported less than 1.2% of its GNP during the period 1960–1989 and ran a steadily positive trade balance after 1980, capturing over 10% of world export sales in 1988 (US Office of Technology Assessment, 1991, p. 4, based on US Department of Commerce and OECD data). These divergent trade patterns had a cumulative impact on political and policy developments.

In addition to its leadership role in the General Agreement on Tariffs and Trade/World Trade Organization (GATT/WTO) process and other globally focused economic initiatives (see discussion in chapter 6), the US has pursued its international objectives through both bilateral and multilateral initiatives (Schott, 1989). Successful agreements were reached with both Israel (1985) and Canada (1988), and the latter was broadened to create the North American Free Trade Area (NAFTA), including Mexico, effective in 1994. The US has also launched multilateral initiatives involving other parts of the Western Hemisphere: the Caribbean Basin initiative and the Enterprise for the Americas initiative. On the other hand, Australia and Japan declined US free trade proposals in the 1980s.

The US made its initial foray into bilateral efforts outside the GATT framework with the 1985 Israel–US Free Trade Agreement, which aimed at the elimination of all tariffs between the two countries within ten years (Greenaway, Hyclak, and Thornton, eds., 1989). This commitment was more symbolic than practical, since US tariffs for many Israeli products were already set at zero under the Generalized System of Preferences (GSP) for developing countries. The basic effects of the agreement were to guarantee continuation of preferential status for Israel after 1990, to eliminate the EC-preference created by the 1975 EC–Israel free trade agreement, and to commit both sides to further tariff reductions in the 1990s. The agreement also stipulated "best efforts" to negotiate rules on services trade.

The greatest importance of the Israel–US pact may have been its role as a model for the subsequent 1988 Canada–US Free Trade Agreement. Both agreements established special administrative bodies for the resolution of disputes among the parties. These resolution procedures were highly important, because tariff reductions have led to increasing emphasis on countervailing-duty and antidumping laws in the US.

5.3.1 NAFTA: US, Canada, and Mexico

The North American Free Trade Agreement (NAFTA) among Canada, Mexico, and the US took effect on January 1, 1994.[6] The agreement eliminates or harmonizes all crossborder tariff and nontariff trade barriers (NTBs) within fifteen years. The three member countries can maintain their own trade barriers against nonmember countries.

The NAFTA countries contain a 1995 population of 386.2 million (table 5-2), significantly less than the EEA population of 441.3 million (table 5-1 above). The aggregate NAFTA GDP of $7.15 trillion compares with an EEA total of $6.9 trillion. As the data in table 5-2 show, the US accounts for a dominant share of both NAFTA population, GDP, trade, and foreign direct investment (FDI).

Eden (1995, pp. 40–41) characterizes the US as the hub of a wheel with separate spokes to Canada and Mexico, which have little contact with each other. Canada and the US are the world's largest bilateral traders. Even before the US–Canada FTA was established, their bilateral merchandise trade (exports and imports) was considerably larger than US trade with either Europe or Japan (Wonnacott, 1987a, p. 2). In 1987, Canada received 23.6% of total US exports and provided 17.9% of total US imports; more than 70% of Canadian exports went to the US, and the US share of Canadian imports was almost as great (Schott, 1988, in Schott and Smith, eds., pp. 9–10, based on US Department of Commerce, 1988).

Canada and the US functioned as a free trade area during 1854–1866, but that arrangement was terminated by the US because of difficulties connected with the Civil War. By 1987, when the most recent negotiations began in earnest, 65% of US exports to Canada and 80% of US imports from Canada already were duty free, with more cuts scheduled under existing GATT agreements (Wonnacott, 1987a, p. 3). However, major problems remained because of high tariffs in certain sensitive industries such as textiles, apparel, footwear, and furniture and because of nontariff barriers. The 1988 agreement committed both parties to reduce all tariffs to zero over a ten-year period, beginning in 1989, and to eliminate nontariff restraints on trade in energy and automotive products.

Table 5-2. Basic Statistical, Trade, and Investment Data for NAFTA Countries (current US$)

	1993		1995		1993
	GDP ($ Billions)	%	Population (Millions)	%	GDP Per Capita
NAFTA	7149.7	100.0	386.2	100.0	n.a.
US	6259.9	87.6	263.8	68.3	24,270
Canada	546.3	7.6	28.4	7.4	18,959
Mexico	343.5	4.8	94.0	24.3	3815

	1993		1994		1992
	Trade Balance ($ Billions)	Exports ($ Billions)	FDI ($ Millions) Inflows	Outflows	% Share of World Manufac- tured Exports
NAFTA	-95.2	854.1	63,458	50,418	n.a.
US	-76.5	647.8	49,448	45,640	11.97
Canada	-3.3	161.4	6032	4778	2.92
Mexico	-15.4	44.9	7978	0.2	n.a.

	US	Canada	Mexico	Japan	Europe
		% Destination of 1991 Exports			
US	–	20	8	11	29
Canada	75	–	0.4	5	8
Mexico	74	5.5	–	4	16 *
		% Origin of 1991 Imports			
US	–	19	6	19	21
Canada	64	–	2	8	11
Mexico	72	0.8	–	6	21 *
		% Destination of 1991 Outward FDI Stock			
US	–	15	3	5	50
Canada	58	–	0.2	2	25
Mexico 1990	63.4	1.5	–	24.5	30.6 *
		% Origin of 1991 Inward FDI Stock			
US	–	7	0.1	21	63
Canada	64	–	0	4	29
Mexico	81.2	1.6	–	n.a.	20.4

Sources: Population and general trade data from *Statistical Abstract of the United States, 1995* (Washington, DC: US Department of Commerce, 1995). Foreign direct investment (FDI) from UNCTAD, *World Investment Report,1995* (New York: 1995). Gross national product (GNP) data from UNCTAD, *Handbook of International Trade and Development Statistics, 1994* (New York: 1995). Trade and FDI structure data from Eden, "Multinationals and Regional Integration: Lessons from NAFTA," in Preston ed., *Multinational Enterprises and the Global Economy* (1995), pp. 44–45.

Notes: For trade and FDI structure data (adapted from Eden), "Other" (not shown) is residual percentage. *Mexico data combines Europe (dominant), Japan, and "Other" (not shown).

This agreement also opened more government procurement contracts to competitive bidding and barred most border restraints on bilateral investment. Implications of the 1988 agreement for automotive trade were particularly important. Automotive products constitute one third of US–Canada merchandise trade, and the 1965 Auto Pact provided for duty-free passage of original equipment parts and new vehicles between the two countries. The 1988 FTA removed tariffs on replacement parts and then committed Canada to ending its embargo on used car imports within five years. Overall, the Canada–US pact was much broader than typical bilateral trade agreements and established precedent-setting rules for service trade and investment between the two countries.

There are profound economic differences between the US and Canada, both advanced countries with closely integrated economies, and Mexico, which must be classified as a newly industrialized country (NIC) type of economy, with both advanced and primitive segments. In 1990, Mexico's GNP per capita was only a tenth of that in the US and Canada, and its real GNP growth rate was only 0.5% compared to 3.3% for its NAFTA partners; its inflation rate of 20% was four to five times higher than theirs. At the same time, Mexico offered a large labor force and low average wages ($2.30 per hour compared to $14.30 in the US and $14.70 in Canada in 1990) (*Deloitte and Touche Review*, May 20, 1991). Hence, the NAFTA partnership was to be based on complementary differences, not strong similarities.

Negotiation of a formal free trade agreement with the US was proposed by Mexico in 1990. At the same time, the Mexican government also announced that it would reprivatize the banking industry (nationalized in 1982) by selling its 66% share in the country's eighteen largest commercial banks. The new agreement was presented as an element within a more general program of liberalization and privatization. From the US perspective, negotiations with Mexico were intertwined with two sensitive political issues: 1) labor immigration from Mexico into the US; and 2) foreign ownership and development of natural resources (especially energy) in Mexico. The energy resources of Mexico are regarded as a national patrimony; in 1938 these resources were nationalized and a state monopoly, Petroleos Mexicanos (PEMEX), was created to control and exploit them.

NAFTA negotiations raised important labor and environmental issues. The supplementary North American Agreement on Environmental Cooperation (NAAEC) took a limited approach based on the assumptions that 1) trade and environmental protection are compatible, and 2) dispute-resolution procedures will handle environmental disputes amicably. NAFTA prohibits reduction of domestic environmental standards or enforcement. There is a joint plan for dealing with pollution along the

Mexico–US border (Schuler, 1994). NAFTA does not create a common market, and hence labor mobility is not directly addressed, although there are measures to facilitate temporary entry for business persons along the lines of provisions in the 1988 Canada–US FTA.

There have already been trade disputes between the US and both Canada and Mexico within the NAFTA framework. The US has been concerned over cheap tomato imports and trucking regulations; Mexico attempted to keep out American tires through labeling and inspection requirements (*The Economist*, February 10, 1996). The US insisted on an agreement limiting its imports of Canadian softwood lumber (Greenberger and Tamburri, 1996). Experience with the NAFTA agreement thus far suggests that it provides a framework for negotiation about specific problems but not necessarily a comprehensive scheme for integration of the three economies.

5.3.2 Asia Pacific Economic Cooperation (APEC)

APEC, an eighteen-nation economic forum circling the Pacific Rim, was established in November 1989 primarily at US initiative. The conglomeration includes the three NAFTA member countries (Canada, Mexico, and US); the six ASEAN member countries (Brunei, Indonesia, Malaysia, the Philippines, Singapore, and Thailand); and Australia, Chile, China, Japan, New Zealand, Papua New Guinea, and the other three Asian NICs (Hong Kong, Taiwan, and South Korea). APEC members jointly accounted for 45.7% of total world exports in 1993, three quarters of which came from Canada, Japan, the US, and the Asian NICs (see table 5-3).

APEC, which now holds an annual summit of government leaders, has not made much progress since formation (Bergsten and Noland, eds., 1993). The 1994 summit set a twenty-five year time horizon for trade liberalization within the Pacific Rim. The key issue with Japan is the large bilateral US trade deficit (Greenwald, 1995). Japan is also particularly sensitive to the issue of "special treatment" for agriculture because its rice farmers are a powerful interest group. It has been suggested that Japan seeks to contain US efforts at trade liberalization within a slow multilateral process and that APEC members are turning from trade liberalization to "economic cooperation" and "flexibility" (Cooper and Williams, 1995; cf. Funabashi, 1995). However, an APEC advisory panel recommended to the 1995 summit that some trade liberalization goals set in the 1994 WTO accord be accelerated and that a voluntary dispute-mediation service be established to supplement WTO. APEC also adopted a Japanese proposal to strengthen the patent systems and industrial product standards of the region's developing countries. China tried unsuccessfully to use its APEC status to get the US to exempt it from the an-

Table 5-3. Basic Statistical, Trade, and Investment Data for APEC Countries (current US$)

	1995 Population (Millions)	1993 GDP ($ Billions)	1993 GDP Per Capita	1994 Merchandise Trade Balance with US ($ Billions)	1994 Exports to US ($ Billions)	1993 World Trade Balance ($ Billions)	1993 % Share of World Exports	1993 Net FDI ($ Millions)
APEC 18	2195.9	13,273	n.a.	-130.12	450.86	-25.0	45.7	n.a.
Japan	125.5	4214.1	33,839	-65.7	119.1	100.3	9.8	-13,640
China	1203	426.7	357	-29.5	38.8	-11.5	2.5	23,115
Chile	14.2	43.7	3160	1	1.8	-0.9	n.a.	410
Asian NICs	72.6	665.0	n.a.	n.a.	n.a.	n.a.	8.2	n.a.
Hong Kong	5.5	109.6	18,866	1.7	9.7	n.a.	n.a.	n.a.
South Korea	45.6	332.8	7542	-1.6	19.7	0.6	n.a.	-540
Taiwan	21.5	222.6	10,680	-9.6	26.7	n.a.	5.7	n.a.
ASEAN 6	368.4	443.5	n.a.	n.a.	n.a.	n.a.	n.a.	n.a.
Brunei	0.3	n.a.	n.a.	0.33	0.05	n.a.	n.a.	n.a.
Indonesia	203.6	144.7	755	-3.7	6.5	3.3	n.a.	2004
Malaysia	19.7	64.4	3348	-7	14	0.6	n.a.	5206
Philippines	81.6	54.4	839	-1.8	5.7	-4.6	n.a.	763
Singapore	2.9	55.1	19,723	-2.3	15.4	1.2	n.a.	6062
Thailand	60.3	124.9	2168	-5.4	10.3	-5.9	n.a.	1081
Oceania	26	330.7	n.a.	n.a.	n.a.	n.a.	1.5	n.a.
Australia	18.3	281.9	15,999	6.6	3.2	-1	n.a.	1540
New Zealand	3.4	43.7	12,539	0.09	1.4	1	n.a.	n.a.
Papua New Guinea	4.3	5.1	1239	-0.04	0.11	1	n.a.	0.6

Sources: Population, GNP, and merchandise trade data from *Statistical Abstract of the United States, 1995* (Washington, DC: US Government Printing Office, 1995). Other trade data from World Bank, *World Data 1995 CD-ROM* (Washington, DC). World trade share from Cooper and Williams, *Wall Street Journal* (1995), based on IMF and APEC sources.

Notes: NAFTA is difference between APEC 18 and countries listed here. For NAFTA data, see table 5-2. 1993 World Bank GNP at factor cost in current US$ 109 billion for Hong Kong (5.8 million population) and US$ 36 billion for New Zealand (3.5 million population). Imports can be computed as difference between trade balance and exports.

nual review of its most-favored-nation (MFN) status. APEC has, as yet, no real institutional setting and not even the initial elements of a formal regime.

5.3.3 Conclusion on US Agreements

The 1992 edition of this book predicted that the NAFTA negotiations, which were then approaching a successful conclusion, would probably terminate this type of activity for the US for the foreseeable future. Continued expansion of such agreements in the direction of both Asia and Europe had been proposed, but these developments did not then seem likely (Schott, 1989). However, in November 1995, the EU foreign ministers voted to proceed toward a possible Trans Atlantic Free Trade Agreement (TAFTA) with the US (Pope and Greenberger, 1995). The next month, the US and the EU signed a broad trade and security accord dubbed the "New Transatlantic Agenda," which promised joint efforts in 150 specific policy areas, including reduction of trade barriers and mutual recognition of safety testing, product standards, and certification procedures (Nelson and Coleman, 1995). As a practical matter, agriculture, steel, and textiles will prove to be the primary areas of interest and conflict. The TAFTA movement was driven by the NAFTA and APEC accords. The EU provides a majority of all FDI in the US, which in turn sends more than 40% of its outbound FDI to Europe. In 1994, EU-US trade amounted to just under $100 billion in each direction, and prospects seem fair for some kind of TAFTA arrangement before the turn of the century (Pope and Greenberger, 1995).

During the 1990s, the US has faced significant difficulties with respect to foreign trade policies. Notable progress has been made with respect to GATT/WTO, APEC, and TAFTA and also in the OECD and Organization of American States (OAS) accords concerning foreign corrupt practices (see Epilogue below). At the same time, there have been major controversies concerning the continuing economic boycotts of Iraq, Libya, and Cuba and over restrictions on trade with Iran and China. In the spring of 1996, the US and China came close to the outbreak of trade war over the issue of intellectual property rights. In addition, there has been a dispute among the US, the EU, and the Andean Pact countries involving bananas. Although GATT panels have twice ruled that the Banana Framework Agreement regulating the marketing of Latin American bananas in the EU violates GATT rules, the EU has ignored those rulings (Mazuera, 1995). This is a US policy concern because of the close links between the US and Latin American banana-exporting countries. In 1996, the US filed a WTO complain against the EU in connection with the latter's ban on imports of meat containing hormones (*Wall Street Journal*, January 29, 1996b). In addition, new product standards developed within the EU have created substantial difficulties for US enterprises (Aeppel, 1996; cf. Sykes, 1995). In recent years, the US has withdrawn from talks concerning liberalization of services trade in banking, telecommunications, and maritime services, claiming a lack of reciprocity by other countries (Bahree, 1996a&b).

The greatest international trade concern for the US involves Japan, which appears to be a reluctant or at least cautious participant in APEC and other multilateral consultations. The US and Japan are making both unilateral and bilateral moves to improve their trade relations, but the development of a general agreement between them does not seem likely at this time. Instead, there have been continuing threats of a trade war between the two countries in recent years.

In spite of all of these difficulties, there is overwhelming US business support for increased trade liberalization and regional integration (cf. Lawrence, 1996, chapter 1). The reason is quite simple. In the mid 1990s, twenty-five of the one hundred largest US multinationals earned 50% or more of their sales abroad; Exxon earned nearly 80%, and Colgate-Palmolive, Coca-Cola, Gillette, Mobil, Ford, and DEC were in the 60%-70% range. In addition, fifteen of the top hundred firms held more than half their assets abroad (*Forbes*, July 17, 1995, cited in Weidenbaum, 1996, p. 3). All of the US regional initiatives involve the areas (the Western Hemisphere, Europe, and the Pacific Rim) where most of these offshore operations are located. Anything that increases the openness of these markets, or increases their prosperity as a result of export activity, is favorable to US corporations.

5.4 OTHER REGIONAL ARRANGEMENTS

The only important regional economic arrangements that can be unarguably described as "successful" at this time are the EU and the Canada–US FTA. NAFTA should also prove successful in the long run, but its initial years of operation have been destabilized by the 1994–1995 Mexican currency crisis. There is no guarantee that regional economic arrangements will prove to be workable or particularly beneficial to their member nations, and none of the developing country arrangements attempted to date have achieved significant benefits, although not all have dissolved. The regional arrangements in the developing world are not really free trade areas, much less customs unions, in the conventional sense. Their focus is primarily on import substitution, export promotion, and the control of economic development (Robson, 1987).

In fact, economic progress in the LDCs may be far more dependent on developments taking place within the WTO and UNCTAD frameworks than on regional initiatives. Establishment within GATT/WTO of the Generalized System of Preferences (GSP), which sets low tariff levels for imports from LDCs entering advanced countries, is among the most important of these developments. In addition, the US, the EU, Japan, and other countries have taken a variety of bilateral and multilateral initiatives aimed at improving the economic development prospects of the LDCs.[7] Nevertheless, some of the regional arrangements that have arisen over the last few decades merit brief attention.

5.4.1   Council for Mutual Economic Assistance (CMEA)

The Council for Mutual Economic Assistance (CMEA), often called COMECON (for Communist Economies), officially dissolved in June 1991; it nevertheless merits brief mention here as a type of regional economic organization quite different from those discussed above (Drabek, 1989, in Greenaway, Hyclak, and Thornton, eds.; Schrenk, 1990; Brine, 1992). The CMEA was basically a Soviet device for economic domination of its satellites, particularly those in Eastern Europe, which were already intimately linked by trade, geographic proximity, and political-strategic considerations.[8]

Most production in these economies originated in state-owned enterprises (SOEs), and export-import activities were handled by government-controlled trading companies. Such organizations found it difficult to deal with market-oriented enterprises and were often noncompetitive on price and quality in international markets. Soviet domination isolated these economies from worldwide developments and increased their interdependence, from which they gained little benefit. There is now a strong movement toward privatization, decentralized market pricing and trading, and dismantling of state administrative apparatus in all of these countries; but this process is inevitably slow and difficult. Even East Germany, the most advanced CMEA economy, has encountered great difficulties in its merger with West Germany. The CMEA experience reveals some of the potential dangers of regional economic arrangements, especially in developing regions, that isolate their members from global economic trends.

5.4.2   Latin America and the Caribbean

NAFTA and the Enterprise for the Americas initiative stimulated discussion of the possibility of an Inter-American Free Trade Zone or Western Hemisphere Free Trade Area (WHFTA) embracing North, Central, and South Americas and the Caribbean. It has been estimated that a full-scale WHFTA would divert a small amount of Latin American trade to the US, reducing Latin American imports from affected third countries by 2.8% while increasing FDI in Latin America by some $60 billion (Hufbauer and Schott, 1994, p. 171).

During the early 1990s, and parallel to its NAFTA negotiations, Mexico negotiated a free trade agreement with Chile, a framework pact with New Zealand, and preferential arrangements with several other Latin American countries (Hufbauer and Schott, 1994, p. 160, n. 1).

During the postwar decades, five regional economic arrangements have been attempted in Latin America and the Caribbean (group memberships are detailed in figure 5-1 above):[9]

The *Latin American Free Trade Association* (LAFTA, or ALALC in Spanish), founded in 1960 and succeeded in 1980 (the two Treaties of Montevideo) by the rather less ambitious *Latin American Integration Association* (LAIA/ALADI). Intraregional trade never rose to 14% of total group exports (Edwards and Savastano, 1989, in Greenaway, Hyclak, and Thornton, eds., p. 194).

The *Central American Common Market* (CACM/MCCA), also founded in 1960. The five member countries account for 7% (35 million) of the 1993 population and 3.3% of the 1993 GNP (constant 1987 US$ 28 billion) of Latin America and the Caribbean (US Department of Commerce, 1995, table 1341; World Bank, *World Data 1995 CD-ROM*). CACM was virtually abandoned in the 1980s due to the political and military disturbances within the region. A major stumbling block was inability to agree on free movement of labor within the region.

The *Caribbean Free Trade Association* (CARIFTA), founded in 1965 and followed by the 1973 *Caribbean Community and Common Market* (CARICOM), consisting of English-speaking island-nations that were formerly members of the British Commonwealth. CARIFTA contained a special Eastern Caribbean Common Market (ECCM) for the less developed members of the community. The CARICOM region contains only 5.9 million people (1.2% of Latin America and the Caribbean) and a combined GNP of only $13.6 billion in constant 1987 US$ (1.6%). The membership is geographically dispersed and their economies are competing rather than complementary. The US Caribbean Basin initiative was intended to provide special financing, investment, and trade preference programs for the benefit of these countries from the US, Canada, Mexico, Venezuela, and international financial organizations. A newly formed Association of Caribbean States that seeks to combine the island-nations of the Caribbean with the mainland countries bordering that sea is so new that little can be said about it here (*The Economist*, August 13, 1994).

The *Andean Group*, or Andean Common Market (ANCOM), formed in 1969 (Cartagena Agreement) by a subset of LAFTA members aiming at comprehensive regional industrial planning within a common external tariff (CET). Intraregional trade never reached 5% of total group exports. The Andean Group accounts for about 21% (100 million) of the population and 17% of the GNP of Latin America and the Caribbean. There is a significant effort to revive the Andean Pact as a freer trade area (*The Economist*, August 13, 1994). Intraregional trade among the five member countries more than tripled, from $1.3 billion in 1990 to $4.7 billion (in current US$) in 1995 (Lash, 1996, p. 2).

The recent *Common Market of the South* or Southern Cone Common Market (Mercado Común del Sur, or Mercosur), which came into effect at the end of 1994 (1991 Treaty of Asunción). The four member countries (Argentina, Brazil, Paraguay, Uruguay). have a combined GNP (constant US$ 1987) of about $432 billion (51.7% of the total GNP of Latin America and the Caribbean) and a combined population of some 204 million (41.8% of the total population). Brazil accounts for 79% of group population and 68% of group GNP, Argentina for 16.8% and 28.7%, respectively. Intraregional trade rose about 300%, from $4 billion in 1991 to $15.8 billion in 1995 (Lash, 1996, p. 2, citing *Investor's Business Daily*, 1995). In June 1996, Chile signed a free trade agreement with Mercosur that will reduce tariffs over eight years starting October 1, 1996. Mercosur was scheduled at that time to make a similar agreement with Bolivia within three months (*Wall Street Journal*, June 26, 1996).

None of the terms (*free trade*, *common market*, etc.) in the titles of these organizations are properly descriptive of their actual characteristics. LAIA, CARICOM, and the Andean Group are tariff preference zones; CACM was intended to be a free trade area. Figure 5-1 above lists Mercosur as a customs union rather than a true common market; it provides for free movement of goods, services, and production factors but not of people. Some schemes intended a common external tariff (CET), and some did not. The basic purpose behind all these schemes has been to increase intraregional trade in order to alleviate perennial foreign-exchange crises. The common strategy has been to enlarge internal markets and restrict imports from hard-currency countries.

Latin America and the Caribbean are characterized by tremendous cultural, political, and socioeconomic variety. The area itself is vast, geographically diverse, and populated by large and dissimilar groups: European (Spanish, German, Italian), Indian, Negro, and mestizo. Spanish, Portuguese, English, French, and Dutch languages are spoken in various parts of the region. There are also tremendous differences in income and degree of urbanization. Mexico City and São Paulo are, or soon will be, among the largest cities in the world (US Department of Commerce, 1990, table 1441), but many parts of the region are rural and primitive. Argentina, Brazil, Chile, and Mexico are usually considered newly in-dustrialized countries (NICs), and some other states in the region qualify as "middle-income" countries, but still others are very poor. Inflation rates vary widely. Mexico and Trinidad-Tobago never joined the Organization of Petroleum Exporting Countries (OPEC); Ecuador joined and withdrew; and Venezuela remains an OPEC member. The countries within the region are not closely integrated with each other; only landlocked Bolivia obtains even half of its exports from its regional neighbors, and most countries are heavily dependent on imports from other parts of the world.

Prior to the Great Depression of the 1930s, there was a general approximation of free trade throughout Latin America; formal trade barriers among countries did not exist. The depression, however, led to widespread implementation of import substitution and protectionist measures. In the 1950s and 1960s, the UN Economic Commission for Latin America (ECLA/CEPAL) promoted industrialization through import-substitution strategies associated with what was intended to be temporary protection against external competition. Not surprisingly, protectionist policies became permanent, and the program tended to establish and preserve inefficient industrial sectors characterized by high capital intensity and low productivity (Edwards and Savastano, 1989, in Greenaway, Hyclak, and Thornton, eds., p. 190). The movement toward various forms of regional economic integration during recent decades has been driven by a desire to obtain larger-scale markets for these industrial sectors while continuing to practice external protectionism. During the late 1960s and 1970s, the importance of export promotion beyond Latin America and the Caribbean also received significant emphasis.

5.4.3 Africa and the Middle East

Probably the least successful efforts at economic integration have taken place in Africa and the Middle East, regions which are characterized by great cultural diversity, weak economic complementarities, and also political-diplomatic turmoil (Boyd, 1991; Robson, 1987). A Regional Co-operation for Development (RCD) scheme organized in 1964 among Iran, Pakistan, and Turkey to achieve limited sectoral industrial integration became moribund with the formation of the Islamic Republic of Iran in February 1979 (Amuzegar, 1993, p. 154). The effort was later revived as an Economic Cooperation Organization (ECO), joined by various smaller states in the region in November 1992.[10] In February 1992, Iran, Russia, and three other lacustrine countries formed a Caspian Sea Littoral States Cooperation Organization.

A wide variety of schemes have been attempted in Africa. After some fifty years of operation in various forms and with varying membership, the East African Community (EAC) finally dissolved in 1978. (At one time, the EAC aimed at a common market with common currency.) In

1981, fifteen countries joined to form the more modest Preferential Trade Area for Eastern Africa. In 1969, a Southern African Customs Union was established among South Africa (which in 1948 had formed a customs union with Southern Rhodesia), Botswana, Lesotho, and Swaziland. The Southern African Development Coordination Conference organized in 1980 aimed only at economic collaboration rather than creation of a formal trade bloc. West African countries, which are culturally very diverse and relatively small in size, have attempted a number of arrangements. The six-member Communauté Economique de l'Afrique de l'Ouest (CEAO), established in 1974, was linked in a monetary union with Benin and Togo. The 1973 Mano River Union (MRU) created a Liberia-Sierra Leone customs union, which later included Guinea. The 1975 Economic Community of West African States (ECOWASI) attempted to unite some sixteen countries including CEAO and MRU members. In Central Africa, varying numbers of countries have been involved in monetary, customs, and other types of cooperative arrangements but with little stability or results. The problems in West and Central Africa closely resemble those of the Caribbean.

Economic cooperation efforts in the Arab Middle East have been strongly affected by the political-diplomatic turmoil within the region and by divisions among the Arab members of OPEC. A Council of Arab Economic Unity was organized in June 1957 but did not meet until 1964. The Arab Fund for Economic and Social Development organized in May 1968 involved the twenty-one members of the Arab League (founded 1945) plus the Palestine Liberation Organization (PLO). The Arab Monetary Fund (April 1976) contained the same membership except for the PLO. None of these efforts has been much more successful than the short-lived 1960s political union between Egypt and Syria (the "United Arab Republic").

5.4.4 ASEAN

The Association of South East Asia Nations (ASEAN) was created by the Bangkok Declaration of August 1967 (Balasubramanyam, 1989, in Greenaway, Hyclak, and Thornton, eds.; Wu, 1991). Its membership consisted of six countries: Brunei (1986), Indonesia, Malaysia, the Philippines, Singapore, and Thailand. (Basic economic data on the five largest members of ASEAN are provided in table 5-3 above.) There are enormous political, economic, and social differences among these countries. Singapore and Brunei are extremely small in size and population; Indonesia is extremely large in both, with Thailand and the Philippines being intermediate. The Philippines is the only Christian country in Asia (with a large Muslim minority in the southern islands); Indonesia is the world's largest Muslim country, and Malaysia is also Muslim. Thailand is a Buddhist country, and Singapore is predominantly

Chinese. Singapore and Malaysia are relatively high income NICs, with substantial FDI and export activities. Indonesia is a member of OPEC, but Brunei (the other oil exporter) is not.

ASEAN is not a fully developed free trade area. It is a loose association of geographically proximate states with mutual political and economic interests. Trade and investment relations are handled largely by administrative regulation. There is very little likelihood of a true customs union developing. Balasubramanyam concludes:

> The ASEAN has had little success in promoting its stated objectives. ... [T]he main stumbling block in the way of progress appears to be the marked differences in the development strategy and economic philosophy of the principal member countries. ... The ASEAN has had little impact on either the magnitude or the pattern of FDI in the region (1989, pp. 185–186).

In spite of this pessimism, there has more recently been a significant increase in intraregional trade, which rose 24% to $110 billion between 1994 and 1995 (Lash, 1996, p. 2, citing *Far Eastern Economic Review*, September 14, 1995).

5.5 REGIONAL REGIMES AND MNEs

Regulation of MNE activities in general and of FDI in particular has been a major concern in most of the regional regimes. Conspicuous examples in the industrial market economies are the OECD guidelines for MNEs and the Canada–US auto pact. Canada has in the past limited FDI by US firms through the screening procedures of its Foreign Investment Review Agency (FIRA), and the investment part of NAFTA may be unstable (Wonnacott, 1987a, p. 9). The EU has generally been open to both internal and external FDI, except for France, which has attempted (unsuccessfully) to restrict US investment. The CMEA was largely closed to FDI; former CMEA countries are now trying to encourage FDI, particularly joint ventures, but hard-currency payment requirements and other restrictions have limited the interest of foreign investors. It should also be noted that the US maintains various restrictions on FDI, including reporting requirements, restrictions or prohibitions on FDI by industry, restrictions on national treatment under various federal programs, and national security restrictions. In fact, according to Lash, "Restrictions of foreign direct investment are as common in the United States as they are in other nations" (1996, p. 9).

Latin American countries have attempted to regulate MNE activities in a variety of ways. The "sectoral programming strategy" of the Andean Group, although never implemented as planned, restricted internal free trade to firms with at least 51% Andean Group ownership, an approach that discouraged FDI. LAIA used company complementation agreements, an approach that tended to reduce tariff duties for the companies involved. Although some twenty-five such agreements were concluded in a variety of industries, including chemicals, pharmaceuticals, electrical appliances, and telecommunications, they did not prove successful in attracting FDI. A recent report by the Association of American Chambers of Commerce in Latin America and Chase Manhattan Bank concluded that the investment climate in Latin America continues to improve (*Deloitte and Touche Review*, May 27, 1996). Foreign investment increased from 1.28% of regional GDP in 1992 to 1.78% in 1994. Economic growth through 1997 was expected to exceed 5% in Chile, El Salvador, and Nicaragua and to be between 1% and 5% in most other countries (including Mexico), except Jamaica, Panama, Paraguay, and Venezuela (the report did not include a number of countries such as Uruguay). Many Latin American governments are working to eliminate impediments to capital flows in order to encourage FDI.

The Andean Foreign Investment Code (1971–1987) illustrated the widespread desire in the developing countries to stimulate local ownership participation. The Andean Code (Declaration 24) subjected FDI and the entry and operation of foreign-owned enterprises to common rules enforced by separate (and nonharmonized) national laws in the member countries. Foreign ownership in enterprises was to be reduced to 49% within fifteen years (twenty in Bolivia and Ecuador); enterprises not meeting this criterion lost tariff preferences. Profit remittance, reinvestment, and use of patents and trademarks to protect industrial technology were all limited, and reporting requirements were increased. New FDI was forbidden in certain nonmanufacturing sectors (e.g., public services, insurance, banking, electricity, telecommunications, and news media). In addition, each country was allowed to restrict foreign ownership in other sectors to 20% of company value. Grosse (1983) analyzed the impact of the Andean Code through management interviews and other relevant data and concluded that the code had a substantial negative impact on MNE entry decisions and operating flexibility. FDI slowed during the first few years of the code, and there was a significant shift in new entry ownership toward host-country joint ventures. Chile withdrew from the Andean Group in 1976 in order to enact legislation more attractive to FDI; and the code itself was replaced in 1987 by a new set of rules aimed at stimulating foreign investment. This change was driven by the foreign debt crisis of the 1980s.

The ASEAN approach has been much more accommodating to FDI and MNEs, although not much more successful in practice until quite recently. While the regional pact provided for industrial complementation agreements along Andean Group lines, MNEs were admitted to the process on both company (as in LAIA) and industrywide levels. The agreement process never functioned successfully, however, because it was largely left to enterprises without government participation, and conflicts among enterprises prevented agreements.

The general experience with regional codes or guidelines for regulating FDI and other MNE activity is that they have tended to work poorly even in the industrial market economies and to fail in other settings. The various "guidelines" developed within the OECD carry no sanctions and have apparently had little influence either on member countries or on MNEs. However, if, as seems likely, regional regimes become stronger and expand their activities in the future, their ability to influence MNE operations will likely increase. Such increased influence will probably be used to stimulate some forms of MNE activity and FDI while restricting others in order to achieve regime objectives.

Notes

1. Associated bodies with separate governing statutes include the International Energy Agency (IEA), the OECD Nuclear Energy Agency (NEA), the European Conference of Ministers of Transport (CERI), the OECD Development Centre, and the Club du Sahel. The Center for Cooperation with Economies in Transition assists the formerly communist states of Eastern Europe in becoming market economies.

2. Key references include Emerson, 1989; Makridakis et al., 1991; Price Waterhouse, 1987; Sapir and Jacquemin, eds., 1990; and Wallace, 1994.

3. Voting rights in the EU are distributed roughly in accordance with the size and importance of various countries, for a total of 87 votes. Germany, France, Italy, and the UK presently have 10 votes each; Spain, 8; Belgium, Greece, the Netherlands, and Portugal, 5 each; Austria and Sweden, 4 each; Ireland, Denmark, and Finland, 3 each; and Luxembourg 2. At least 62 votes are required to approve Commission proposals, and both 62 votes and at least ten member countries to approve other proposals.

4. The present Parliament (the next election is due in 1999) consists of 626 members, distributed roughly according to country size. Germany, unified in 1991, has 99 seats; France, Italy, and the UK, 87 each; Spain, 64; the Netherlands, 31; Belgium, Greece, and Portugal, 25 each; Sweden, 22; Austria, 21; Denmark and Finland, 16 each; Ireland, 15; and Luxembourg, 6. Members of Parliament sit by pan-European party membership rather than in national groups; there are some 100 political parties organized most recently into eight political groups.

5. ECOSOC membership (222 total) was distributed as follows: France, Germany, Italy, and the UK, 24 each; Spain, 21; Belgium, Greece, the

Netherlands, Portugal, Sweden, and Austria, 12 each; Denmark, Ireland, and Finland, 9 each; and Luxembourg, 6.

6. Key sources are Greenaway, Hyclak, and Thornton, eds., 1989; Schott, 1989; Schott and Smith, eds., 1988; Smith and Stone, eds., 1987; and Wonnacott, 1987a&b.

7. The most important economic aid came from the Development Assistance Committee (DAC), a subset of the OECD countries (US Department of Commerce, 1995, tables 1413 and 1414). In 1987, DAC members provided $66.4 billion in LDC aid from public and private sources (excluding military flows); in 1992, they provided $115.8 billion. About 51.5% came from EU and EFTA members, 14% from Japan, and 32.6% from the US and Canada. Per capita assistance ranged in 1993 between highs of $267 from Denmark and $264 from Norway and a low of $25 from Portugal; the US contributed $48, Japan $91, and Canada $93. Official OPEC development assistance (a narrower category than official flows) fell from a high of $9.7 billion in 1980 to $1.2 billion in 1992 (other aid categories are not readily available) and averaged some $3.2 billion per annum during the eight years from 1985 to 1992. CMEA's European members provided $5 billion in 1987 compared to OPEC's $3.3 billion.

8. The six East European members were: Bulgaria, Czechoslovakia, East Germany, Hungary, Poland, and Romania. (Albania was a member only during 1949–1951.) Cuba, Mongolia, and Vietnam were non-European members of CMEA but with little apparent involvement in its activities. Yugoslavia was never a member but was accorded equal economic status.

9. See Lewis, 1984, in Nunez del Arco, Margain, and Cherol, eds.; and Edwards and Savastano, 1989, in Greenaway, Hyclak, and Thornton, eds.

10. Afghanistan, Azerbaijan, Kazakhstan, Kirgizstan, Tajikistan, Turkmenistan, and Uzbekistan. At more than 300 million population, ECO was then the world's second largest economic bloc after the European Community.

References

Aeppel, Timothy. 1996. "Europe's 'Unity' Undoes a U.S. Exporter," *Wall Street Journal*, April 1.

Amuzegar, Jahangir. 1993. *Iran's Economy Under The Islamic Republic*. London: I.B. Tauris.

Andic, Fuat. 1984. "Tax Harmonization and Economic Integration," in Nunez del Arco, Margain, and Cherol, eds., *The Economic Integration Process of Latin America in the 1980s*. Washington, DC: Inter-American Development Bank, Institute for Latin American Integration, pp. 205–228.

Bahree, Bhushan. 1996a. "U.S. Is Leaving Maritime Trade Talks Amid Lack of Market-Opening Offers," *Wall Street Journal*, May 24.

Bahree, Bhushan. 1996b. "U.S., EU Offer to Open Phone Markets In Bid to Restart Talks on World Pact," *Wall Street Journal*, November 14.

Balandi, Gianguido. 1996. "Introduction to Social Europe," *European Letter*, Issue No. 1, January. Rome and Brussels: Istituto Europeo di Studi Sociali-Associazone Europea (IESS-AE).

Balasubramanyam, V.N. 1989. "ASEAN and Regional Trade Cooperation in Southeast Asia," in Greenaway, Hyclak, and Thornton, eds., *Economic Aspects of Regional Trading Arrangements*. New York: New York University Press, pp. 167–188.

Bergsten, C. Fred, and C. Randall Henning. 1996. *Mismanaging the World Economy: The Demise of the G-7*. Washington, DC: Institute for International Economics.

Bergsten, C. Fred, and Marcus Noland, eds. 1993. *Pacific Dynamism and the International Economic System*. Washington, DC: Institute for International Economics.

Boyd, Gavin. 1991. *Structuring International Economic Cooperation*. London: Pinter Printers.

Brine, Jenny. 1992. *Comecon: The Rise and Fall of an International Socialist Organization*. New Brunswick, NJ: Transaction Publishers.

Cooper, Helene, and Michael Williams. 1995. "U.S. Limits APEC-Summit Expectations: Major Trade Moves Are Unlikely at Osaka Talks," *Wall Street Journal*, November 11.

Deloitte and Touche Review. 1991. "Future Growth in North American Trade," May 20, p. 5.

Deloitte and Touche Review. 1996. "Foreign Investment Climate in Latin America Improving," May 27, p. 4.

Dobson, Wendy. 1991. *Economic Policy Coordination: Requiem or Prologue?* Washington, DC: Institute for International Economics.

Drabek, Zdenek. 1989. "CMEA: The Primitive Socialist Integration and Its Prospects," in Greenaway, Hyclak, and Thornton, eds., *Economic Aspects of Regional Trading Arrangements*. New York: New York University Press, pp. 235–254.

The Economist. 1994. "After NAFTA, AFTA," August 13, pp. 15–16.

The Economist. 1996. "Rotten Tomatoes," February 10, pp. 74–75.

Eden, Lorraine. 1995. "Multinationals and Regional Integration: Lessons from NAFTA," in Lee E. Preston, ed., *Multinational Enterprises and the Global Economy*. College Park, MD: Center for International Business Education and Research, University of Maryland, pp. 39–61.

Edwards, Sebastian, and Miguel Savastano. 1989. "Latin America's Intra-Regional Trade: Evolution and Future Prospects," in Greenaway, Hyclak, and Thornton, eds., *Economic Aspects of Regional Trading Arrangements*. New York: New York University Press, pp. 189–234.

Emerson, Michael. 1989. *The Economics of 1992: The E.C. Commission's Assessment of the Economic Effects of Completing the Internal Market.* New York: Oxford University Press.

European Documentation. 1982. *The European Financial Common Market.* Luxembourg: Office for Official Publications of the Communities.

European Documentation. 1989. *Europe Without Frontiers: Completing the Internal Market.* Luxembourg: Office for Official Publications of the Communities, third edition.

Forbes. 1995. "100 Largest U.S. Multinationals," July 17, pp. 274–276.

Funabashi, Yoichi. 1995. *Asia-Pacific Fusion: Japan's Role in APEC.* Washington, DC: Institute for International Economics.

Greenaway, David, Thomas Hyclak, and Robert J. Thornton, eds. 1989. *Economic Aspects of Regional Trading Arrangements.* New York: New York University Press.

Greenberger, Robert S., and Rosanna Tamburri. 1996. "U.S. Defends Quota on Canada Lumber As Necessary Means to Avert Trade War," *Wall Street Journal,* February 20.

Greenwald, John. 1995. "Heading for a Crash: The U.S. Levies Duties That Would Double the Price of Japanese Luxury Cars and Set Off a Trade War," *Time,* May 29, p. 29.

Grosse, Robert. 1983. "The Andean Foreign Investment Code's Impact on Multinational Enterprises," *Journal of International Business Studies,* vol. 14, no. 1 (Winter), pp. 121–133.

Gumbel, Peter, and Thomas Kamm. 1995. "Decision Point: EU Nations Near Vote on Fate of Single Currency," *Wall Street Journal,* December 13.

Haggard, Stephan. 1995. *Developing Nationals and the Politics of Global Integration.* Washington, DC: Brookings Institution.

Hufbauer, Gary C., and Jeffrey J. Schott. 1994. *Western Hemisphere Economic Integration.* Washington, DC: Institute for International Economics.

Investor's Business Daily. 1995. "World Economy in Brief," September 13, p. B1.

Kamm, Thomas, and Maureen Kline. 1995. "The Treaty's Goals Look Far Away to Italians Who Aren't Sure if They'd Rather Be In or Out," *Wall Street Journal,* December 13.

Kenen, Peter B., ed. 1994. *Managing the World Economy: Fifty Years after Bretton Woods.* Washington, DC: Institute for International Economics.

Kobrin, Stephen J. 1995. "Regional Integration in a Globally Networked Economy," *Transnational Corporations,* vol. 4, no. 2 (August), pp. 15–33.

Lash, William H. 1996. *The Exaggerated Demise of the Nation State.* Center for the Study of American Business, Washington University, St. Louis, MO.

Lawrence, Robert Z. 1996. *Regionalism, Multilateralism, and Deeper Integration.* Washington, DC: Brookings Institution.

Lewis, Vaughan A. 1984. "Regional Integration and Theories of Regionalism in the Commonwealth Caribbean," in Nunez del Arco, Margain, and Cherol, eds., *The Economic Integration Process of Latin America in the 1980s*. Washington, DC: Inter-American Development Bank, Institute for Latin American Integration, pp. 27–42.

Machlup, Fritz, ed. 1976. *Economic Integration: Worldwide, Regional, Sectoral; Proceedings of the Fourth Congress of the International Economic Association (1974)*. New York: Halsted Press.

Makridakis, Spyros G., et al. 1991. *Single Market Europe: Opportunities and Challenges for Business*. San Francisco, CA: Jossey-Bass.

Marshall, Matt. 1996. "Germany Won't Meet EU Debt Target, Imperiling Schedule for Single Currency," *Wall Street Journal*, June 13.

Mazuera, Daniel. 1995. "A Trade Dispute Gone Bananas," *Wall Street Journal*, November 17.

Nelson, Mark M., and Brian Coleman. 1995. "U.S. and EU Sign Trade, Security Pact, Boosting Trans-Atlantic Cooperation," *Wall Street Journal*, December 4.

Nunez del Arco, Jose, Eduardo Margain, and Rachelle Cherol, eds. 1984. *The Economic Integration Process of Latin America in the 1980s*. Washington, DC: Inter-American Development Bank, Institute for Latin American Integration.

Pope, Kyle, and Robert S. Greenberger. 1995. "Europe Seeks Trade Pact With U.S. Similar to Nafta," *Wall Street Journal*, November 27.

Price Waterhouse. 1987. *European Communities*. New York: Price Waterhouse.

Robson, Peter. 1987. *The Economics of International Integration*. London: Allen & Unwin, third revised edition.

Sapir, Andre, and Alexis Jacquemin, eds. 1990. *The European Internal Market: Trade and Competition*. New York: Oxford University Press.

Schelpe, Dirk. 1991. "A Statute for a European Company," *The CTC Reporter*, no. 31 (Spring), pp. 17–19.

Schott, Jeffrey J. 1988. "The Free Trade Agreement: A US Assessment," in Schott and Smith, eds., *The Canada-United States Free Trade Agreement: The Global Impact*. Washington, DC: Institute for International Economics, pp. 1–35.

Schott, Jeffrey J. 1989. *More Free Trade Areas?* Washington, DC: Institute for International Economics.

Schott, Jeffrey J., and Murray G. Smith, eds. 1988. *The Canada-United States Free Trade Agreement: The Global Impact*. Washington, DC: Institute for International Economics.

Schrenk, Martin. 1990. "Future of the CMEA," *Socialist Economies in Transition*, vol. 1, no. 1 (April), pp. 3–5.

Schuler, Douglas A. 1994. "The NAFTA and the Environment: Trade, Diplomacy, and Limited Protection," unpublished paper, Jesse H. Jones Graduate School of Administration, Rice University, Houston, TX.

Shoup, Carl S., ed. 1967. *Fiscal Harmonization in Common Markets*. New York: Columbia University Press, two volumes.

Smith, Murray G., and Frank Stone, eds. 1987. *Assessing the Canada-U.S. Free Trade Agreement*. Halifax, Canada: Institute for Research on Public Policy.

Smith, Roy C., and Ingo Walter. 1991. *The First European Merger Boom Has Begun*. Center for the Study of American Business, Washington University, St. Louis, MO.

Smolowe, Jill. 1991. "European Community: Blueprint for the Dream," *Time*, vol. 138, no. 25 (December 23), pp. 29–30.

Sykes, Alan O. 1995. *Product Standards for Internationally Integrated Goods Markets*. Washington, DC: Brookings Institution.

US Department of Commerce. 1988. *Advance Report of U.S. Merchandise Trade: December 1987*, FT 900 ADV, 12 February, Bureau of the Census.

US Department of Commerce. 1990. 1995. *Statistical Abstract of the United States*. Washington, DC: US Government Printing Office.

US Office of Technology Assessment, US Congress. 1991. *Competing Economies: America, Europe, and the Pacific Rim; Summary*. Washington, DC: US Government Printing Office.

Wallace, William. 1994. *Regional Integration: The West European Experience*. Washington, DC: Brookings Institution.

Wall Street Journal. 1995. "U.N. Urges EU to Slow Monetary-Union Schedule," December 5.

Wall Street Journal. 1996a. "Markets in Europe Are Reacting To Doubts About Single Currency," January 29.

Wall Street Journal. 1996b. "U.S. Files WTO Complaint Against EU on Meat Ban," January 29.

Wall Street Journal. 1996. "Russia Seeks to Join OECD With Surprise Application," May 29.

Wall Street Journal. 1996. "Latin Bloc, Chile Sign Pact," June 26.

Weidenbaum, Murray. 1996. *Neoisolationism and Global Realities*. Center for the Study of American Business, Washington University, St. Louis, MO.

Wonnacott, Paul. 1987a. *The United States and Canada: The Quest for Free Trade*. Washington, DC: Institute for International Economics.

Wonnacott, Paul. 1987b. *The US-Canadian Free Trade Agreement: A View from South of the Border*. Toronto, Canada: University of Toronto, Institute for Policy Analysis, Policy and Economic Analysis Program.

Wu, Friedrich. 1991. "The ASEAN Economies in the 1990s and Singapore's Regional Role," *California Management Review*, vol. 34, no. 1 (Fall), pp. 103–114.

6

TRADE, MONETARY, AND
INVESTMENT REGIMES

The most extensive and complex international economic regimes that have evolved during the postwar period are those governing trade, currency exchange, and financial relationships among and between the economically active countries of the world. For most of the period, the former USSR and its satellites were not formal participants in these regimes, although they have never been entirely excluded. It now appears that most of them are, or will soon become, actively involved. In any event, the great bulk of world commerce and financial activity has been governed by these regimes, and they should therefore be considered *global* in character. Although their functional scope is limited, their effects on the entire system of international business and economic activity are complex and pervasive.

Even before the beginning of World War II, there was widespread international opinion, particularly in the US and Great Britain, that a totally new system of monetary and trade relationships should be developed. It was generally believed that international trade conflicts and exchange disequilibria were principal causes of worldwide economic instability during the interwar period and, ultimately, of the war itself. Establishment of a trade regime based on unrestricted international competition, with the elimination of country preferences and exchange controls, became a particular objective of US policy. A second, although transient, concern was the need to facilitate reconstruction in the war-damaged economies. And a third concern, continuing down to the present, was the promotion of long-term economic and social development in the less developed countries (LDCs) of the world.

A series of international conferences, begun while the war was still in progress, explored these issues and examined possible alternatives for dealing with them. Eventually the dual objective of stable currencies and liberal trade came to be embodied in two institutions: the International Monetary Fund (IMF) and the General Agreement on Tariffs and Trade (GATT). (The latter is now incorporated into the World Trade Organization, WTO.) These two institutions, although very different in character, shared a common objective: *mutually beneficial multilateral trade should be encouraged to the greatest extent possible*. Unrestricted international competition, facilitated by stable currency-exchange arrangements, was the means adopted to achieve this goal.

Reliance on competition and freedom of contract was not, however, adopted as the guiding principle with respect to international investment and capital flows. One reason for this posture was a fear that some countries, primarily LDCs but initially including the war-damaged economies as well, would not be able to obtain sufficient support for long-term reconstruction and development projects from existing sources. The International Bank for Reconstruction and Development (IBRD, or World Bank) was created to provide a pool of funds, supplied by cooperating governments, for loans to countries needing this type of assistance. The second reason for rejecting open competition as the paramount principle for capital flows was a general recognition that various states (and not, as it turned out, only the poorer ones) might wish to control either inward or outward capital flows in order to pursue their own economic development objectives.

The policy arrangements adopted during the immediate postwar period did not take into account the possibility that a worldwide foreign investment boom, accompanied by explosive growth in the number and size of multinational enterprises (MNEs), would soon follow. Only now, half a century later, are some elements of a comprehensive international investment regime beginning to emerge. Over the intervening decades, however, the growth of investment has impacted the trade and exchange regimes in varied and important ways. Foreign investment is both a substitute and a stimulus for trade; hence, the growth of investment may "solve" some trade problems while giving rise to others. In addition, both investment and trade operate through the same international monetary system, often with opposite effects on currency values; in particular, equilibrating movements in exchange rates in response to trade imbalances may be offset by capital flows. Hence, as a practical matter, it is not possible to analyze the operation of trade and payments systems without attention to investment activity as well.

In this chapter we describe the evolution of the closely related regimes for trade and monetary exchange during the past half century and then examine recent developments that may eventually produce a comprehensive policy regime for international investment.

6.1 THE TRADE REGIME: GATT AND WTO[1]

The principle of international economic relations broadly supported by the victorious nations of World War II was unrestricted freedom for, and indeed maximum encouragement of, mutually beneficial multilateral trade. However, development of a set of institutional arrangements and behavioral norms to implement this principle was not a simple matter. The fundamental problem was (and still is) that individual countries have traditionally protected various domestic industries and interests from foreign competition and/or promoted their development through subsidies and other devices, for a variety of entirely understandable reasons: long-term development goals, concern for politically important interests or disadvantaged groups, and national defense considerations. The phasing out of these protection/promotion policies inevitably creates costly economic and political dislocations in domestic economies. In fact, the trade regime has repeatedly confronted various forms of "new protectionism" that work directly against the long-term goal of liberalization.

The concept of unrestricted multinational free trade was embodied in US bilateral trade agreements during the 1930s and was reflected in the Atlantic Charter (1941) and the Lend-Lease Agreement (1942). A US proposal for establishment of an International Trade Organization (ITO) under UN auspices was circulated for international discussion in 1945. As with the related (and logically secondary) process of establishing an international monetary regime, a series of international conferences and negotiations took place at various levels, and in 1947 a codification of trading relations among an important group of trading nations was signed in Geneva. This document, the General Agreement on Tariffs and Trade (GATT), was viewed as a transitional step toward the ITO. The ITO proposal reached its final form in the Havana Charter, which was signed by more than fifty countries in 1948. However, by that time differences among the wartime allies and concerns about special trade relationships on the part of both advanced and less developed countries had undermined the immediate postwar consensus. Even in the US, the original sponsor, the ITO proposal provoked great opposition, and President Truman eventually withdrew the proposal from Congressional consideration in 1950.

The result was that GATT, which was never intended to be anything other than a transitional device and which took the form of a treaty rather than a formal organization, became the primary expression of international commitment to a liberal trade regime for nearly half a century (Irwin, 1995). In 1994, at the conclusion of the Uruguay Round of GATT negotiations (the eighth round since 1947), the World Trade Organization (WTO), a modified version of the ITO originally proposed in 1945, was finally established by agreement among more than one hundred participating countries (see figure 6-1).

Scope	Worldwide trade, including services, agricultural goods, and intellectual property as well as manufactures.
Purpose	Promote unrestricted, multilateral trade through both a) establishing rules and commitments binding on member countries, and b) maintaining an environment for continuing negotiation among trading parties.
Organizational Form	Ministerial Conference, representing all signatories, meets every two years. General Council is operating unit, managing Dispute Resolution and Trade Policy Review units and subsidiary committees.
Decision and Allocation Modes	Intention is to continue GATT policy of decision by consensus, but voting is on a "one vote per country" basis. Large majorities or unanimity are required for major policy actions. Dispute-resolution procedures are binding on members under certain circumstances.
Strength and Change	WTO arrangement is too recent to provide much evidence. Current disputes primarily involve US and EU; implementation of broadened coverage (beyond manufactured goods) will take time.

Figure 6-1. The WTO Trade Regime.

Brazil and India initially opposed a new round of negotiations, which required a majority vote by the GATT membership. The major issues in the round (in addition to formation of the WTO itself) were: 1) liberalization of trade in services, including protection of intellectual property; 2) reductions in agricultural protection; and 3) the LDC demand for a standstill and rollback of US and European Union (EU) measures that were believed to contravene GATT rules (Golt, 1988; see also Kahler, 1995, pp. 34–47). The WTO embodies the same international policy commitments as the GATT, but the distinction between the two is profound (cf. Hoekman, 1995). The WTO, which will have about 160 members when accession procedures are completed, is a formal international organization with specific membership requirements and sharp distinction between member and nonmember status. Moreover, WTO rules are binding among all members; formal dispute-resolution procedures are required; and sanctions (fines, retaliation, exclusion) for non-compliance may be imposed. The new WTO assumed responsibility for administering three new major agreements: the GATT Agreement of 1994, the General Agreement on Trade in Services (GATS), and the Agreement on Trade-Related Aspects of Intellectual Property Rights (TRIPS). Taken together, these agreements expand the scope of the trade regime to include not only manufactured goods but also agricultural commodities, some internationally traded services, and intellectual property (Jackson, 1995). There were also efforts at an agreement on Trade-Related Investment Measures (TRIMS). Specific policy developments with respect to many of these topics will be ongoing for many years within the WTO framework, and some agreements will continue to be "plurilateral" (i.e., binding only among their individual signatories, as was the case with GATT) rather than universal among all members. Nevertheless, the economic welfare gains from expanded multilateral trade within the WTO framework are expected to be substantial. Lash (1996, p. 2) cites estimates from various OECD, World Bank, and GATT studies that a 30% across-the-board cut in tariffs and subsidies on all commodities (including raw materials) should increase estimated global gross income between $213 billion and $274 billion by the year 2002 (in 1992 dollars), or between 0.75% and 1%.

6.1.1 Key Concepts and Issues

The postwar commitment to trade liberalization initially embodied in the GATT and expanded in the WTO involves two key concepts: 1) the reduction of trade barriers; and 2) the elimination of discrimination and preferences among trading partners. These two ideas are quite distinct, since it is possible (indeed, historically typical) to reduce barriers or grant preferences for some trading partners while maintaining, or even increasing, them for others (thus maintaining or increasing discrimination). The principle of nondiscrimination is therefore the fundamental idea, a fact reflected in its priority position in article 1 of the original GATT agreement. The principle of nondiscrimination is formally expressed as "most favored nation" (MFN) treatment: the most favorable treatment accorded any trading partner will be extended to others. Reciprocal MFN agreements were initially developed by the US during the interwar period. When reductions in trade barriers are negotiated in a multilateral reciprocal MFN setting, the efficiency-increasing and welfare-enhancing effects of liberalization are extended to all participants.

Three major types of obstacles have delayed and complicated creation of a fully liberalized international trade regime over the postwar decades:

1. Traditional industry protections and trade-partner preferences; these were the types of restrictive arrangements to which the postwar trade negotiations were initially addressed.
2. Concern that LDCs cannot overcome historic disadvantages without preferential treatment (i.e., discrimination in their favor) in their dealings with more advanced countries.
3. Establishment of regional and other "customs union" and "free trade" agreements, which by their nature violate MFN principles since participants in such agreements favor each other over outsiders.

The last of these obstacles has proved least troublesome, since the new regional group agreements evolving over the postwar period have provided for greater liberalization among their own members rather than increased restrictions on others (see chapter 4 above). However, there are currently about eighty active subglobal agreements registered with the GATT/WTO, and only *one* of these has been found to be in *full* conformity with GATT/WTO requirements. Of the one hundred and twenty current members of the WTO, more than half (accounting for a much larger portion of world trade) are also signatories to regional or other subglobal agreements, and many of these involve discriminatory practices of one sort or another (Sampson, 1996). Hence, the potential drag of subglobal agreements on full multilateralism may not be insignificant. (The relatively greater appeal of global rather than regional trade agreements is emphasized by McMillan, 1994. The impact of divergent product standards, both national and plurilateral, on multilateral trade is analyzed in detail by Sykes, 1995; see especially the appendix on technical barriers and the Uruguay Round.)

Concern that LDCs would not be able to compete successfully in a completely nondiscriminatory trading system was a major factor undermining worldwide support for the initial (1948) ITO proposal. After a number of years of discussion and negotiation, a set of criteria for preferential trade treatment for these countries, known as the Generalized System of Preferences (GSP), was developed. The idea is that all countries meeting certain criteria would be accorded the same preferential treatment by all other countries participating in the agreement. The GSP system, although it involves discrimination, is considered to be consistent with the liberal trade regime's fundamental goal of worldwide economic development and growth. The principal problems encountered have been connected with the reluctance of GSP countries to "graduate" (i.e., lose GSP status) as their levels of economic development and trade competitiveness increase.

Paradoxically, traditional industrial protection and discriminatory practices have accounted for both GATT's greatest achievements and for continuing problems that now confront the WTO. The MFN principle has been universally recognized, and tariff levels have been repeatedly reduced; the 1994 GATT agreement includes further reductions as well as the elimination of tariffs on more than 40% of all manufactured goods. In fact, the GATT process has been criticized for an overemphasis on numerical tariff reductions, without regard to their significance or scope, and for underestimating the role of nontariff barriers (NTBs). More important, however, has been the persistence of protection for historical political interests in advanced countries (e.g., agriculture in Western Europe and Japan as well as in the US), and the appearance of "new protectionism" for some important manufacturing industries, particularly in the US. Since the "new protectionism" tends to rely on nontariff barriers, quotas, "voluntary" restraints, etc., these developments conflict both with the basic principles of trade liberalization and with the historical GATT emphasis on tariffs as the principal form of trade restriction. The conventional arguments favoring an emphasis on tariffs are: 1) tariffs are "transparent" (i.e., the amount of restriction can be readily observed) and hence are convenient objects of negotiation; and 2) tariffs can be easily revised through across-the-board adjustments (i.e., percentage reductions), and hence do not require case-by-case negotiations. These observations are accurate, but a half century of tariff reductions has not eliminated the vast web of restrictions and practices restraining world trade.

GATT ceased to function effectively during the 1980s. Its weak legal status and its inability to impose sanctions or resolve disputes arising from either "old" or "new" forms of protectionism were continuing handicaps (Schott, 1990). Moreover, as a result of significant economic and technological change throughout the world, adoption of new industrial policies, including protectionist practices, became more, rather than less, widespread. Also, growth of new regional economic groupings created alternative sources of pressure and benefit within the trade regime. The WTO clearly has firmer legal status and stronger formal authority than the GATT, but it remains to be seen whether or not the new mechanisms will be able to respond to current forces and tendencies more effectively.

6.1.2 Product and Commodity Agreements Within the Trade Regime

Within the broad international commitment to free trade embodied in the GATT/WTO arrangements, there is also a set of subsidiary regimes involving explicit and significant commitment to an opposite notion, the principle of restricted competition or "managed trade" (Waldmann, 1986). Volatility in demand, supply, and price of agricultural commodities and other raw materials has led to the development of many different types of international stabilization arrangements, some of which date back to the prewar era. Inclusion of agricultural products and raw materials, essentially exempt from previous GATT policies, within the WTO framework represents a considerable advance. WTO members are required to convert all nontariff agricultural trade barriers into tariff form as a prelude to a series of multilateral rate reductions in the future. However, transitional adaptations within these politically sensitive areas will inevitably be slow. One of the most notorious restrictive schemes tolerated under GATT, the Multifiber Agreement (MFA), is scheduled to be phased out over a ten-year period as a result of the 1994 negotiations. (For an insightful analysis of the MFA experience, see Cline, 1990. The MFA and the Integrated Program for Commodities, or IPC, are examined briefly in the 1992 edition of this book at pp. 172–175.) However, in recent years, bilateral and multilateral agreements have been used to limit competition, imports, and/or exports in a number of important manufacturing sectors and product lines, and WTO rules contain certain "safeguards" that may allow many of these practices to persist over time. (The complex motivations of firms and governments involved in these "strategic trade policy" actions are well explored in Yoffie, 1993.)

6.2 THE MONETARY REGIME[2]

Commitment to a system of worldwide multilateral free trade, even if such an objective is only partially achieved, necessarily involves a parallel commitment to an international monetary system that contributes to, or at least does not impede, this objective. Establishment of an international monetary system, however, inevitably involves a loss of national autonomy with respect to foreign-exchange arrangements and monetary policies. A country can participate fully in the open international trading system only to the extent that its currency (or, equivalently, its output of goods and services) is acceptable to its various trading partners and, ultimately, to the international community as a whole. Hence, establishment of an open trading system requires parallel creation of a supportive system of currency exchange, including both a means of setting initial exchange rates and a mechanism for stabilizing and/or adjusting rates in response to changing developments over time.

A fundamental question about any international arrangement established for this purpose is the extent to which such rate settings and adjustments will be "automatic" or "discretionary," that is, whether they will occur without case-by-case policy intervention or, on the other hand, will require specific and detailed negotiations and agreements. Although little serious consideration was given in the postwar discussions to a return to the international gold standard, the theoretically "automatic" adjustment mechanism of the gold standard is generally regarded as a point of reference for the evaluation of other international monetary regimes. A brief description of the gold standard therefore provides an appropriate starting point for our analysis.

6.2.1 The Gold Standard[3]

Gold, along with other precious metals and commodities, has been used as a store of value and means of payment since ancient times, but its only lengthy period of use as the central element in the international monetary system was 1870–1914. After serving as a de facto standard for about a century, gold was formally established as the basis for the value of the British pound sterling in 1821. As Britain became the world's leading economic and military power during the nineteenth century, other countries voluntarily adopted similar arrangements (sometimes, as in the US, over considerable domestic opposition), and a worldwide system of currency valuation and exchange in terms of gold evolved. The absence of centralized discussions and formal agreements in the establishment of the nineteenth-century gold-standard regime is one of its most curious features; as Cooper remarks, the nineteenth-century gold standard "was in a sense an accident of history" (1987, p. 44).

The essential idea of the gold standard is that the value of each country's currency is established in terms of a specific quantity of gold. According to the oversimplified textbook explanation, the system operates as follows: foreigners coming into possession of a particular currency in amounts in excess of their immediate needs (as a result of export sales greater than corresponding imports, for example) may convert the currency to gold and return it to their own country, reconverting it there into the national currency. This operation will draw down gold stocks in one country and increase gold stocks in the other. If gold flows of this sort are substantial and persistent, the money supply and prices will decline in the gold exporting country and increase in the gold importing country; and these relative price movements will continue until the basic disequilibrium in import-export relationships is corrected. Thus, in theory, the gold standard tended to stabilize international economic relationships in two important ways:

1. Establishment of currency values in terms of gold provided security for international transactions and facilitated easy conversion of one currency into another, eliminating the need for actual gold movements and stimulating multilateral trade.

2. In the event of persistent disequilibrium and substantial gold flows, the money supply and price effects resulting from changes gold reserve holdings would ultimately induce corrective adjustments within the countries involved.

Although these theoretical features of the gold standard are clearly demonstrable in the abstract case of a two-country, two-currency world, actual experience with the gold standard was substantially different. For a variety of reasons, not all due to the operation of the gold standard itself, prices and trade volumes, production, and employment in the major trading countries were quite unstable throughout the gold-standard era. The time periods required for supposedly reequilibrating adjustments proved to be long; and the domestic economic adjustments involved would, according to Cooper, be considered "intolerable" in the contemporary world (1987, p. xiii). He notes that the late nineteenth-century reign of the gold standard ended in something that was then called the "Great Depression" until the worldwide economic collapse of the 1930s (which followed a brief return to gold in the 1920s) took over that title. In a more technical analysis, Cooper shows that the gold standard did not produce price stability, either short- or long-term, in the US or Great Britain and that the unemployment rate in both countries was higher during the gold-standard decades than during a comparable time period following World War II (Cooper, 1987, chapter 2). Meltzer reaches similar conclusions but points out that there is "a higher probability that the long-term price level would remain constant under the gold standard" than under postwar arrangements (1986, p. 150). The fear that the gold standard would have a permanently depressing effect on both prices and the level of economic activity throughout the world was, in fact, one of the reasons for its rejection in the postwar discussions.

6.2.2 The Bretton Woods Institutions

Dissatisfaction with international trade and monetary arrangements during the interwar period and the desire to create a framework for unrestricted international trade in the postwar era led to the development of a variety of proposals for new exchange arrangements to be put in place at the close of World War II. After considerable consultation among the wartime allies (which at that time included the USSR), the UN Monetary and Financial Conference convened at Bretton Woods, New Hampshire, in July 1944, to address two interrelated problems: 1) creating an orderly basis for international currency exchange, including both stabilization and adjustment mechanisms; and 2) providing loans to support reconstruction in war-damaged countries and economic growth and development in poorer countries. These two different purposes led to the creation of two different institutions: the International Monetary Fund (IMF) and the International Bank for Reconstruction and Development (IBRD, or World Bank). As was noted at the time, the names of these institutions are somewhat confusing, since the IMF was established to carry out exchange, reserve, and short-term loan functions normally associated with a "bank," while the IBRD is essentially a "fund" for providing long-term loans. The term *World Bank* is particularly unfortunate, since the IBRD was intended from the beginning to provide financial assistance only to a select group of countries (initially war-damaged, and later less developed) and for very limited purposes. It performs none of the functions, such as currency issue and monetary policy control, that would be associated with a worldwide central bank. From the time of their creation, the two Bretton Woods institutions have evolved in very different ways. In particular, as its exchange stabilization role has declined (see below), the IMF has become increasingly involved in the affairs of developing and transitional countries (e.g., Mexico, Poland). The IBRD, although playing a highly significant role in some countries and with respect to some important facets of worldwide economic development, is in fact a peripheral element of the worldwide trade and monetary exchange systems. (There is further discussion of the IBRD in connection with international investment below.)

6.2.3 Regime Operation: From Fixed to Floating Rates

The basic idea reflected in initial plans for the IMF was to create a system of international currency exchange that would have the desirable properties of the theoretical gold standard while avoiding its destabilizing and deflationary effects. In a modification of the "gold-exchange" standard that operated briefly during the interwar period, gold convertibility of key currencies (ultimately only the dollar) was to be maintained, and exchange rates among currencies would be established from this reference point. The result was a set of fixed exchange rates pegged to the dollar, which became the key reserve currency and the source of international liquidity. The exchange rates for all other currencies were to be stabilized during periods of short-run disequilibrium not by movements of gold but by loans from a reserve fund established at the outset by contributions from all member countries. In the event of substantial and persistent disequilibrium in a particular currency, revaluations would be negotiated among the member contributors. In principle, the IMF system with fixed exchange rates created the same fungibility between domestic and foreign currencies that had characterized the gold standard; and, since currency revaluations were expected to be rare, the stability of contracts provided by the gold standard was anticipated as well. (The current profile of the monetary regime is shown in figure 6.2.)

Scope	Exchange rates and mechanisms among nations engaged in world trade and finance.
Purpose	Establish orderly process for monetary exchange (including setting, stabilizing, and modifying exchange rates) to promote growth of world trade and investment.
Organizational Form	International Monetary Fund (IMF): A formal organization controlled by a Board of Governors representing the membership and operated by a professional secretariat. The actual "fund" consists of the contributions of member countries, established by quota.
Decision and Allocation Modes	Weighted voting on policy issues, based on relative contribution. Loans from stabilization fund largely controlled by professional staff within policy guidelines. Currency revaluations negotiated between major involved parties and IMF staff.
Strength and Change	Initial scheme aimed at maintenance of pegged exchange rates ended in early 1970s, when the current "floating rate" system was introduced. Result has been a changed *role* for IMF but not a decline in its importance.

Figure 6-2. The International Monetary Regime. Alongside the IMF, periodic conferences among the major trading nations, referred to as the Group of Five (G5) or the Group of Seven (G7), depending on the number of participants, have attempted to stabilize or revise exchange rates among major international currencies, with varying degrees of success.

Initial establishment of both specific exchange rates and the reserve fund was facilitated by the facts that the dollar had already become the de facto international currency standard and that the US was the largest contributor to the reserve fund itself. Subsequently, economic recovery in other major trading nations and inadequacy of the total gold/currency reserve in the light of expanding world trade led to the creation of a new form of reserve credit, *Special Drawing Rights (SDRs)*, in 1967. SDRs are defined as a "basket" of major currencies, but in fact they are simply internal accounting units used to describe the indebtedness of various members to the reserve fund and to settle accounts among them.

Creation of SDRs both reflected and facilitated the declining role of both gold and the dollar in the international monetary system and contributed to worldwide inflationary processes already underway, largely as a result of US budget and trade deficits. In response to fears that European countries would demand conversion of their dollar reserves into gold, the US unilaterally altered the worldwide monetary regime by ending the gold convertibility of the dollar and imposing a 10% surcharge (in effect, a temporary tariff) on a wide range of imports. This marked the end of the de facto "dollar standard" (i.e., the gold exchange standard pegged to the dollar) of the postwar era. By 1973, a worldwide system of flexible exchange rates, supervised by the IMF and the Group of Seven (G7) countries and referred to as "managed float," had evolved.

The developments of the early 1970s marked the end of arrangements that had provided unusual international monetary stability for more than a decade but that had also become increasingly fragile over time. The new system of flexible rates is clearly more volatile and not necessarily less fragile, since its effectiveness depends upon stabilizing cooperation among the G7 countries (see G7 discussion in chapter 5 above). The role of the IMF in this new regime has changed but not diminished. In the mid 1970s, just at the time of these major changes, the worldwide increase in oil prices greatly increased the need for short-term payments financing, in which the IMF played a role. Subsequently, as noted above, the IMF has become increasingly involved in advising and monitoring individual countries and facilitating their entry into full participation in the global economy. The IMF now includes more than 150 members and provides focus and support for an orderly international monetary system, an essential requisite of global economic stability and growth.

Thus, in spite of very significant structural modifications in response to changing circumstances, the objectives and norms of the postwar monetary regime are essentially unchanged. The fact that these goals are being pursued without reference to the fixed exchange rates and stabilization loans that were the IMF's principal initial features can be interpreted as a sign of the regime's long-term success. Eichengreen (1994) believes that the ultimate policy choice has to be between *freely* floating rates (with no reference to "pegs," "bands," or "managed" levels) and some forms of monetary union, probably based on "current areas," such as the EU or the North American Free Trade Area (NAFTA).

6.3 INTERNATIONAL INVESTMENT: THE SEARCH FOR A REGIME

The role that foreign direct investment (FDI) would play in the postwar international economic order was not anticipated when the foundations of the trade and payments regimes were put in place. Historically, foreign financing of economic development occurred either within the framework of colonialism or in the form of portfolio investment. To finance construction of the North American railroads, for example, British investors bought shares or provided loans to domestic enterprises, taking little if any control over actual operations. Prior to World War II, FDI was confined almost entirely to natural resource exploitation (e.g., oil, metals) and specialized agriculture (e.g., bananas). Nestle, Singer, and Unilever stood out as the rare large MNEs in manufactured products.

Postwar interest in international investment was initially focused on the reconstruction of war-damaged economies and, secondarily, on the creation of favorable development conditions in postcolonial states. As its name implies, the International Bank for Reconstruction and Development (IBRD, or World Bank) was created in response to these concerns. Like the IMF, the World Bank initially dealt exclusively (and still deals principally) with governments. It provides financing for types of projects (large-scale and long-term) for which private financing is difficult, if not impossible, to obtain; and, again like the IMF, World Bank assistance is often tied to substantial resource and policy commitments by the receiving country. The initial focus of World Bank activity was on the replacement of war-damaged infrastructure, and infrastructure projects (port facilities, power systems, etc.) continued to receive primary emphasis when attention shifted to development of poorer nations and regions. Agricultural and rural development projects have been emphasized more recently (van Meerhaeghe, 1987, pp. 67–100).

The IBRD was augmented by the creation of two related institutions: 1) the International Finance Corporation (IFC, 1956), intended to increase the funds available for private-enterprise investment in LDCs; and 2) the International Development Agency (IDA, 1960), intended to improve LDC loan terms. The provision of technical assistance for the design and execution of investment projects has become an increasingly important World Bank function over time. The impact of the World Bank on worldwide economic development and integration during its half century of existence is literally incalculable, since the roughly $200 billion made available through its operations has been multiplied many times through the activities of domestic governments and private investors (van Meerhaeghe, 1987, pp. 67–100; Gavin and Rodrik, 1995).

By the 1980s, it became obvious that international production (made possible by international investment) had surpassed international trade as the source of worldwide economic growth and that FDI patterns dictated the level and patterns of trade rather than the other way around (Behrman, 1993). Ostry (1995) refers to FDI as "the engine of transformation of the global economy"; and an annual *World Investment Report*, prepared by the Division on Transnational Corporations and Investment of UNCTAD, provides definitive documentation of FDI patterns and impacts. National governments have been quick to respond to these developments, often in conflicting and inconsistent ways (cf. Kapstein, 1994). Hence, the need for greater multilateral understanding and harmonization of investment policies has increased right along with the growth in FDI itself. Julius (1990) strongly emphasizes that a policy environment providing "neutrality or non-discrimination" between 1) both domestic and foreign investors, and 2) both trade and investment, will maximize potential worldwide efficiency gains from FDI.

6.3.1 Investment Regime Proposals

The IBRD was never conceived as the core element of an international investment regime, and (in spite of the creation of the IFC) it has not evolved in that direction. The difference between IBRD–related activities and a comprehensive international investment regime was emphasized in the widely cited article "Toward a GATT for Investment" by Goldberg and Kindleberger (1970). Their list of investment-related concerns meriting international policy attention is quite broad and includes some issues, such as taxation and competition, subsequently covered in UN discussions and elsewhere (see chapter 4 above). They also identified a number of investment-related issues, such as the impact of exchange controls, export controls, and varied national standards of securities regulation on MNE activities, that have not yet received systematic international attention.[4] Figure 6-3 presents an outline of the possible elements of a comprehensive international investment regime.

In spite of the broad sweep of their analysis, Goldberg and Kindleberger did not emphasize the international investment issue that has been the principal focus of action over the subsequent decades: insurance against political risks. The US developed a foreign investment guarantee program to encourage private investment in the reconstruction of Europe after World War II. This program gradually expanded to include other countries, and in 1959 it was modified to focus exclusively on investment in developing countries. The Overseas Private Investment Corporation (OPIC), was established in 1971, with various revisions thereafter. Several other major investor countries, led by Germany and Japan, have also developed national investment insurance schemes; there are some private providers as well (Shelp, in Goodwin and Mayall, eds., 1980).

Scope	Worldwide international investment, including rights/responsibilities of both governments and and investors.
Purpose	Establish ground rules for relations between and among nations and enterprises in order to promote international investment; reduce unilateral controls on capital flows; protect foreign investment against default and expropriation.
Organizational Form	(1) World Bank: Provides long-term loans and technical assistance for major projects in less developed countries. (Only IMF members may join.) Supplemented by IDA and IFC.
	(2) MIGA: Provides insurance against political risks for investments among signatory countries. (Only World Bank members may join.)
	(3) Possible multilateral code, evolving from issues raised by proposed UN Code of Conduct on Transnational Corporations, OECD Declaration on International Investment and Multinational Enterprise, and subsequent FDI agreement negotiations; and regional codes (EU, NAFTA, APEC, Andean Group, etc.).
Decision and Allocation Modes	(1) World Bank: Policy controlled by governing board; detailed decisions made by secretariat.
	(2) MIGA: Policy set in basic agreement; administered by staff.
	(3) Future multilateral arrangements to be determined. Policy set by initial agreement and all-party assemblies, with staff implementation (following WTO model), seems likely.
Strength and Change	No comprehensive investment regime is yet in place; critical missing elements are common international understandings about accounting standards, corporate governance, repatriation of funds, securities regulation, tax treatment, etc.

Figure 6-3. Elements of an International Investment Regime.

Proposals for some kind of *multilateral* insurance arrangements have circulated for several decades. Such arrangements appeared to be needed because of conflicts and gaps in national and bilateral schemes; also, multilateral arrangements would be appropriate for investor and/or recipient groups that were themselves multinational. A major sticking point, however, was LDC resistance to the use of international mechanisms for dispute resolution. Such mechanisms are obviously critical, since the principal risk to be insured is expropriation, and the point of an insurance scheme is to provide some recourse for the foreign investor other than decisions of domestic governments and courts (Holthus, Kebschull, and Menck, 1988).

After many years of debate and discussion under World Bank auspices, the Multilateral Investment Guarantee Agency (MIGA) became operational in April 1988. Both advanced and developing countries join MIGA voluntarily, accepting their roles and responsibilities when they do so. (Advanced countries supply capital to the insurance fund in accordance with an established formula.) MIGA guarantees eligible investments against noncommercial risks of several types, including:

1. Transfer risks arising from currency restrictions (the first concern raised by Goldberg and Kindleberger, 1970);
2. Loss from legislative or administrative actions, whether or not such actions constitute formal expropriation;
3. Government repudiation of contracts; and
4. Armed conflict and civil unrest.

MIGA is intended to supplement, but not supplant, national and private investment insurance programs. It is also intended to take an active role in research, technical assistance, and other functions that would contribute to increased foreign investment in LDCs ("The Legal Framework: MIGA Launched," 1988).

More than one hundred countries have joined MIGA, and contracts have been issued covering billions of dollars worth of investments in diverse locations. However, experience with MIGA has been too brief for any conclusions to be drawn as to its effectiveness and impact. If it meets the needs of advanced-country investors and developing-country recipients, then one would expect its operations to expand accordingly. As an additional agency within the complex of the World Bank and the IMF, MIGA might over time become the nucleus for a regime that would address securities regulation, corporate governance, and other investment-related issues on a multinational basis. On the other hand, MIGA's resources may prove inadequate, or its settlement procedures may fail to satisfy the various parties involved.

As noted in chapter 4 above, the OECD has recently initiated an effort to fill the FDI regime gap with a proposed Multilateral Agreement on Investment (Witherell, 1995). Negotiations within the OECD, although complex enough in themselves, are clearly easier than in UN or World Bank contexts, since all members are relatively advanced countries. However, non-OECD countries will be consulted during the negotiation process; and the OECD FDI agreement, once completed, will be open to signatory by non-OECD members (Lachica, 1995). The main focus of the OECD agreement is expected to be nondiscrimination, with a primary emphasis on *national treatment* (i.e., the principle that foreign and domestic enterprises and investments will be treated equally). *Transparency* (i.e., the principle that regulations, and their implications, must be clear to all parties) will also receive significant emphasis. Finally, the agreement will contain specific conciliation and dispute settlement provisions. As noted in chapter 4 above, it is contemplated that the OECD agreement will be *legally binding*, not simply recommendatory, on all signatories. In addition to this current OECD initiative, several regional economic groupings, including the EU, NAFTA, Asia Pacific Economic Cooperation (APEC), and the Andean Group, have also attempted to develop FDI codes (Graham, 1994). In fact, many nations now have adopted policies, both domestic and plurilateral, governing both FDI and portfolio investment and, in general, promoting liberalization of investment regimes and high standards of protection for foreign investor interests (Parra, 1995). As Gray (1995) notes, these principles have become integral elements of the "modern structure of international economic policies" in nations in which created assets and proprietary technology play and important role. The strongest multinational action to date is probably the Basel Accord of 1988, which set common capital standards for major banks doing business across national borders. Initially signed by representatives of twelve countries whose banks account for 90% of all international banking activity, these standards have now been adopted in all of the world's major banking centers (Herring and Litan, 1995, pp. 107–113 and passim).

6.4 THE GLOBAL ECONOMIC REGIMES: EVALUATION

In the context of this analysis, the international economic regimes described above require evaluation from three perspectives. First: Are these regimes substantive or merely institutional; that is, do they have genuine effects on international business and economic relationships within their functional scope? Second: How are these regimes related to growth of the world economy and the success of MNEs during the postwar decades; is there a cause-effect relationship in either direction? Third: What does experience with these regimes tell us about the general nature of regimes, their origins and evolution, and the likely future direction of development, particularly with reference to an investment regime?

With respect to the substantive impact of the regimes (that is, in what way is the world different because of their existence?), a definitive conclusion is not possible, since we lack a second environment in which to conduct parallel experiments. However, it is indisputable that, by any measure or comparison, world trade has grown more rapidly, and the benefits of trade have been more widely distributed among regions, nations, and industries, during the postwar decades than at any other time in world history. Hence, it is hard to believe that the postwar money and trade regimes have failed in their primary purpose, which was and is to expand the volume and extend the benefits of worldwide multilateral trade.

Strange argues that "the 'golden years' of growth in the 1950s and 1960s are better explained by the steady expansion of credit ... than by the reduction in the barriers to trade or the observance of rules regarding exchange rates" (1988, p. 105). However, there is some circularity in this claim, since creation of the trade and exchange regimes preceded, facilitated, and to some extent brought forth the credit expansion. With specific reference to the trade regime, it is indisputable that average tariff levels have been reduced and duties in many specific areas eliminated altogether. And numerous empirical studies confirm that the postwar monetary regime has led to greater stability (or at least no greater instability) in several indicators of economic performance as compared to a similar time period under the nineteenth-century gold standard (cf. Cooper, 1987; and several papers in Campbell and Dougan, eds., 1986). If there is a long-term tradeoff between inflation and unemployment, as many people believe and as the gold standard/IMF-era comparisons suggest, then the postwar experience (more inflation and less un-employment) is certainly in the direction that would be chosen by most contemporary regime participants. At a minimum, the trade and mone-tary regimes, taken together, may be said to have promoted restraint in the management of international economic relations, both by individual countries and by multinational groups, and to have reduced uncertainty, which "may well be the single most important" barrier to the growth and development of the international economy (Finlayson and Zacher, 1983, p. 314).

The evolution of the postwar trade and exchange regimes has been peculiarly associated with the growth of MNEs in both numbers and scale. On the one hand, trade liberalization and ease of currency exchange created a favorable setting for the expansion of international business activity in all forms, and particularly for FDI. Since the theory of the MNE involves the optimization of investment, facilities, production, and marketing among various locations, it follows that ease of movement for both capital and output, reductions in exchange controls and tariffs, etc., tend to facilitate MNE expansion. On the other hand, the growth of

MNEs takes a large amount of international economic activity out of the "market" arena and into the internal control of individual firms. Once MNE structures are established, local revenues become available for expenditure in various jurisdictions and local capital sources become accessible as well; the need for international financial transfers is correspondingly reduced. In a sense, the growth of the MNEs, nurtured within the framework of convertible currencies and liberalizing trade, has created a situation that makes the framework itself less important. The apparent "weakening" of the monetary regime, in particular, may be in fact a reflection of the "strengthening" of the forces that have grown up within it, both the increasing volume of foreign investment of all types and the vast amount of foreign currency trading taking place within the "floating rates" environment.

With respect to the theoretical analysis of the creation and evolution of regimes, formation of the postwar trade and monetary regimes unquestionably owes much to the economic and political dominance of the US. However, the frameworks of both regimes have remained intact even as the US abandoned its primary supporting role and, indeed, took actions (such as the 1971 break with gold and the more recent "new protectionism") that conflicted with fundamental regime commitments. It seems clear that the US will be an active defendant against trade violation complaints within the WTO framework. The trade and exchange regimes seem to depend more on mutuality of interests and fundamental commitment to principles among their participants, not on hegemonic power.

With respect to the possibilities for a comprehensive international investment regime, Herring and Litan note that progress to date has depended heavily on an international sense of "crisis" and that "multilateral efforts [of this type] take time, often a lot of time, to bear fruit" (1995, p. 95). On the one hand, increasingly integrated inter-national financial markets require common norms and standards for efficient operation, but on the other, no matter what degree of formal cooperation the various authorities and enterprises involved may achieve, cheating and shirking will often give rise to microlevel advantage, and "effective supervision faces severe limits" (Herring and Litan, 1995, p. 147). Herring and Litan's implicit prediction for the evolutionary pattern seems to be a combination of 1) situation-specific agreements, such as the Basel Accord, and 2) regional arrangements, such as those within EU and NAFTA, both of which spread globally through a process of natural adaptation (analogous to the gold-standard experience) rather than through formal multilateral negotiation and adoption.

Notes

1. The structure and evolution of GATT and WTO are described in innumerable publications. Major analyses of the world trading system from an "international regimes" perspective include Kihl and Lutz (1985), Low (1993), and papers by Finlayson and Zacher, Lipson, and Ruggie, all in Krasner (ed., 1983).

2. Out of the very large literature on the international monetary system, principal references for this section include: Bordo (1995), Cooper (1987), Campbell and Dougan, eds. (1986), Classen (1990), Eichengreen (1994), Williamson and Miller (1987). Papers by Cohen and Ruggie, both published in Krasner (ed., 1983), specifically deal with the international monetary system from a "regimes" perspective.

3. Principal sources for this section include Cooper (1987, chapter 2); papers by Meltzer and Schwartz, both in Campbell and Dougan (eds., 1986); and Eichengreen, in Cooper et al. (eds., 1989).

4. More contemporary views of the requirements for an international investment regime are presented in Brewer, 1993 and 1995; Brewer and Young, 1995; and Herring and Litan, 1995.

References

Behrman, Jack N. 1993. "World Investment Report 1993: Transnational Corporations and Integrated International Production," *Transnational Corporations*, vol. 2, no. 3 (December), pp. 149–162.

Bordo, Michael D. 1995. "Is There a Good Case for a New Bretton Woods International Monetary System?," *American Economic Review*, vol. 85, no. 2 (May), pp. 317–322.

Brewer, Thomas L. 1995. "International Investment Dispute Settlement Procedures: The Evolving Regime for Foreign Direct Investment," *Law and Policy in International Business*, vol. 26, no. 3 (Fall), pp. 633–673.

Brewer, Thomas L. 1993. "Government Policies, Market Imperfections, and Foreign Direct Investment," *Journal of International Business Studies*, vol. 24, no. 1 (First Quarter), pp. 101–120.

Brewer, Thomas L., and Stephen Young. 1995. "Towards a New Multilateral Framework for FDI: Issues and Scenarios," *Transnational Corporations*, vol. 4, no. 1 (April), pp. 69–83.

Campbell, Colin D., and William R. Dougan, eds. 1986. *Alternative Monetary Regimes*. Baltimore, MD: Johns Hopkins University Press.

Classen, Emil-Maria, ed. 1990. *International and European Monetary Systems*. New York: Praeger.

Cline, William R. 1990. *The Future of World Trade in Textiles and Apparel*. Washington, DC: Institute for International Economics, revised edition.

Cohen, B.J. 1983. "Balance-of-Payments Financing: Evolution of a Regime," in Krasner, ed., *International Regimes*. Ithaca, NY: Cornell University Press, pp. 315–336.

Cooper, Richard N. 1987. *The International Monetary System*. Cambridge, MA: MIT Press.

Eichengreen, Barry. 1989. "Hegemonic Stability Theories of the International Monetary System," in Richard N. Cooper et al., *Can Nations Agree? Issues in International Economic Cooperation*. Washington, DC: Brookings Institution, pp. 255–298.

Eichengreen, Barry. 1994. *International Monetary Arrangements for the 21st Century*. Washington, DC: Brookings Institution.

Finlayson, J.A., and Mark Zacher. 1983. "The GATT Regime and the Regulation of Trade," in Krasner, ed., *International Regimes*. Ithaca, NY: Cornell University Press, pp. 273–314.

Gavin, Michael, and Dani Rodrik. 1995. "The World Bank in Historical Perspective," *American Economic Review*, vol. 85, no. 2 (May), pp. 329–334.

Goldberg, P.M., and C.P. Kindleberger. 1970. "Toward a GATT for Investment: A Proposal for Supervision of the International Corporation," *Law and Policy in International Business*, vol. 2, no. 2 (Summer), pp. 295–325.

Golt, Sidney. 1988. *The GATT Negotiations, 1986–90: Origins, Issues and Prospects*. London: British-North American Committee.

Graham, Edward M. 1994. "Towards an Asia-Pacific Investment Code," *Transnational Corporations*, vol. 3, no. 2 (August), pp. 1–27.

Gray, H. Peter. 1995. "The Modern Structure of International Economic Policies," *Transnational Corporations,"* vol. 4, no. 3 (December), pp. 49–66.

Herring, Richard J., and Robert E. Litan. 1995. *Financial Regulation in the Global Economy*. Washington, DC: Brookings Institution.

Holthus, Manfred, Dietrich Kebschull, and Karl Wolfgang Menck. 1988. *Multilateral Investment Insurance and Private Investment in the Third World*. New Brunswick, NJ: Transaction Books.

Hoekman, Bernard. 1995. *Trade Laws and Institutions: Good Practices and the World Trade Organization*. Washington, DC: World Bank, International Trade Division.

Irwin, Douglas A. 1995. "The GATT in Historical Perspective," *American Economic Review*, vol. 85, no. 2 (May), pp. 323–328.

Jackson, John H. 1995. "The World Trade Organisation: Watershed Innovation or Cautious Small Step Forward?," *The World Economy*, vol.18, Global Trade Policy Supplement, pp. 11–31.

Julius, DeAnne. 1990. *Global Companies and Public Policy: The Growing Challenge of Foreign Direct Investment*. New York: Council on Foreign Relations Press for The Royal Institute of International Affairs.

Kahler, Miles. 1995. *International Institutions and the Political Economy of Integration*. Washington, DC: Brookings Institution.

Kapstein, Ethan B. 1994. *Governing the Global Economy: International Finance and the State*. Cambridge, MA: Harvard University Press.

Kihl, Y.W., and James M. Lutz. 1985. *World Trade Issues: Regime, Structure, and Policy*. New York: Praeger.

Krasner, Stephen D., ed. 1983. *International Regimes*. Ithaca, NY: Cornell University Press.

Lachica, Eduardo. 1995. "OECD Nations Ask Outsiders to Join Investment Treaty," *Wall Street Journal*, November 9.

Lash, William H. 1996. *The Exaggerated Demise of the Nation State*. Center for the Study of American Business, Washington University, St. Louis, MO.

"The Legal Framework: MIGA Launched." 1988. *The CTC Reporter*, no. 25 (Spring), pp. 19–21.

Lipson, Charles. 1983. "The Transformation of Trade: The Sources and Effects of Regime Change," in Krasner, ed., *International Regimes*. Ithaca, NY: Cornell University Press, pp. 233–272.

Low, Patrick W. 1993. *Trading Free: The GATT and US Trade Policy*. New York: Twentieth Century Fund Press.

McMillan, Charles J. 1994. "Globalization: Multilateral vs. Regional Approaches to Trade Policy," *Business and the Contemporary World*, vol. 6, no. 3, pp. 137–153.

Meltzer, A.H. 1986. "Some Evidence on the Comparative Uncertainty Experienced Under Different Monetary Regimes," in Campbell and Dougan, eds., *Alternative Monetary Regimes*. Baltimore, MD: Johns Hopkins University Press, pp. 122–153.

Ostry, Sylvia. 1995. "Investment: The Engine of Transformation of the Global Economy," *Business and the Contemporary World*, vol. 7, no. 3, pp. 126–138.

Parra, Antonio R. 1995. "The Scope of New Investment Laws and International Instruments," *Transnational Corporations*, vol. 4, no. 3 (December), pp. 27–48.

Ruggie, J.G. 1983. "International Regimes, Transactions and Change: Embedded Liberalism in the Postwar Economic Order," in Krasner, ed., *International Regimes*. Ithaca, NY: Cornell University Press, pp. 195–232.

Sampson, Gary P. 1996. "Compatibility of Regional and Multilateral Trading Agreements: Reforming the WTO Process," *American Economic Review*, vol. 86, no. 2 (May), pp. 88–92.

Schott, J.J., ed. 1990. *Completing the Uruguay Round*. Washington, DC: Institute for International Economics.

Schwartz, Anna J. 1986. "Alternative Monetary Regimes: The Gold Standard," in Campbell and Dougan, eds., *Alternative Monetary Regimes*. Baltimore, MD: Johns Hopkins University Press, pp. 44–72.

Shelp, Ronald K. 1980. "Private Sector Investment and Political Risk: A Comparative Study of OPIC and Other Schemes," in Geoffrey Goodwin and James Mayall, eds., *A New International Commodity Regime*. New York: St. Martin's Press, pp. 186–228.

Strange, Susan. 1988. *States and Markets*. New York: Basil Blackwell.

Sykes, Alan O. 1995. *Product Standards for Internationally Integrated Goods Markets*. Washington, DC: Brookings Institution.

van Meerhaeghe, M.A.G. 1987. *International Economic Institutions*. Dordrecht, The Netherlands: Kluwer Academic Publishers, fifth revised edition.

Waldmann, Raymond J. 1986. *Managed Trade: The New Competition Between Nations*. Cambridge, MA: Ballinger.

Williamson, John, and Marcus H. Miller. 1987. *Targets and Indicators: A Blueprint for the International Coordination of Economic Policy*. Washington, DC: Institute for International Economics.

Witherell, William H. 1995. "The OECD Multilateral Agreement on Investment," *Transnational Corporations*, vol. 4, vol. 2 (August), pp. 1–14.

Yoffie, David B. 1993. "Beyond Free Trade, Firms, Governments, and Global Competition," *Transnational Corporations*, vol. 2, no. 3 (December), pp. 171–174.

7

SEA AND AIR
TRANSPORT REGIMES*

Among the institutional and behavioral arrangements governing various aspects of international business, those dealing with sea and air transport are among the most interesting to examine from a "regimes" perspective. Strange notes that, although it is easy to view "the political economy of transport systems" as a matter of only marginal significance, the truth is that the governance and operation of international transport has become increasingly salient. Both the volume of world trade and the amount of world transport activity have been growing much faster than world production for several decades, and transport services are spanning ever greater distances at ever greater speeds (Strange, 1988, p. 137). As the world becomes smaller and more interdependent, the forces of shrinkage and linkage become more, not less, important.

In spite of their obvious differences in technology and purpose (air transport primarily involves the movement of people, sea transport the movement of goods), these two industries have many common features. Their economics is dominated by the pressures of highly cyclical demand; the equipment involved is costly and has few alternative uses, and the cost of trips is much the same, whether the equipment is full or empty. In ad-

*We are indebted to Dr. Martin Dresner, University of Maryland, for updating this chapter for the revised edition.

dition, both activities have very significant network and systemic attributes; they serve multiple geographic points from central and interlinked nodes. Each industry also involves technological aspects requiring fairly high levels of expertise; and both safety/performance aspects and intercarrier standardization are important features.

Although both sea and air transport services are generally operated by business enterprises (whether private- or state-owned) rather than by political management, both industries are subject to substantial policy attention by national governments. Krasner (1985, chapter 8) emphasizes that international sea transport has evolved over several hundred years on the basis of market-oriented principles and norms, whereas the air transport regime has been "authoritarian" (i.e., primarily under government control) from its very beginnings. This distinction is broadly accurate but may give insufficient weight to the important role of domestic government policies in developing and supporting commercial shipping activities in the major sea transport countries. These mutually tolerated and interwoven domestic transport policies created an international regime that was at least partially governed by nonmarket forces even before the new and more authoritarian intergovernmental agreements of the late 1960s. On the other side, the international air transport regime is becoming increasingly market-oriented. Hence, the sea and air regimes, although having very different histories, are somewhat more alike today than they have ever been in the past. Our research also suggests that these two regimes have followed a common evolutionary pattern over the post-1945 era that has not been clearly observed in prior studies.

7.1 THE OCEAN SHIPPING REGIME[1]

Ocean shipping is one of the very few international business activities that has no substantial domestic counterpart. Telecommunications, banking, commercial trade and investment, and, at least for US carriers, air transport, all take place primarily within sovereign states and only secondarily between them. By contrast, even for the US, where ocean shipping is a significant mode of *domestic* transport, international shipments account for roughly two thirds of total ocean tonnage and much higher percentages of total ton-miles and value of shipments. (Very few US domestic ocean shipments involve high-valued manufactured goods.)

Surprisingly, however, the overwhelmingly international character of ocean shipping has not led to the development of a strong international network of intergovernmental and interenterprise understandings and agreements. On the contrary, and in contrast to the ubiquitous state interest in both air transport and telecommunications, the international shipping industry has evolved in an atmosphere of almost complete private ownership and control. National policies toward ocean shipping have a history going back to Columbus, Vasco da Gama, and Sir Francis Drake. However, both historically and at present, these policies have tended to support, promote, and protect rather than restrict the operations of home-country entrepreneurs and carriers.

Shipping was the subject of one of the first international conferences concerned with the conduct of routine business activity, the International Marine Conference, convened by the US in 1889. The agreement coming out of that conference dealt only with navigational issues, and the US proposal for creation of an international maritime commission received little attention. Subsequent international conventions and agreements have addressed safety issues, working conditions, skill qualifications, and other operating concerns, but fundamental economic issues (particularly entry into the industry, the critical issue upon which all others depend) were not addressed multilaterally until 1958. The current international policy regime for ocean transport involves a combination of essentially private interenterprise agreements, national policies, and international conventions, the latter dealing with both economic and noneconomic issues affecting the industry. (Principal elements of the regime are summarized in figure 7-1.)

7.1.1 Background and Regime Characteristics

Many factors explain the absence of a strong regulatory tradition, both domestic and international, in ocean shipping. One is certainly the long historical evolution of the industry and the prominence of both entre-preneurial initiative and colonialist ambitions in its development. A second factor is the diversity of the industry, particularly the seg-mentation of markets in both geographic and product or service dimensions. These functional differences give rise to differences in cost and demand conditions among carriers and shippers, which in turn inhibit uniform approaches to policy issues and even handicap the carriers' own efforts to reach and maintain agreements among themselves. Third, the ocean shipping industry lacks the prominent natural monopoly features that characterize many transport and communications activities and that typically give rise to some form of state intervention.

As a result of the natural openness of ocean shipping to competitive forces, the national policies of most states involved in the industry have, both historically and more recently, emphasized the promotion of domestic carriers and the suppression of competition. According to the traditional home-country perspective, the shipping industry deserves promotion as a contributor to national wealth and power and as a bulwark in the country's defense system. Any cost burdens arising from maritime industry support can be shifted to trading partners or third-country ship-

Description	Liner Conferences	IMO/UNCTAD
Institutional identification	Conference agreements (1880s–present)	IMO (1958) UNCTAD Code (1974/1983–present)
Purpose and Scope		
Purpose	Restrict competition	IMO: Noneconomic aspects UNCTAD: Permit/control entry
Scope	Entry, capacity, schedules, rates	IMO: Technology, safety, data entry UNCTAD: Participation
Organizational Form		
Structure	Enterprise-level, decentralized (some government recognition)	Multilateral (governments)
Power/concentration	Decentralized/concentrated within trade routes	Increasingly diffused among both carriers and governments
Decision and Allocation Modes	Negotiated (within multiple cartels)	Market/administrative
Strength and Change		
Peak strength	Up to early 1970s	1980s
Current (1980–1990)	Medium, and declining	Medium
Why change?	Economic, technological, and political change; new sources of competition; new industry participants	

Figure 7-1. The Ocean Shipping Regime.

pers. Even the US, in spite of its traditional commitment to market competition, has long provided the domestic shipping industry with subsidies (for ship construction and labor training as well as for operations) and with protection from foreign competition as well as some exemption from domestic antitrust requirements. Other major shipping countries have typically been more restrictive of foreign competitors and have tolerated strong anticompetitive agreements among carriers.

The historic means of suppressing competition in ocean shipping is the "liner conference," a nongovernmental organization of scheduled (non-bulk) carriers serving a specific trading route. The conference system developed in the late nineteenth century with the advent of steam ships, which made it possible to offer regularly schedule service along established routes. "Closed" conferences are classic cartels that limit membership, allocate business, and pool revenues and costs; "open" conferences set rates but do not formally restrict membership (although they may discourage entry in other ways). US law requires that all conferences serving American ports (which means conferences carrying about 20% of the value of total world trade) be "open"; most others are "closed." There have been three to four hundred active conferences operating in the worldwide shipping trade in recent decades.

The purpose of liner conferences was and is to control entry and to discourage the intense price competition that often arises in industries or markets with low barriers to entry. Although liner conferences are, in principle, highly restrictive business arrangements, their effectiveness has varied constantly as a result of changes in demand, technology, and industry capacity and in response to political developments.

7.1.2 Strength and Change

The immediate post–1945 decades were high points of conference effectiveness. The world shipping industry recovered rapidly from the war, but total carrying capacity maintained a rough balance with demand. The conference system was able to preserve a minimum rate structure and take advantage of periods of high demand to achieve substantial profits. However, by the early 1970s, the conference system gradually began to weaken as a result of changes in economic, technological, and political conditions. On the economic side, rate agreements lacking full cartel status are difficult to monitor, and the sanctions and remedies available to control violations relatively weak. The US "open conference" requirement thus had significant impact on the worldwide cartel environment; the cartel compliance of US carriers, with more than 90% of their international tonnage operating under foreign "flags of convenience" to escape domestic labor and safety requirements, has tended to be erratic.

Moreover, even the strongest conference rate agreements involve only conference members. Independent liner operators may solicit business among the same routes and shippers, and the tendency to violate or bypass conference agreements increased steadily as the switch to larger container-carrying vessels resulted in worldwide overcapacity in the industry. In addition, a substantial and increasing amount of tonnage is carried in bulk, in which case an entire vessel filled with a single commodity makes a point-to-point voyage at a negotiated price. Bulk cargo, both freight and tanker, now accounts for about three fourths of all ocean shipping tonnage and perhaps a quarter of all shipments by value.

Additional economic, technological, and regulatory trends weakening the power of the conferences include: 1) vertical integration by large multinational enterprises (MNEs) into the carriage of their own merchandise in their own vessels (Kindleberger, 1985); 2) development of land routes that provide alternatives to traditional ocean shipments; 3) increasingly aggressive organizations of shippers who use combined bargaining power to negotiate favorable freight rates or develop alternatives to conference rate shipments; 4) actions by the European Commission to restrict collective price-setting practices by conference members; and 5) pending revisions to US legislation that would sanction confidential contracts between shippers and shipping lines and eliminate requirements for the public filing of shipping rates.

As a result of all of these developments, although the traditional conference structure appears to constitute a classic cartel, its actual effects have been uneven with respect to nations and carriers, types of shipments, and trade routes, and also highly variable over time, declining (except for peaks associated with the oil crises) since the early 1970s.

The international political environment also changed in ways that eventually produced new multinational policy initiatives concerning ocean shipping. Three features of the postwar environment were of critical importance in this process: 1) US political and economic leadership in the noncommunist world, which gave traditional US resistance to restrictive business practices in international trade an increased importance; 2) European economic recovery, along with traditional European government support of the liner conference system; and 3) appearance of numerous postcolonial states (the less developed countries) on the world scene and their strong drive toward economic independence and development.

The first important international policy developments arising out of this context were the International Maritime Organization (IMO) and the 1958 Geneva Convention on the High Seas. The IMO was established in 1958 under UN auspices to serve as custodian for a number of existing international conventions and subsequently source of new agreements concerning noneconomic aspects of the maritime industries (i.e., safety, pollution, data collection). These concerns were greatly increased in the postwar years because of the increase in ocean traffic and in the size of vessels. The High Seas Convention, an output of the first UN Conference on the Law of the Sea (UNCLOS), addressed issues of national registration and attempted to reduce the use of "flags of convenience" as a means of avoiding operating costs required to meet advanced country (and international) safety and labor standards. This latter objective did not have US support and was not attained. Both of these developments reflect the power of the US with respect to international shipping policy, in spite of the fact that US carriers (both national flag and "flag of convenience") account for less than 10% of total world shipping tonnage.

The most important international policy development involving ocean shipping, however, arose from the third feature of the postwar environment, the desire for economic independence and development among the less developed countries (LDCs). This desire became focused in the demand for a New International Economic Order (NIEO), eventually formalized in UN resolutions in 1974; and a major vehicle for the creation of NIEO was the UN Conference on Trade and Development (UNCTAD), first convened in 1964 and ultimately established as a permanent UN agency. Ocean shipping (its cost, service, and national control) had been of concern to many of the LDCs during their years of colonial status, and UNCTAD became the focus of these concerns from its inception. The ultimate goal of the LDCs can be described as *participation* in the operation and management of the world shipping industry, particularly insofar as their own imports and exports were affected. The practical dimensions of such participation would include both: 1) reservation of some portion of LDC shipments to national carriers, many of which might be state-owned; and 2) generally increased LDC government involvement in the heretofore private (and largely First World–dominated) arena of international shipping.

After a decade of debate, the UNCTAD Code of Conduct for Liner Conferences was adopted in 1974 and came into force in 1983 when it was ratified by nations accounting for more than 25% of the relevant tonnage. Since fifty-eight nations were required to reach this level of coverage, the abstention of several major shipping states as well as of the principal states offering "flags of convenience" (Liberia and Panama), is apparent. European Community (EC) member countries ratified the code only after it was agreed that intra-OECD shipments would be excluded from coverage and that the entire EC would be considered one "national state" for purposes of cargo allocations. The former USSR and other East European countries also retained substantial flexibility even after becoming signatories to the code.[2]

The UNCTAD Code responds directly to LDC concerns with their historically unfavorable position vis-à-vis ocean shipping. Recognizing that the existing liner conference system could not be easily displaced, the code requires that "national shipping lines" of any nation served by a conference be automatically allowed to join the conference as a full participant; moreover, the consent of such "national lines" to all major conference decisions affecting the relevant country is required. Conferences are also required to consult with shippers about rates and related matters. Since many of the LDC enterprises involved in these relationships, whether as carriers or as shippers, are state-owned enterprises or closely related to national governments in other ways, these provisions effectively include LDC governments within the information and decision-making systems of the relevant conferences. Moreover, designated carriers of the LDCs are guaranteed actual participation in the provision of shipping services through the most widely discussed aspect of the code, the "40-40-20" formula for allocating shipments. Unless mutually agreed otherwise, the code requires that all conference shipment revenues between two nations shall be equally divided between their national line carriers, except that third-country carriers have the right to carry "a significant part, such as 20%" of the total. Although the language of the code applies to *conference* shipments only, the intent of most LDCs seems to be that the "40-40-20" formula would apply to all *liner* shipments, whether conference or independent; bulk shipments, however, are not involved in the arrangement.

A multilateral effort is now underway to bring international shipping into the framework of World Trade Organization (WTO) rules. This initiative would liberalize international maritime services, for example, limiting states' rights to restrict maritime traffic to their own flag carriers. As of summer 1996, the talks were deadlocked, with the US unwilling to relinquish authority to the WTO and wanting to maintain its right to take unilateral action against protectionist nations or shipping lines (Damas, 1996).

7.1.3 Impact of the Current Regime

The combination of cartel rate setting through the conferences and government allocation of cargo under the UNCTAD Code might be expected to yield a rigidly controlled international shipping regime. However, basic economic and technological trends tending to widen the scope for competitive forces in the industry remain at work. Continuing increases in economies of scale, at both the vessel and the enterprise level, make small-scale operations increasingly uneconomic; some LDCs have found that their only viable strategy is to lease their 40% cargo rights back to some international carrier. In addition, the US responded to the changed environment of the 1970s with the Shipping Act of 1984.

This legislation strengthened the participation of American carriers in the liner conferences in certain respects but weakened their power in others. In brief, the Shipping Act increased somewhat the immunity of conference agreements from US antitrust requirements and authorized the use of "service contracts," which tend to foreclose entry of competitors, between conferences and individual shippers or shipper associations. At the same time, however, the Shipping Act strengthened the rights of conference members to take "independent action" (i.e., individual rate-setting) and more flexible approaches to price and service decisions. Required registration of all US trade conference agreements with the Federal Maritime Commission (FMC) appears to convert that agency into an enforcement arm of the cartels; however, the FMC also has a watchdog role in that it can disapprove such agreements. The overall effect of the 1984 Act has been a subject of continuing debate up to the present (Grifman, 1988).

In short, although the UNCTAD Code adds another noncompetitive dimension to the *liner conference* portion of worldwide ocean shipping, and this dimension involves both some increase in the number of market participants and some protection of their interests, neither the code nor the conferences to which it is linked can completely alter the effect of basic economic forces (economies of scale, overcapacity, demand in-stability, ease of entry, etc.) that account for the fundamentally com-petitive structure of the ocean shipping industry.

7.2 THE AIR TRANSPORT REGIME[3]

International commercial air transportation presents a perfect example of the complex network of contacts and activities, involving both enterprises and governments, that characterizes the contemporary multinational business environment. As Kasper notes, "An airline hub diagram could just as easily illustrate a telecommunications network, a marine cargo transport system, or even a financial clearing house operation," and the current policy regime is "a hodge-podge of multi-lateral and bilateral agreements" among governments and enterprises (1988, pp. 8 and 45). During the post-1945 period, international air transport has been affected by extreme forms of nationalistic protection and international cartelization; at the same time, economic and techno-logical trends, as well as domestic political developments in a number of countries, have stimulated competitive forces and liberalized international air transport policies.[4]

The international air transport regime consists of three main elements:

1. Bilateral agreements among governments that allocate international air routes to their respective *national* control.

2. The International Air Transport Association (IATA), a price-setting cartel of airlines, recognized by but not directly involving governments.

3. The International Civil Aviation Organization (ICAO), an intergovernmental organization that deals with technical and safety issues and has important informational functions.

7.2.1 Background

Since the principle of sovereignty over national air space was established following World War I, it has been assumed that government approval is required before a foreign plane can land on its territory. At the outset, individual carriers simply negotiated the relevant permissions on their own, but during World War II federal interest in airline operations and the increase in international flights caused the US government to assume responsibility for these negotiations on behalf of US firms. (Prior to World War II, Pan Am was the only US airline significantly involved in international flights, and only a few other carriers were operating anywhere in the world.)

In 1944, representatives of Allied and nonbelligerent governments met in Chicago to consider alternative postwar policy regimes for international air transport. Conflict between a US commitment to a relatively open international air transport regime (i.e., essentially the idea that carriers should be free to offer service, with a minimum of government intervention) and a desire on the part of other nations, led by the United Kingdom, to protect and promote the development of their own national carriers, prevented the development of global policies with respect to the allocation of routes and other commercial aspects of air transport. As a result, the "Convention on International Civil Aviation" (usually referred to as the "Chicago Convention") reflected agreement on technical and safety issues alone and did not address commercial traffic issues.

The Chicago Convention came into force in 1947 when it was ratified by the required twenty-six national governments; ICAO was formed to carry out the purposes of the convention on a continuing basis. Although the major work of ICAO relates to technical issues, its activities are commercially important for two reasons: 1) technical standards and arrangements affect costs and often provide foundation or ancillary elements of commercial agreements; and 2) absence of any other official international body has led ICAO to assume very significant informational and administrative functions. ICAO apparently was and is seen as a vehicle to prevent complete US dominance of the international air transport regime; at the same time, the US Federal Aviation Administration (FAA) has been a dominant technical force within ICAO during most of its history.

Since neither the Chicago Convention nor ICAO embodied any understanding about route allocations, regularization of international commercial air transport service was left in the hands of the various governments and carriers involved. The primary national participants in international commercial air transport at the end of World War II were the US and the UK, the former having the major fleet of planes and the latter controlling landing rights at important locations around the globe. Representatives of these two nations met in Bermuda in 1946 and worked out an agreement involving bilateral exchange of landing rights along specific routes. In effect, the two nations agreed to permit routes to be flown by each other's national carriers between specific destinations (e.g., New York and London). The national governments involved then allocated these routes among their own airlines as they saw fit. The Bermuda Agreement became the model for the eventual worldwide network of bilateral arrangements. The agreement did not establish fares on the designated routes but essentially assumed the existence of a separate international fare-setting mechanism that was, in fact, already in operation: the International Air Transport Association (IATA), established as an intercarrier organization in 1945.

7.2.2 Post–World War II Regime Characteristics

Although bilateral intergovernmental route agreements and the international airline fare-setting cartel are formally distinct institutions, they are in fact complementary elements of a single international policy regime for commercial air transport. ICAO is this regime's supporting technical branch. (See figure 7-2 for a summary of regime characteristics.) Bilateral agreements define international airline routes in terms of departure points, intermediate points, destinations, and "beyond points" (i.e., extensions). A single "route" may include numerous permutations of these features and may thus involve service to various third countries as well as between the two nations directly participating. Most agreements not involving the US also specify the service capacity (size of planes, number of flights) to be provided by the contracting parties, while many US agreements only provide for ex *post* government review of capacity levels. IATA recognizes a number of air transport regions (e.g., North America–Europe), and "rate conferences" comprised of the carriers serving each such region or subunit thereof determine among themselves the fares to be charged for service along specific routes. The power of this classic cartel arrangement is constrained, however, by several considerations. Not all IATA members providing service in a specific area necessarily participate in the relevant rate conferences, and, as noted above, the volume of non-IATA traffic can also be substantial. IATA rate agreements must also be submitted to the various governments involved for approval. Although such agreements are generally approved, if one is not approved, or if no agreement is reached among the carriers, then the

Description	Bermuda	IATA/ICAO
Institutional identification	Bilateral agreements (1946–present)	IATA (1945–present) ICAO (1947–present)
Purpose and Scope		
Purpose	Establish and allocate	IATA: Cartel system to set fares ICAO: Standardize technology/procedures
Scope	Routes, entry, capacity	IATA: Rates, commercial practices ICAO: Technical issues
Organizational Form		
Structure	Governmental/bilateral/ decentralized	IATA: Interenterprise ICAO: Intergovernment Both: multipartite/ centralized
Power/concentration	Origin: US/UK dominance Later: Bilateral power	IATA: Dispersed among participants ICAO: Originally US (FAA) dominated; now dispersed
Decision and Allocation Modes	Bilateral negotiations	IATA: Cartel agreements ICAO: Technical negotiations
Strength and Change		
Peak strength	1946–1977 (declining)	IATA: 1946–1977 ICAO: Continuously strong to present
Current (1980–1990)	Low	Medium
Why change?	Change essentially due to changes in number/power/ interests of actors, particularly: (1) Entry and increasing capacity, especially on US– Europe routes (2) Domestic deregulation and pressure for international liberalization (3) Mergers and joint agreements	

Figure 7-2. The Air Transport Regime.

conference is declared "open" and individual carriers submit their own rate filings to relevant national authorities. For all of these reasons (and because of underlying changes in the volume, economics, and technology of air travel), the actual cartel power of IATA has varied considerably both among regions and over time.

7.2.3 Strength and Change

The 1946 Bermuda Agreement between the US and the UK became the model for a worldwide intergovernmental system of air route allocations through a very natural process. At the end of World War II, the US had a large and comparatively well-developed domestic airline industry, and a single US carrier (Pan Am) accounted for almost all international commercial travel. The UK was the only other significant participant in the industry, with the advantage of control of important landing sites in colonies around the world (e.g., Newfoundland, Bermuda, India, and Hong Kong), as well as the position of London as the gateway for North American flights to Europe. Commercial air transport was an infant industry in most other countries.

Once the US and UK had reached agreement about conditions of mutual access, similar agreements were made by other nations desiring foreign landing rights for their carriers. And as the air traffic of these third countries developed, the "Bermuda" model, with various modifications, was extended throughout the world. The power of IATA developed in a parallel manner, since US and UK airlines were initially the dominant members. In fact, Pan Am alone accounted for over half of all international commercial travel until the late 1950s.

The Bermuda-IATA regime remained essentially stable for more than three decades and continues in place in most of the world up to the present time. However, the strength of the regime has varied among regions and routes and was gradually being eroded by economic and technological change before it was substantially modified in 1978. The basic change-inducing factors include:

1. A vast expansion in the volume of international air travel during the 1960s and 1970s, with a corresponding increase in total carrying capacity. For example, available international tonne-kilometers increased from five in 1960 to sixty-four in 1980. In addition, under the umbrella provided by the IATA fare structure, nonscheduled (charter) international services expanded rapidly during the 1960s and accounted for almost 40% of total international service in the early 1970s.

2. Increases in the size of planes and changes in the technology of related support activities (e.g., computerized reservation systems) that resulted in differential cost structures and capabilities between carriers.

3. Increases in the number of airlines providing international commercial air transport, many of which are government-owned or subsidized and enjoy monopoly status within their home jurisdictions.

These changes brought a number of different pressures to bear on the Bermuda-IATA regime. Growth in demand increased the opportunity for competition and weakened the power of the cartel. Success of independent charters on densely traveled and vacation routes caused some IATA carriers to expand their own charter activity, while others responded with deep fare discounts. Economies of traffic density increased pressures for high-capacity operations, stimulating fare reductions. At the same time many of the new international airlines were small, with relatively high costs, and required monopoly-cartel protection (as well as government subsidies) in order to operate at all. By the mid 1960s, a majority of IATA member airlines were based in developing countries, and most of these enterprises were small, state-sponsored monopolies established for reasons of national prestige. This change in membership greatly increased the role of governments in the cartel and strengthened support for its activities. (However, some important new national airlines, particularly those of Singapore, Malaysia, Thailand, and Hong Kong, remained for a time outside the cartel and competed vigorously and successfully for international traffic.) The net result of all of these developments was a strengthening of competitive forces on the one hand and a strengthening of support for anticompetitive restrictions, on the other.

These conflicting developments fragmented IATA's structure and strained its cohesiveness. Although fare reductions succeeded in stemming the growth of charters, which now account for only about 10% of total traffic, the price-setting power of the cartel was clearly being eroded. At the same time, concerns of governments (European as well as Third World) for the welfare of their national carriers increased the restrictiveness of bilateral access agreements, including limitations on flight capacity and frequency as well as provisions for revenue pooling. By the mid 1970s, even the US became sufficiently concerned with carrier protection to accept British proposals for capacity and entry controls in a second Bermuda Agreement (Bermuda II, 1977).

However, the expansion of national protectionism embodied in Bermuda II proved to be short-lived. US domestic policy was moving in the direction of deregulation across the board, with the airline industry a major focus of activity. It was felt in Washington, DC, that US international airline policy should parallel domestic policy. Hence, by 1978, the restrictive Bermuda II became essentially a dead letter, and the US negotiated in quick succession over twenty new "liberal" bilateral agreements forbidding government restrictions on airline pricing, capacity, and entry (including charters). The inclusion of asymmetric access (greater foreign access to US destinations) was used to induce acceptance of these liberalizations by foreign negotiators.

Although there was a pause in the signing of liberal agreements during the 1980s, the US embarked on a renewed effort to sign these agreements in the 1990s. By 1995, the US had signed new liberal agreements (now called "open skies" agreements) with nine European countries and Canada. The net result of all of these developments has been a considerable liberalization of the international air transport regime over the past two decades, although the combination of bilateral government agreements and an enterprise-level cartel remains in place. In some markets, particularly the heavily traveled North Atlantic, competition has increased to the point that IATA fare setting is irrelevant; in other regions IATA has designated "fare zones," leaving room for flexibility on specific fares. Some current US agreements contain a "double disapproval" feature that allows airlines to set whatever fares they choose unless *both* governments deny permission.

Recently, many carriers have entered into international alliances to market international air services jointly. (Examples include KLM-Northwest Airlines, British Airways-USAir, and Swissair-Delta-Singapore Airlines.) The most comprehensive of the alliances allow for joint advertising, price-setting, and airport operations. The US government has, in general, been willing to grant antitrust immunity to these alliances as long as routes operated by alliance members are covered by a liberal bilateral agreement. The development of these alliances are creating multinational entities that partially escape home-country control and that may be harmed rather than helped by restrictive national policies.

In addition, liberalization of international airline competition is an important aspect of Europe 1992. Through a series of liberalization "packages," the European Union's Council of Ministers and other governmental and judicial bodies have sought to transform intra-European flights from a series of restrictive transborder routes to a single, liberalized continental market. The packages have involved freeing entry onto routes, the removal of national ownership restrictions on airlines, and even cabotage rights (i.e., the right for a carrier of country A to operate between two points in country B). Although these new rules are scheduled to be phased in throughout the 1990s, there have been implementation delays as governments with weaker airlines seek ways to protect their carriers from unlimited competition.

7.3 CONCLUSION

This analysis of the international regimes for air transport and ocean shipping leads us to two substantive conclusions:

1. These regimes "matter," in the sense that they influence the actions of enterprises and governments, and hence the content and outcome of international business activity.
2. These regimes display a common evolutionary pattern over the postwar decades that has not been clearly observed in previous analyses.

This concluding section summarizes our findings on these two substantive issues.

7.3.1 The Impact of Regimes

The question of whether or not regimes "matter" requires some explication: Do regimes "matter" as compared to *what*? It is impossible to imagine exactly what the international business environment would be like if none of the institutional developments of the postwar decades had taken place; and, in any event, some forms of government involvement and international cooperation/conflict would inevitably exist in these and many other industries. Hence, the relevant question is: Do the regimes examined here have discernible direct consequences? We address this issue in terms of the four specific questions derived from the Haggard and Simmons (1987) analysis (see earlier discussion in chapter 2).

1. Has the regime altered the situation so that cooperation (conflict) among enterprises and states becomes more (less) likely? Our answer to this question is "yes" in both cases, although it is difficult to draw a net balance between the forces of cooperation and conflict involved. On the one hand, both regimes are based on principles of cooperation, usually with cartel aspects. At the same time, these sophisticated and complex arrangements also increase the possibilities for conflict, both between regime participants and outside parties and, even more conspicuously, among the participating governments and enterprises. Hence, the general conclusion seems to be that more, and certainly very different, possibilities for both cooperation and conflict arise in each industry because of the existence of the regimes. In particular, although market forces are now of great importance in both cases, the basic regime structure in air transport and the postwar developments in shipping have tended to shift the focus from market forces to the political arena.

2. Has the regime altered actors' goals and behavior options? Again, our answer is affirmative in both cases; the reasoning is presented in section 7.3.2 below.

3. Has the regime tended to weaken national boundaries? Our answer is negative in both cases. The UNCTAD Code clearly strengthened national interests; and the contemporary weakening of national identity among the airlines is occurring at the expense of, not because of, the international policy regime. However, it should be noted that, although the weakening of national boundaries is assumed to be desirable by some regime enthusiasts, this view is neither unambiguous nor universal. Indeed, Krasner (1985) appears to believe that more "authoritarian" regimes are probably more desirable from the viewpoint of LDCs, and such regimes necessarily involve the strengthening, rather than the weakening, of national authority in some respects.

4. Did the regime strengthen coalitions? The answer is affirmative in both cases, although the coalitions stimulated were typically less than universal and not necessarily benign. Both the Bermuda-IATA regime and the liner conferences were established as coalitions, and they in turn stimulated countervailing coalitions aimed at getting a share of the pie.

Our overall conclusion is that both the sea and air transport regimes do "matter," in the sense that their respective industries involve different constituents and operate in different ways than they would if no similar institutional and behavioral arrangements were in place. However, this conclusion is neither as obviously benign as some regime analysts may have anticipated nor as clearly malign as some critics may have feared. Our positive conclusion is that these regimes have had very significant effects; the normative analysis of these effects (whether they are on balance desirable or undesirable, and from whose perspective) is a question we leave to others.

7.3.2 The Evolutionary Pattern

The first phase of regime evolution common to both of these cases is an increase in government participation within the system of market relationships and agreements previously worked out among enterprises. The initial enterprise-level arrangements are, of course, IATA and the ocean liner conferences. Increased government participation involves both 1) increases in the *number* of governments participating, and 2) more extensive government *involvement*, particularly more government initiative in stimulating and directing enterprise-level activities. Illustrative examples are the international air transport agreements leading up to Bermuda II and the UNCTAD Code.

Increased government involvement and nationalistic protectionism lead directly to an increase in the number of enterprise participants in the industry. Some of these are new competitors (whether state- or private-owned) attracted by cartel price umbrellas; others are created by governments to achieve national representation in international markets. Examples are charter flights and new national airlines, bulk ocean carriers, and UNCTAD national freight allocations. These increases in the number of actors, both government- and private-sponsored, in each industry place fundamental strains on the system of government controls and protections. On the one hand, there are more potential sources of competitive behavior within the industry; on the other hand, many of the new participants can exist only within a protected environment, and increases in their numbers lead to demands for increased protection. The result in the case of airlines, where the cycle is essentially complete, has been the outbreak of competition from both new and old sources, partial abandonment of the protective regime, and a wave of failures, mergers, and new international investments that is still (1996) in progress. In ocean shipping, the growth of bulk carriage (which escapes coverage by both the conferences and the UNCTAD Code) and the leasing of small UNCTAD-guaranteed shipment rights to larger established carriers are comparable developments.

A cursory survey of international economic relationships in a wide variety of industries and areas suggests that this three-phase pattern of evolution has been fairly typical of the post–World War II era. Certainly there has been an increase in government involvement in all aspects of international business and economic activity. And, because of the increase in the number of economically active governments in the world as well as for other reasons, there have been substantial increases in the number of enterprises and actors in most industries as well as increases in inter-industry competition. Hence, tension inevitably increases between protective-controlling regimes, on the one hand, and ever more numerous and diverse enterprises and governments (each of which is a potential source of competition, and some of actual rivalry) on the other hand. The likely outcome, most clearly observed here in the case of international air transport, is a weakening of regime controls and a period of shakeout and consolidation among the potential competitors, both states and enterprises.

Notes

1. This section is based primarily on Stopford, 1988; White, 1988; and Garvey, 1984; see also Waldmann, 1980, chapter 5, and Jenkins, 1996. Comments and suggestions from Professor George A. Garvey, School of Law, Catholic University, are gratefully acknowledged.

2. Important references on the UNCTAD Code include Juda, 1983; Kyle and Phillips, 1983; and Larsen and Vetterick, 1981; as well as Stopford, 1988, chapter 4.

3. This section is based primarily on Dresner, 1989; Jonsson, 1987; Kasper, 1988; and Taneja, 1988; as well as on various official documents.

4. The theory that international regimes are created by a powerful hegemon or coalition and decline when hegemonic power wanes has been tested in three case studies of international airlines. Jonsson (1987) found the theory inadequate and developed an alternative "process model" of regime transformation. Busza (1987) found the theory helpful but introduced a shift in the importance of goals (from national security interests to carrier interests) on the part of the hegemon (US) as a major explanatory factor. In the most rigorous study, Dresner (1989) found the hegemonic stability theory to be supported by three instances of regime change and not supported in one.

References

Busza, Eva. 1987. *The Civil Aviation Cartel.* Unpublished master's thesis, University of British Columbia.

Damas, Philip. 1996. "WTO Talks Hit a Snag," *American Shipper*, April, p. 22.

Dresner, Martin. 1989. *The International Regulation of Air Transport: Changing Regimes and Price Effects.* Unpublished doctoral dissertation, University of British Columbia.

Garvey, George E. 1984. "Regulatory Reform in the Ocean Shipping Industry," *George Washington Journal of International Law and Economics*, vol. 18, no. 1, pp. 1–54.

Grifman, Phyllis, ed. 1988. *The Shipping Act of 1984: A Debate of the Issues.* Los Angeles, CA: Sea Grant Program, University of Southern California.

Haggard, Stephan, and Beth A. Simmons. 1987. "Theories of International Regimes," *International Organization*, vol. 41, no. 3 (Summer), pp. 491–517.

Jenkins, Holman W. 1996. "Antitrust Pirates the High Seas," *Wall Street Journal*, December 3.

Jonsson, Christer. 1987. *International Aviation and the Politics of Regime Change.* New York: St. Martin's Press.

Juda, Lawrence. 1983. *The UNCTAD Liner Code.* Boulder, CO: Westview.

Kasper, Daniel M. 1988. *Deregulation and Globalization: Liberalizing International Trade in Air Services.* Cambridge, MA: Ballinger.

Kindleberger, Charles P. 1985. "Multinational Ownership of Shipping Activities," *World Economy*, vol. 8, no. 3 (September), pp. 249–265.

Krasner, Stephen D. 1985. *Structural Conflict: The Third World Against Global Liberalism.* Berkeley and Los Angeles, CA: University of California Press.

Kyle, Reuben, and Laurence T. Phillips. 1983. "Cargo Reservation for Bulk Commodity Shipments: An Economic Analysis," *Columbia Journal of World Business*, vol. 18, no. 3 (Fall), pp. 42–49.

Larsen, P.G., and V. Vetterick. 1981. "The UNCTAD Code of Conduct for Liner Conferences," *Law and Policy in International Business*, vol. 13, no. 1 (Spring), pp. 223–280.

Stopford, Martin. 1988. *Maritime Economics*. London: Unwin Hyman.

Strange, Susan. 1988. *States and Markets*. New York: Basil Blackwell.

Taneja, Nawal K. 1988. *The International Airline Industry*. Lexington, MA: D.C. Heath.

Waldmann, Raymond J. 1980. *Regulating International Business through Codes of Conduct*. Washington, DC: American Enterprise Institute for Public Policy Research.

White, Lawrence J. 1988. *International Trade in Ocean Shipping Services*. Cambridge, MA: Ballinger.

8

TELECOMMUNICATIONS
AND OTHER SERVICES

As the previous chapter demonstrated, arrangements for facilitating and monitoring international transportation by sea and air have evolved over many decades. Other regimes involving postal, telegraph, and broadcast linkages among countries have also been in operation for many years. However, technological changes in telecommunications and the growth of other types of international services, particularly financial services, during recent decades have placed new demands on existing regimes and have led to new and more comprehensive approaches to international communications and services linkages. The issues raised by these developments, and the contemporary regimes responses' to them, are surveyed in this chapter.

8.1 MONITORING AND REGULATING INTERNATIONAL SERVICES

Internationally traded services present some of the greatest conceptual difficulties, as well as the severest problems of monitoring and controlling, within the entire sphere of international business activity. However, there is no question that international service trade is large and growing; in 1992, services represented some 22% of total trade in both goods and services, an increase of five percentage points (and almost three times in total value) since 1980, according to Hoekman (1994). A rough estimate from UNCTAD data indicates increasing trade in services over time, although differing in detail from Hoekman's data (see table 8-1). The need for international agreements concerning service industries has been a major subject of discussion in business and policy circles since the early 1980s, and service industry issues were a major focus of the Uruguay Round of General Agreement on Tariffs and Trade (GATT) negotiations that resulted in the present World Trade Organization (WTO).

Table 8-1. Content of World Exports, 1975–1993 (current US$)

	1975		1985		1993	
	$ Billions	% Share	$ Billions	% Share	$ Billions	% Share
World Total	950	100	2104	100	4553	100
Services	129	14	311	15	933	20
Merchandise	821	86	1793	85	3620	80

Source: Estimated from World Bank, *World Data 1995 CD-ROM* (Washington, DC).

Notes: "Exports" defined as goods and nonfactor services. "Services" computed as difference between "World Total" and "Merchandise" and may therefore include unallocated exports.

Services have been defined by *The Economist* as "things one can buy or sell, but not drop on one's foot" (UNCTC, 1990). The complete list of service industries as defined by the UN International Standard Industrial Classification system is shown below (UNCTC, 1989, p. 4; for a summary of critical issues in many of these areas, see UNCTAD, 1989):

Wholesale trade

Retail trade

Restaurants and hotels

Transport (railway, urban, other land, pipeline, water, air, etc.)

Storage and warehousing

Communications

Financial institutions (banks and other institutions providing financial services, except for insurance companies)

Insurance

Real estate

Business services (including legal services, accounting, and auditing; data processing; engineering, architectural, and technical services; advertising; other business services, such as credit-rating agencies and employment agencies; news-gathering and reporting agencies, business management, and consulting services; fashion designers; detective agencies and protective services)

International and extraterritorial bodies (including international organizations, foreign embassies, and other extraterritorial units)

Machinery and equipment rental and leasing

Public administration and defense

Sanitary and similar services

Social and related community services (including education services; research and scientific institutes; medical, dental, other health, and veterinary services; business, professional, and labor associations; religious organizations)

Recreational and cultural services (including motion picture production, distribution, and projection; radio and television broadcasting; theatrical producers and entertainment services; all other amusement and recreational services)

Personal and household services (including repair services; laundry and cleaning services; social escort services; and shopping services)

One reason that services have not been conventionally included within the framework of international economic negotiations is their invisible, often nebulous, character. International service transactions may take place without any contact with geographic borders (through telecommunications, for example). They may also occur through the movement of *persons* who subsequently receive services (e.g., tourism) or provide services (e.g., professional work) in another jurisdiction. Such activities do not fit easily into conventional concepts of "trade," although they may have substantial effects on the incomes and international accounts of the enterprises, individuals, and countries involved. At the same time, services are the lubricants of international trade and investment and a major vehicle for the transfer of technology and management processes among countries.

A second major problem in the measurement of international service activities is that their value is often embedded in the value of merchandise, equipment, or investments to which the services themselves are applied. The most recent UN estimate is that service activities account for 50% to 60% of the current world stock of foreign direct investment (FDI) and about 60% of the annual FDI flow (UNCTC, 1990, p. 2).

8.1.1 Policy Concerns in the Service Sector

The sources of national and international policy concern with respect to services are multiple and interrelated (cf. Clegg, 1993; Daniels, 1993; Feketekuty, 1988). The most important is that, although precise definitions and magnitudes are subject to debate, it is generally believed that the volume of international service industry activity is large and growing and that this growth has powerful and pervasive impacts on other business sectors and entire economies. Simply obtaining basic information about international services and their possible impact on domestic economies has become a major concern in itself.

A second issue is that many service industries (e.g., broadcasting, financial services, insurance) are tightly regulated within individual national states. Some are state monopolies, and in others participation is limited in whole or part to nationals. The connection between such national policies and the operations of foreign competitors performing similar functions is highly problematic, particularly when the magnitude and consequences of the activities involved are imprecisely known.

A third concern is that service industry activities are intimately linked with ownership and use of intellectual property, including artistic creations, data collections, operating routines, and communication activities. Enterprises and governments seek to control service activities both to *obtain* access to intellectual property originating elsewhere and to *prevent* or *control* access to their own intellectual property holdings by other interests.

Finally, many states and enterprises see the service sector as a major area for prospective growth, and hence seek to integrate service industries into national development policies and to stimulate and protect nationally based service activities, particularly those involving financial services. Fears that foreign domination of service activities might damage domestic growth prospects, and possibly lead to cultural domination as well, strengthen these considerations.[1]

The complexity of the above issues strongly suggests that development of a policy framework for international services is not an easy task; and this impression is reinforced by a wide range of scholarly opinion. All authorities agree that the key element is the extension of basic GATT principles to the service sector (Feketekuty, 1988; Krommenacker, 1984). However, Kahler emphasizes that the "embeddedness" of service activities in national regulatory and political systems, and the lack of transparency in these domestic arrangements, create significant barriers (1995, pp. 35–38). Krommenacker (1984) recommends the development of an international agreement on "telematics" (a combination of telecommunications, data processing, and information services) as a critical development that might provide a focus and model for other service industries developments. These, however, are among the activities most embedded in domestic policy systems, as well as generating national security concerns. Walter (1988) emphasizes the need to remove national protections for financial services that, combined with insurance, account for by far the largest aggregate value of internationally traded services. However, the obvious competitive advantages of the advanced industrial countries, particularly the US, in these areas gives rise to serious reservations on the part of other governments and enterprises.

Experience with international service trade in the context of US bilateral agreements with Israel, Canada, and Mexico is likely to have considerable influence on larger developments. Both the US–Israel and US–Canada agreements, while virtually eliminating barriers to merchandise trade and investment, basically stipulated "best efforts" to negotiate future arrangements for services. These agreements also created special administrative bodies for dispute resolution. The importance and diversity of services within this particular set of trading partners, and the strong US advantage in service industry activities, make these negotiations a microcosm of global service trade problems and opportunities and have been reflected in the more recent GATT/WTO negotiations.

8.1.2 Services and the GATT/WTO[2]

The difficulties and complexities noted above strongly indicate that a comprehensive policy regime for international service industries is not likely to emerge in the near future. On the other hand, these service industry issues are simply new versions of the concerns that have been at the center of international policy regime evolution over the past half century. Since international service activities and their consequences, both welcome and problematic, are of growing importance in the economy, it seems that the evolution of a policy regime for international trade in services, although probably on a piecemeal rather than comprehensive basis, can be predicted with some confidence.

In fact, one of the major results of the Uruguay Round of trade negotiations was the development of a General Agreement on Trade in Services (GATS). The GATS provisions apply to all measures imposed by any signatory country that affect the consumption of services originating in any other signatory country and cover several possible modes of supply: crossborder services not requiring physical movement (e.g., telecommunications); services involving movement of the consumer to the supplying country (e.g., tourism), or of the supplier to the consuming country (e.g., consulting); and services originating in one country but sold by a legal entity in another (e.g., banking).

Although GATS represents a breakthrough in terms of coverage, it does not in itself advance the cause of trade liberalization in services in any significant way. The GATS agreement sets forth "general obligations and disciplines" of the signatories and pledges them to pursue two traditional GATT norms: nondiscrimination and transparency. In GATS, as within GATT, the concept of nondiscrimination includes both national treatment and most favored nation (MFN) principles. However, application of these principles is more limited, since each signatory can present a *negative* list of services that will be excluded from coverage in its particular case, and over sixty GATS signatories have done so. Financial services and transportation (two of the most important areas of international service activity) are, not surprisingly, among the most frequently listed items. However, in spite of its weaknesses, GATS is significant because it expands the scope of multinational agreement to these important areas and embodies a commitment to future liberalization within them.

8.2 THE INTERNATIONAL TELECOMMUNICATIONS REGIME

The international telecommunications regime is one of the oldest formal multilateral policy systems affecting business; it is also one of the most clearly "global" in character. The International Telegraph Union (ITU) was organized under the sponsorship of the French Emperor Napoleon III in 1865. "Telecommunications" replaced "Telegraph" in the ITU name in 1932, and it became a specialized agency of the UN in 1947. Yet, as a result of changing technology, exploding levels of utilization, and changing political circumstances, there is at the present time no set of coherent international policies in place governing interconnections, access, investment, or trade in this important arena of business and technology (Aronson and Cowhey, 1988). A century-old system based on technological standardization, national monopoly, and international cartel arrangements is collapsing in the face of technological change, changing national regulatory policies, and the emergence of new forms and forces of competition.[3]

8.2.1 Background and Regime Characteristics

Telecommunications involves an interwoven system of equipment, services, and information content (see figure 8-1). Two distinct technologies (telephone and broadcast) are utilized, often in combination, to produce both transient contacts (e.g., conversations, broadcasts) and permanent records (e.g., facsimile copies, data records). And, with a combination of telecommunications and computer services, there are also possibilities for qualitative change in the transmitted material through data processing and other forms of "value added service." International and domestic communications services are indissolubly interlinked, and domestic services are universally regulated and frequently state-owned. Efficient international telecommunications requires technological compatibility among systems; indeed, compatibility, plus the avoidance of interference, was the major principle of the telecommunications policy regime during its first century. However, technological compatibility facilitates contacts that may be in conflict with other national policies (e.g., control of national security information, censorship of political and cultural viewpoints, etc.). Hence, even at a technical level, the concerns of the international telecommunications regime expand to include issues of system utilization and communications content as well as equipment and channels (Dizard, 1988).

8.2.2 Purpose, Form, and Allocation Mode

From its nineteenth-century origins up to the present, the primary focus of the ITU has been on technological cooperation, including standardization of both procedures and equipment. Emphasis shifted from telegraph to radio in 1906, and spectrum allocations under ITU auspices began in 1927. The ITU has been for many decades the administrative authority for the "global commons" of worldwide communications space. (The evolution and structure of the ITU are exhaustively described in White and White, 1988.) Major policy decisions of the ITU are made at periodic World Administrative Radio Conferences (WARCs) attended by several thousand delegates from more than one hundred countries. WARC decisions are made on a "one-nation, one-vote" basis and require national ratification and enforcement. The most significant operating body of the ITU is the Consultative Committee for Telephones and Telegraph (CCITT), which, according to Aronson and Cowhey, has evolved from a purely technical body into "a virtual telephone cartel for PTTs" (1988, p. 14). Compliance with ITU regulations has been very high because of the common interests among the national PTTs (post, telephone, telegraph providers) and also because any nation had to conform to international standards in order to participate in the worldwide communications system. The circumstances that favored voluntary compliance are now being altered by changes in technology and national policies.

Description	Cable	Satellite	All Modes
Institutional identification	Joint operating agreements	INTELSAT	ITU/CCITT
Technology	Point-to-point	Network	All technologies
Purpose and Scope			
Purpose	Market access to monopoly facility	Administer access	Set technical standards; resolve increasingly complex issues
Scope	Entry, rates, technology	Entry, rates, technology	Expanding to include all issues
Organizational Form			
Structure	Private (no government aspect)	Enterprise-level (US COMSAT and national PTTs), multipartite, under government auspices	Multilateral (governments); Annex on Telecommunications attached to GATS Agreement
Power/concentration	Companies/countries with critical locations and capabilities	US technology initially assured control	Political; uncertain
Decision and Allocation Modes	Market, with government approval	Administrative	Administrative, negotiated
Strength and Change			
Peak strength	1800s–present	1965–1980	ITU: 1900s–1960s
Current	High	Medium, declining	ITU/CCITT strong but GATT/WTO now involved as well
Why change?		Satellite technology did not eliminate cable; new competition is developing in satellites; increasingly complex issues emerging.	

Figure 8-1. The Telecommunications Regime.

As with air transport at a later date, the North Atlantic region was initially the major focus of international telecommunications development. The first undersea telegraph cable linking North America and Europe was laid in 1866, and the number of such cables increased steadily for several decades. These undersea cables were owned and operated by private firms that controlled the entire communications circuit and negotiated connections with domestic carriers at either end. Two-way radio (voice) transmission across the Atlantic was initiated by AT&T in 1915 and offered commercially in 1927. Although this technology ultimately proved unreliable, it introduced a new policy feature of permanent importance. For national security and spectrum scarcity reasons, both the US and European nations were unwilling to grant broadcast licenses to foreign enterprises. Therefore, two-way radio links were based on operating agreements between domestic carriers in each country, with each carrier formally in control of only a "half-circuit" of the international communications link. When later technology permitted the laying of transatlantic telephone cables, the principle of half-circuit joint operation was maintained. (International one-way broadcast communication is limited, of course, only by the power of transmitters and receivers, and by overt interference in broadcast signals, i.e., "jamming" to prevent their reception.)

Development of satellite technology in the 1960s opened an entirely new phase of international telecommunications. The vast potential capacity of satellite systems appeared just as increasing world economic integration was greatly increasing the demand for communications services and computerization was generating enormous new collections of material available for transmission. In addition, satellite technology permitted the creation of global networks, within which multiple stations send and receive information simultaneously. However, because satellite communication involves conventional broadcast technology for the up-down links, the issue of national control arose here just as it had with radio a half century earlier.

In the light of all these considerations, the concept of an internationally-owned and -operated satellite system with nationally-owned earth stations in each participating country evolved. The US was at the time the only country other than the former USSR able to launch satellites and a leader in other aspects of satellite technology as well. Hence, US leadership was critical in the formation of the International Telecommunications Satellite Organization (INTELSAT), headquartered in Washington, DC, as an arrangement for joint ownership and management of space communications technology by the authorized agencies of the 139 cooperating governments: the Communications Satellite Corporation (COMSAT) for the US and national PTTs for most of the others.

8.2.3 Strength and Change

The first century of the international telecommunications regime was dominated by considerations of technical efficiency, including the introduction of improved technologies as they became available. During the 1970–1990 decades, however, increased congestion in the communications environment, and increased concern with the economic and political implications of international communications, have generated pressures for change that will necessarily involve other fundamental principles. In the 1960s, it was generally believed that satellite technology would displace cable and that INTELSAT's structure and service capacity would make it the global monopolist of satellite operations. Both of these beliefs, however, proved unfounded. Fiber optic technology has revitalized cable operations; and, although considerable excess capacity remains in the INTELSAT system, a number of competitive alternatives and proposals have arisen. Some of these alternatives bypass common carrier communications channels entirely. Orion, a private US satellite firm, established direct linkages among users in various countries (usually units of a single multinational entity) who install their own transponders for direct contact with the satellite; a similar arrangement for a firm specializing in service to international financial institutions was approved by the US Federal Communications Commission (FCC). In addition, various groups of nations have proposed new systems targeted toward their special needs: Arabsat (Arab countries consortium); the European Communications System (ECS); and Palapa-B (Indonesia and neighboring countries). A number of private firms and consortia are now entering the low-level satellite transmission business, sometimes on a regional rather than global scale. In addition, many developing countries believe that both broadcast frequencies and orbital locations should be allocated without regard to immediate use considerations in order to break the pattern of communications dominance by the advanced countries and to preserve their own possibilities for future development (Soroos, 1982, p. 157). Such proposals call into question the traditional "first come, first served" approach to space allocation within the world communication environment and suggest an alternative approach based on national jurisdiction and interest. The latter approach would reflect the same kind of national sovereignty considerations that apply to overflight airspace and territorial waters.

In the midst of all of these developments, the fundamental jurisdictional concept of international communications law has also been challenged. From the very beginning of international communication among persons (which took place, of course, by post), it has been assumed that each sovereign state had the right to control the flow of communications into and out of its territory, and most states have in fact exercised such control at one time or another. In recent years, however, the concept of a basic human right to communicate, including contact across national boundaries, a concept enunciated in the 1948 UN Universal Declaration on Human Rights, has gained a certain amount of general support. The ITU formally recognized such a right in 1973, and comparable ideas are included in numerous bilateral treaties and conventions. Although these declarations are primarily aimed at freedom of personal communication and open access to public news and information, the principle of unrestricted communication almost necessarily implies the disregard of content, particularly since the same facilities and systems are used for all purposes. On the other hand, the concern of various governments and enterprises with the control of transborder data flows and the maintenance of cultural independence creates a strong set of offsetting pressures.[4]

The important point with respect to policy about the content/data aspects of communications is that one set of forces are pressing for greater freedom and openness, while another is pressing for greater control and restriction. Both sets of forces, however, increase the pressure for further regime development, since the issues involved cannot be resolved by national policies or bilateral agreements alone. The complex interlinkage of government and organizational interests and concerns involved in these issues (particularly the functional needs of multinational enterprises and financial institutions) demands their resolution through multiparty negotiations. The likely outcome would seem to be gradual evolution of an communications policy regime of increasing openness.

The institutional setting for the new international communications regime remains uncertain and characterized by a "diversity of forums" (Kahler, 1995, p. 66). It seems clear that INTELSAT will evolve as a competitive player, not as a global communications monopoly and still less as a vehicle for international policy-making. There have been recent discussions concerning the possible partial privatization of INTELSAT (Cole, 1996). The future roles of ITU and CCITT are equally problematic, although no one expects them to go out of business. The problem is that international telecommunications issues are becoming increasingly politicized, and the ITU is not an ideal forum for political debate. The Annex on Telecommunications attached to the 1994 GATS Agreement covers access to, and use of, public telecommunication networks but leaves the opening of basic telecommunications sectors to ongoing negotiations.

The only firm conclusion to be drawn is that, within the multidimensional policy environment of international communications, "GATT, favored site for the liberalizers, has assumed a far more central place" (Kahler, 1995, p. 67). Inclusion of telecommunications services within the new

GATT/WTO framework is particularly appropriate, since unlike other important service activities (e.g., finance), in telecommunications there is an intimate link between equipment (a conventional GATT concern) and service performance. Hence, although both ITU and INTELSAT will continue to perform significant roles, it seems likely that GATT/WTO will provide the integrating focus for the international telecommunications regime over the coming decades. This shift of focus should have substantive as well as procedural significance, increasing the emphasis on international, as opposed to domestic, considerations within the regime. International objectives, such as interference-free broadcasting and the expansion of satellite networks, often conflict with the objectives of member governments, which tend to stress the importance of national boundaries and policy objectives. Technological change has already eroded these limitations; the policy framework seems certain to change accordingly.

Notes

1. Nearly one hundred members of the WTO agreed to a 1996–1997 accord (effective August 1, 1996) for opening their domestic markets to foreign banking and financial services enterprises. The US agreed only to limited participation, because it regarded access offers by other countries as insufficient. New talks were scheduled to begin in late 1997 (Bahree and Goldsmith, 1995).

2. This summary of GATS provisions is based on Hoekman, 1994; Jackson, 1988; Kahler, 1995.

3. Key sources are Noam, 1989; *The Economist*, 1991; Dowling, Boulton, and Elliott, 1994; Kahler, 1995, pp. 65–67. See Bahree (1996) for latest information on opening of telecommunications markets to foreign competition.

4. Space does not permit significant discussion of these issues here; important references include UNESCO, 1978; Branscomb, ed., 1986; Blatherwick, 1987; Taishoff, 1987.

References

Aronson, J.D., and Peter F. Cowhey. 1988. *When Nations Talk*. Cambridge, MA: Ballinger.

Bahree, Bhushan. 1996. "U.S., EU Offer to Open Phone Markets In Bid to Restart Talks on World Pact," *Wall Street Journal*, November 14.

Bahree, Bhushan, and Charles Goldsmith. 1995. "WTO Countries Agree to Relax Curbs on Foreign Banking, Financial Services," *Wall Street Journal*, July 27.

Blatherwick, David E.S. 1987. *The International Politics of Telecommunications*. Berkeley and Los Angeles, CA: Institute of International Studies, University of California.

Branscomb, Anne W., ed. 1986. *Toward a Law of Global Communications Networks*. New York: Longman. See especially articles by Branscomb, Herzstein, and Glasner.

Clegg, Jeremy. 1993. "Investigating the Determinants of Service Sector Foreign Direct Investment," in Howard Cox, Jeremy Clegg, and Grazia Iettro-Gillies, eds., *The Growth of Global Business*. London and New York: Routledge, pp. 85–104.

Cole, Jeff. 1996. "Intelsat's Privatization Beams In Rivals' Cries of Foul," *Wall Street Journal*, October 17.

Daniels, W.P. 1993. *Service Industries in the World Economy*. Oxford and Cambridge, England: Basil Blackwell.

Dizard, Wilson P. 1988. "International Regulation: Telecommunications and Information," in Carol C. Adelman, ed., *International Regulation: New Rules in a Changing World Order*. San Francisco, CA: Institute for Contemporary Studies, pp. 115–136.

Dowling, Michael J., William R. Boulton, and Sidney W. Elliott. 1994. "Strategies for Change in the Service Sector: The Global Telecommunications Industry," *California Management Review*, vol. 36, no. 3 (Spring), pp. 57–88.

The Economist. 1991. "A Survey of Telecommunications," October 5.

Feketekuty, Geza. 1988. *International Trade in Services: An Overview and Blueprint for Negotiations*. Cambridge, MA: Ballinger.

Hoekman, Bernard. 1994. "Tentative First Steps: An Assessment of the Uruguay Round Agreement on Services," unpublished conference paper, World Bank, Washington, DC.

Jackson, John H. 1988. *International Competition in Services: A Constitutional Framework*. Washington, DC: American Enterprise Institute for Public Policy Research.

Kahler, Miles. 1995. *International Institutions and the Political Economy of Integration*. Washington, DC: Brookings Institution.

Krommenacker, Raymond J. 1984. *World-Traded Services: The Challenge for the Eighties*. Dedham, MA: Artech House.

Noam, Eli M. 1989. "International Telecommunications in Transition," in Robert W. Crandall and Kenneth Flamm, eds., *Changing the Rules: Technological Change, International Competition, and Regulation in Communications*. Washington, DC: Brookings Institution, pp. 257–297.

Soroos, Marvin S. 1982. "The Commons in the Sky: The Radio Spectrum and Geosynchronous Orbit as Issues in Global Policy," *International Organization*, vol. 36, no. 3 (Summer), pp. 665–677.

Taishoff, Marika N. 1987. *State Responsibility and the Direct Broadcast Satellite*. London: Frances Pinter.

UN Centre on Transnational Corporations (UNCTC). 1989. *Foreign Direct Investment and Transnational Corporations in Services*. New York: UNCTC.

UN Centre on Transnational Corporations (UNCTC). 1990. *Transnational Corporations, Services and the Uruguay Round*. New York: UNCTC.

UN Conference on Trade and Development (UNCTAD). 1989. *Trade in Services: Sectoral Issues*. New York: UNCTAD.

UN Educational, Scientific, and Cultural Organization (UNESCO), International Commission for the Study of Communications Problems. 1978. *Interim Report on Communication Problems in Modern Society*. Paris: UNESCO.

Walter, Ingo. 1988. *Global Competition in Financial Services: Market Structure, Protection and Trade Liberalization*. Cambridge, MA: Ballinger.

White, Rita L., and Harold M. White, Jr. 1988. *The Law and Regulation of International Space Communication*. Boston, MA: Artech House.

9

ENVIRONMENTAL REGIMES*

International efforts to control and protect the water, air, and land resources of the globe are numerous, diverse, incomplete, and in many cases highly controversial. In spite of their varied subjects and purposes, most of these efforts are based on the idea that the natural environment of the earth constitutes, in some sense, a "commons," a collection of resources to be shared among all of the earth's inhabitants, present and future. The familiar "tragedy of the commons" is that excessive use of "free" common resources by some may ultimately lead to reduced welfare for all. This result, one of the classic examples of "market failure," arises because each user rationally seeks to maximize current individual benefit from use of the common resources without regard to collective or long-term costs. Policy regimes, whether local, national, or international, designed to deal with this type of problem attempt to alter the behavior of individual users in order to increase the aggregate benefits available to all users over the long term. Whether such corrective regimes can, in fact, be designed and implemented, and whether other "tragedies" or "failures" will occur as a consequence, are matters of considerable controversy. In addition, in many areas of environmental concern, there is substantial uncertainty about the actual impact of specific resource uses on the flow of potential benefits, both present and future, and these uncertainties add significantly to the complexity of the policy debate.[1]

*We are indebted to Dr. Kenneth L. Conca, University of Maryland, for assistance in updating this chapter for the revised edition.

Although the idea is widely accepted that some features of the planet earth, both global and regional, should be viewed as "commons," there is no general agreement as to which specific domains are encompassed by this concept and what kinds of collaborative arrangements should govern their appropriate use. The high seas, for example, have been historically viewed as a "commons," beyond control or expropriation by private persons and individual states. On the other hand, territorial jurisdiction is a fundamental characteristic of the nation state; and the extension of national sovereignty to cover adjacent natural domains (airspaces and coastal waters) is also conventionally accepted. And when common uses and nation-based activities overlap (as, for example, in the disposal of wastes), national authority is typically called upon to protect common-access resources. After extensive discussion and debate, the Stockholm Conference on the Human Environment (1972) eventually incorporated both "commons" and national perspectives into the following statement of principle:

> Nations ... have the sovereign right to exploit their own resources ..., and the responsibility to insure that activities within their jurisdiction or control do not cause damage to the environment of other States, or of areas beyond the limits of national jurisdiction (Declaration of the United Nations on the Human Environment, Principle 21, Stockholm, 1972. This statement reappears virtually verbatim as "Principle 2" of the Rio Declaration; cf. UN Conference on Environment and Development, UNCED, 1992a, *Agenda 21: The United Nations Programme of Action from Rio*).

The evolution of international environmental regimes during recent decades has affirmed the validity of both national domains and common environmental resources and has extended each in individual cases. The existence of a "global commons" has been formally recognized in international agreements such as the Moon Treaty (1979) and the Rio Declaration (1992). At the same time, nation-state jurisdiction over some portions of the heretofore "common" natural environment (e.g., fisheries) has also been regularized and extended. Numerous and pressing environmental issues remain to be resolved by arrangements that combine national interests and "commons" considerations.

The fact is that relatively few environmental problems are truly "global" in character, and a "commons" is a difficult entity to manage under the best of circumstances. On the other hand, it is clear that "the entire ecology of the planet is not arranged in national compartments" (Kennan, 1970, pp. 401–402). Hence, it is universally agreed that some kinds of international understandings and agreements are required to deal with environmental issues that involve more than one political juris- diction. The United Nations Environmental Program (UNEP), which was created at the 1972 Stockholm Conference, was not intended to be, and has not become, the basis for a comprehensive international environmental regime. However, it "proved indispensable to the process of arriving at an international consensus to protect the ozone layer," according to the chief US representative involved (Benedick, 1991, p. 40). It also laid the ground work for the "Earth Summit" in Rio de Janeiro in 1992.

9.1 THE NATURE OF ENVIRONMENTAL REGIMES

Environmental regime initiatives arise from concerns about fundamental relationships between population and human activity, on the one hand, and the natural status and resources of the planet, on the other. Some authorities view the fundamental planetary population/resource balance with great alarm (cf. *Global 2000 Report*, 1980; Brown et al., 1990), while others emphasize that human history to date reveals diverse and largely successful responses to resource availabilities and shortages (Simon and Kahn, 1984). Without taking sides in this extensive and often acrimonious debate, it is easy to agree with Pirages that "more and better anticipatory thinking" may be of value (1989, p. 5). This perspective suggests an emphasis on information gathering and on the development of cooperative modes of problem exploration, activities that have, in fact, been major purposes of international environmental regime development over the past quarter century. If the international trade and exchange regimes discussed in chapter 6 above present the clearest examples of formal and integrated regime development over the postwar decades, the environmental initiatives discussed here present sharply contrasting examples of tentative and fragmented responses to problems that are comparably complex, diverse, and interconnected (cf. Young, 1989b).

Environmental concerns differ from many other international policy issues not only in their variety and dispersion; they may also be mitigated, as well as exacerbated, by the independent actions of individuals, enterprises, and industries. The American Assembly notes that in the "environmental challenge ... success or failure will not hinge on the actions of governments alone. It will rest equally on the beliefs and actions of billions of individuals, and on the roles played by national and multinational business" (1990, p. 6). The role of particular enterprises and industries in recognizing and responding to specific environmental problems is of special importance, and many firms and industries have taken innovative initiatives in this regard.[2]

9.1.1 The Scope of International Environmental Policies

Topics differing widely in both substance and scope appear on the various lists of "international environmental issues" found in the literature (cf. MacNeill, Winsemius, and Yakushiji, 1991; United Nations, 1993). Most analysts begin with a broad perspective on population, poverty, and the uneven distribution of resources, climate, and productive capacity throughout the globe. The impact of national security concerns and activities, particularly the production and use of nuclear weapons, is also frequently emphasized. The *Final Report* of the 1990 American Assembly session on "Preserving the Global Environment" identified three main concerns: human population growth; deforestation and loss of biological diversity; and global atmospheric change (American Assembly, 1990).

One way to understand the status and development of environmental regimes, particularly those relevant to the activities of international business, would be to organize the diverse themes from the literature around the following four categories of resources and their uses:

1. Renewable resources and their products (agriculture, forests, fisheries).
2. Minerals and other nonrenewable resources and their products.
3. Secondary impacts of resource use on the ambient environment (air, water, climate).
4. Access to and use of hitherto unappropriated environmental domains (the seabed, polar regions, outer space).

Another approach would be to follow the logical flow of economic activity, beginning with access to and control of resource sites, through exploitation (production or extraction), processing, utilization, waste disposal, and ancillary impacts.

The UNCED (1992b) survey of international environmental policies lists 124 multilateral agreements, more than half of which were primarily regional in scope. (Bilateral agreements, some of which, such as those between US–Canada and US–Mexico, are of great importance, were not included.) The agreements analyzed were extraordinarily diverse, as the list in figure 9-1 indicates. Of course, most of these agreements do not form the basis for comprehensive policy regimes; and many need to be considered collectively, in related groups (such as the freshwater river agreements), in order to discern their global importance.

Moreover, in spite of their number and diversity, it is clear that many environmental concerns and many business-environment interactions are not yet addressed through these mechanisms. The 1992 Earth Summit, not covered by this survey, broadened the scope of international environ-

Type of Agreement	Number	Examples
General environmental concerns	11	Stockholm Declaration on the Human Environment (1972)
Nature conservation and terrestrial living resources	16	Antarctic Treaty (1959) International Tropical Timber Agreement (1983)
Atmosphere and outer space	6	Convention on Long-range Transboundary Air Pollution (LRTAP, 1979)
Marine environment and pollution	23	UN Convention on the Law of the Sea (UNCLOS, 1982)
Marine living resources	14	Convention for the Regulation of Whaling (1946), and many regional fisheries agreements
Transboundary freshwaters	24	Declaration Concerning the Industrial and Agricultural Use of International Rivers (1933) and many regional agreements
Hazardous substances	10	FAO Code of Conduct on the Distribution and Use of
Nuclear safety	5	Treaty Banning Nuclear Weapon Tests in the Atmosphere (1963)
Working environment	7	ILO Conventions on radiation protection, cancer, asbestos, etc.
Liability for environmental damage	8	Numerous agreements on civil liability for nuclear damage, oil pollution, etc.

Source: UN Conference on Environment and Development (UNCED), *The Effectiveness of International Environmental Agreements*. London: Grotius, 1992.

Figure 9-1. Types of International Environmental Agreements, with Illustrative Examples.

mental collaboration to some extent but reached a significant agreement only in the area of climate change (see further discussion below). The 1994 General Agreement on Tariffs and Trade/World Trade Organization (GATT/WTO) agreement, discussed in chapter 6 above, assigned the new WTO specific responsibility to take into account the environmental impact of trade policy developments, and these environmental issues are frequently included in regional trade negotiations. (For a broad survey of trade-environment relationships and policy issues, see Low, 1992.) Our overview of environmental regimes in this chapter concentrates on those that are business-related and of "global" status, even though often encountered in subglobal or regional contexts: the ambient environment, the oceans, the polar regions, and outer space.

9.2 THE AMBIENT ENVIRONMENT: AIR, WATER, AND CLIMATE

The climate of planet earth is one of the few environmental concerns that is unarguably "global"; in fact, the ubiquity of the climate may be its only undebatable characteristic. Climate results from the interaction between natural phenomena (both the planetary surface of land and water and the external forces of temperature and weather) and human activity; and the latter may alter climatic conditions directly (either inadvertently or intentionally), or by their indirect impact on climate-creating resources and processes.

Human activities (production, consumption, and environmental alteration) with potential climatic impact take place for the most part within individual national jurisdictions, and the effects of local pollution of air and water may be confined to one or a few adjacent countries and appropriately dealt with by their own national policies and regional agreements among limited numbers of participants. Activities of the Joint (US–Canada) Committee on the Great Lakes or the MEDPLAN for the Mediterranean are of this character. Haas notes that the MEDPLAN "serves as a model for arrangements for nine other regional seas in which over 130 states ... take part" (1990, p. xx). These regional environmental regimes share many characteristics with the regional economic regimes discussed in chapter 5 above and indeed are sometimes integral elements of them. (The environmental aspects of the NAFTA agreement were particularly controversial; cf. Hufbauer and Schott, 1992, pp. 131–153; see also Kahler, 1995, pp. 102–107).

Regional economic development and integration, while generally desirable, often raises new environmental issues. For example, increasing road traffic poses a significant threat, including both noise and air pollution effects, to the Alpine environment of Austria (Solsten and McClave, eds., 1994, pp. 155–156). Between 1970 and 1990, freight transported through Austria increased fivefold, from 4 million to 20 million tons, much of it moving among second and third countries through the Alpine passes. Austria limits the size of international trucks traversing the country and is seeking to shift freight from trucks to rail. The Austrian agreement with the European Economic Area (EEA) provided for separate negotiations on traffic volume that resulted in a 1992 accord limiting traffic volume and allowing rules protecting Alpine areas. Completion of the Rhine-Main-Danube Canal in 1992 made possible water communication from Rotterdam to the Black Sea, and inland waterway traffic in Europe may triple by the year 2000. Pipeline linkages are also expanding. All of these developments raise new environmental issues that require international response.

Increased knowledge of the forces making for climate change (including the fact that these forces may arise from numerous and diverse sources, no one of which in itself may have great local significance or independent impact) has led to a series of new and "global" international initiatives concerned with air, water, and climate over the past couple of decades. Figure 9-2, adapted from Hahn and Richards (1989), tabulates the principal features of five of the most important of these agreements. As the detailed data show, these agreements involve significant numbers of countries (and from various parts of the world); they deal with a wide range of global and regional environmental concerns; and they commit signatories to varied responses: cooperation and monitoring in some instances, specific reductions in environmental discharges in others. None of them contain provisions for international enforcement or sanctions. (Unlike withdrawal of privileges at the International Monetary Fund or World Bank, there is no way to deny a nonconforming nation access to use of the global environment.)

The Framework Convention on Climate Change was the key formal achievement of the 1992 Earth Summit. The ultimate objective of the convention is stated to be the stabilization of greenhouse gas concentrations in the atmosphere, with the intention of slowing or eliminating the potential for long-term global warming. The 154 signatories to the convention pledged themselves to provide information, promote relevant research, and take climate change into account in developing relevant domestic policies. In addition, industrial countries throughout the world have pledged themselves to limit the emission of greenhouse gases, with the intention of returning to global 1990 aggregate emission levels. Various countries introduced various qualifications about the scope and timing of these actions, both in general and within their specific jurisdictions, and less developed countries (LDCs) insisted that they could meet their convention commitments (chiefly data collection) only if associated costs were covered by advanced countries. No firm deadlines for meeting the overall objectives of the convention were established (Douglass and Weidenbaum, 1996; Lang, 1994; Young, 1994, chapter 2).

	Convention on Long-Range Transboundary Air Pollution (1979)	Sulfur Emissions Protocol (1985)	Nitrogen Oxides Emissions Protocol (1988)	Vienna Convention On Protection of the Ozone Layer (1985)	Montreal Protocol (1987)
Problem addressed	Reduction of transboundary air pollution	Reduction of SO_x emissions (acid rain)	Reduction of NO_x from mobile and stationary sources (acid rain and ground level ozone)	Protection of ozone layer from CFCs	Reduction of CFC use
No. of signatories[a]	34	21	25	41	46
Lag time from negotiation to need for action	4 years	8 years	2 years	No significant action required	19 months
Type of action required	Monitoring, R&D, exchange	30% reduction in SO_x from 1980	Limitation of NO_x to 1987 (or earlier levels)	Research only	Restriction of CFC consumption
How monitored/enforced	No enforcement	Self-monitored	Self-monitored with reports to executive body	No monitoring	Self-monitored with penalties to be determined at a later meeting
Scope of problem	Regional/global	Regional	Regional	Global	Global
Country-specific concerns addressed	Yes	No	Yes	No	Yes
Initiating body	UNECE[b]	UNECE[b]	UNECE[b]	UNEP[c]	UNEP[c]

[a] Number of signatories includes all countries that had signed the treaty, whether or not they had ratified, plus the number of countries that had deposited documents of accession, as reflected in US State Department records as of February 15, 1989.

[b] UNECE = UN Economic Commission for Europe (Geneva).

[c] UNEP = UN Environmental Program.

Source: Hahn and Richards (1989), table 2, p. 342.

Figure 9-2. Major Multilateral Air Pollution Agreements.

9.2.1 The Likelihood of Agreement

Hahn and Richards conclude from their analysis of climate-related regimes that the likelihood of multilateral agreement in any specific case increases in response to: 1) scientific consensus as to the causes and seriousness of the problem; 2) increased public concern; 3) the perceived "fairness" of the proposed arrangements; 4) increased short-term political benefits; and 5) the existence of previous and related agreements (1989, pp. 433–434).

The importance of the "fairness" issue is well illustrated by controversies about the treatment of countries that have taken substantial steps toward environmental protection prior to the establishment of relevant international policies. The US, in particular, has argued that its preagreement actions with respect to sulfur oxide emissions and chlorofluorocarbons (CFCs) entitle it to "credit" in subsequent policy implementation. Such "credit" would arise, for example, if policy goals are set in terms of *levels* of discharge (that an environmentally advanced country might already have achieved). By contrast, no "credit" will arise (and, indeed, very difficult and costly tasks may be required) if goals are set in terms of *percentage reductions* from current levels. On the other hand, countries that are less environmentally advanced oppose the granting of credit for past actions, since this approach gives them primary responsibility for the next phase of global improvements.

The importance of the final factor listed (existence of other related agreements) can scarcely be overstated, since acceptance of and (favorable) experience with current regimes undoubtedly contributes to the development of new agreements. The US signed only ten multilateral environmental treaties during the four decades ending in 1969 but then signed nine during the 1970s and seven more during 1980s (Hahn and Richards, 1989, p. 425). There is every reason to believe that the number of such agreements, and the necessary interconnections among them, will continue to increase. French concludes a survey of recent developments by emphasizing that, although continued progress will unquestionably be difficult, "the notion that 'pollution is the price of progress' has become antiquated. ... [P]eople on every continent are discovering that pollution control is a sound investment" (1990, p. 42). Optimism about the possibility of enlarging the scope of global environmental consensus is also reflected in the American Assembly report (1990) on this topic.

The role of individual industries and enterprises in the evolution of regimes with respect to air, water, and climate (and, in a related set of developments, with respect to worker and consumer safety as well) has been problematic. There is plenty of evidence of tendencies to "export pollution," both directly in the form of hazardous wastes and indirectly by shifting environmentally troublesome activities out of countries where protective national regimes are in place and into less restrictive settings (cf. Pearson, ed., 1987). On the other hand, many US-based multi-nationals claim to have adopted US standards throughout their worldwide operations. Evidence as to the accuracy of these claims is spotty, but there is certainly some "export of standards," for the sake of operating efficiency if for no other reason, within most large multinationals. (Varied remarks from speakers at the Conference on Global Environmental Accords held at MIT in collaboration with the Business Council for Sustainable Development support this view; cf. Choucri, ed. 1994.)

9.3 EXPLOITING THE OCEANS[3]

Much of the international concern with water as an environmental issue is focused on regional water resources (river systems, enclosed seas, and littoral areas) where the primary issues are: 1) pollution, and 2) conflicting modes of use, access, and control. In dealing with these problems, the prior existence of national jurisdictions and the interests of numerous and diverse constituents are taken as given at the outset. By contrast, since the seventeenth century, the open oceans of the world (the "high seas") have been considered beyond the control of individual governments and equally open to all users and uses (i.e., part of a "global commons").

Until late in the nineteenth century, it was generally believed that the resources of the oceans, specifically including fisheries, were literally inexhaustible. However, changes in population and technology altered this perspective, and in 1899 the King of Sweden called a conference of nations concerned with the North Sea and Baltic fisheries. In 1901, the International Council for the Exploration of the Seas (ICES), the first international body concerned with marine conservation, was formed. Throughout the present century, there has been widespread and increasing recognition that the resources of the oceanic "global commons" (both living organisms, particularly fish and mammals, and undersea minerals) should be subject to some kind of international understandings.

One might imagine, particularly in light of policy developments concerning the ambient environment discussed in the preceding section, that any international regimes evolving in this area would involve increased regulation of oceanic resource use within a "global commons" framework. However, with one important exception (deep sea mining), the opposite is the case. The main international policy theme with respect to oceanic resources in the postwar half century has been the reduction of the "global commons" through the expansion of the territorial rights of nation states. As a result of these extensions of national authority, more than half of the asserted boundaries of states in the territorial sea involve conflicting claims (Cuyvers, 1984, p. 63). Many of these claims are currently of little consequence, although some (for example, Greece versus Turkey) involve strong nationalistic and commercial interests, and others may become more significant as fish populations shift and technologies for marine resource exploitation change (cf. Sanger, 1986, chapters 5 and 6).

9.3.1 Renewable Resources: Fisheries

The interests of particular national fishing industries in the exploitation of specific fishery resources (e.g., US and Canada in the North Atlantic; Chile, Peru, and Ecuador in the Southeastern Pacific) have been long recognized in treaties and other agreements among the parties directly concerned. Growing competition in world fishing and the possibility that new "industrial fishing" techniques could exhaust entire fish populations led to more general international concern with the exploitation of fishery resources even prior to World War II.

The first suggestion that potential damage to the resources of the oceanic commons might be avoided through expanded national jurisdiction, rather than increased international control came in 1945 when President Truman unilaterally announced that US jurisdiction over undersea minerals extended to the limits of the so-called "continental shelf" and asserted the right to establish fishing conservation zones on the high seas adjacent to US coasts. Chile, Peru, and Ecuador followed quickly with expanded claims for whaling rights in the open ocean; and the decision of the International Court of Justice in the *Anglo-Norwegian Fisheries* case (1951) opened the way for the development of new concepts of jurisdiction and territoriality on the high seas. The first UN Conference on the Law of the Sea (UNCLOS), intended to deal with these and many other marine environment issues, was convened in 1958; successive UNCLOS sessions and follow-up conferences have continued down to the present.

The critical principle of the UNCLOS conferences with respect to fisheries involves recognition of "Extended Fisheries Jurisdiction" (EFJ), the right of coastal states to control access and use of important fishery resources beyond the limits of their territorial waters. Countries with EFJ in a specific area have the authority to limit access to their own nationals, levy charges on the fishing fleets of other countries, and prescribe the harvesting methods employed and the amount and type of fish that may be harvested. The EFJ concept recognizes the fact that the oceanic commons with respect to fisheries is regional rather than global in character and embodies a property rights approach to managing it. The underlying assumption is that users (nations and enterprises) with the strongest interest in the future productivity of oceanic resources will make the wisest decisions with respect to their preservation and use. Unfortunately, natural developments (e.g., storms, movements of other

sea organisms) and inadequate national policies and enforcement programs, along with inefficient harvesting, have frustrated the process of
optimal collective management in some instances.

Whatever the effects of the EFJ concept on the long run productivity of
world fisheries, and however difficult it might be to achieve these or
better results through other means, the current international policy
regime has transferred large and valuable resources from long-recognized
open access (i.e., a "commons") to national jurisdiction and control.
Some of the world's best fishery resources are involved, and the results
(such as allocation of the rich Georges Bank area of the North Atlantic to
the US and Canada, for example) do not necessarily favor poor or
developing countries. The world fishing catch is generally believed to be
at or approaching its biological limits at the present time; hence, the EFJ
arrangement, whatever its merits, has serious implications for the future
international distribution of income and wealth.

9.3.2 Nonrenewable Resources: Undersea Minerals

The US proclamations of 1945 put forth important claims for coastal
state jurisdiction over the resources of the seabed (specifically oil and gas)
as well as over living organisms. These claims, along with the varied and
conflicting claims of many other countries in all parts of the world,
eventually led UNCLOS III to recognize the concept of "Exclusive
Economic Zones" (EEZs) extending up to two hundred miles beyond the
conventional territorial limits of coastal states. Within these zones,
which remain parts of the high seas as far as navigation and overflight are
concerned, coastal states have broad discretionary authority, including the
granting or withholding of exploration and extraction rights to their own
nationals and others. Thus, although the physical dimensions of EFJs and
EEZs are unrelated, their functions are analogous; they grant some, but
not all, jurisdictional control over portions of the open sea to individual
coastal states.

There is, however, a sharp distinction between EEZ and EFJ concepts
with respect to their implications for areas *outside* their respective
collective boundaries. It is universally agreed that living organisms (fish,
mammals, plant life, sponges) outside EFJ boundaries are subject to
capture by any party with the necessary capability. However, the same
principle is *not* universally applied to undersea mineral resources beyond
the limits of all EEZs. The status of such resources is, in fact, one of the
most controversial issues on the entire international policy agenda. Three
distinct legal positions, each of which involves an analogy between the
seabed and some other planetary domain, are put forward:

1. The high seas and the underlying seabed constitute a legal unity that is not subject to appropriation by any state or other entity; in this view the seabed is an intrinsic element of the "global commons" of the oceans.

2. The sea and seabed are distinct; the seabed, like any unclaimed land, is subject to national appropriation.

3. There is no conventional legal recognition of the bed of the open sea; hence the legal status of the seabed, like that of outer space, may be determined by competent international authorities without concern for precedent.

The third of these positions was apparently accepted by an overwhelming majority of UN member states (including the US) in 1958 when they declared the seabed outside all national jurisdictions to be part of "the common heritage of mankind." (If the seabed were considered a dimension of the sea itself, there would have been no reason for a vote.) The difference between the first and third concepts became critical in 1982 when another UN majority (this time *not* including the US) approved establishment of an International Seabed Authority (ISA) to control the conditions under which seabed mineral resources can be exploited.

The issue of jurisdiction over the deep seabed has become significant because of increased interest in long-known manganese nodules and other mineral deposits on the floor of the open ocean, and the belief that technologies capable of exploiting these deposits are or will soon become available. Although exploitation of these resources is not economically justified at present, there has been strong interest in resolving the jurisdictional issues well in advance. Schachter believes that general international acceptance of the "common heritage" concept implies a further understanding that there should be some sharing of the benefits of seabed exploitation among "all mankind" (in Pontecorvo, ed., 1986, p. 53). And Krasner declares that UNCLOS III, signed by more than one hundred countries in 1982, "gave the coup de grace to an older, weakening regime whose central principle was that the oceans belong to no one," and were thus subject to the rule of capture (1985, p. 231).

However, the remark of a Canadian representative very early in the seabed mining negotiations that "everyone accepts the concept of an international regime, but what isn't agreed are its powers" (Sanger, 1980, p. 167) remains true up to the present. Several governments (particularly the US, UK, and Germany) favor exploitation of undersea deposits by private enterprises, with some portion of the revenue going into a trust fund for the use of LDCs. On the other hand, as noted above, an overwhelming majority of UN member states endorsed the creation of the ISA, which would have an operating branch known as the "Enterprise" to carry out actual mining activities. The current scheme requires that companies wishing to undertake undersea mining submit two similar mining sites to the ISA, one of which will be approved for private exploitation and the other reserved for exploitation by the "Enterprise" for the benefit of developing nations. These arrangements are unacceptable to the nations most likely to be capable of engaging in undersea mining, and the whole matter is currently at an impasse, which may not be resolved until actual mining operations are imminent or in progress (Cuyvers, 1984, pp. 65–66; Young, 1989a, chapter 5, particularly pp. 125–141).

9.3.3 Pollution of the Sea

Pollution of the sea arises from many sources: discharge of industrial and organic waste from land sources, economic activity and transport on the sea itself, marine accidents and natural disasters. Unlike previous marine conventions, UNCLOS III (1982) included significant attention to the protection and preservation of the marine environment. The principal emphasis is on the development of guidelines for national policies (particularly including responsibilities of flag states for the status and operations of vessels under their registry); there was also some endorsement of pollution control authority for coastal states and port states. These principles, both their substance and their modes of implementation, are still in the early stages of evolution (cf. Brubaker, 1993; Mitchell, 1994). Pollution of the sea is, of course, a principal concern of the MEDPLAN and other regional agreements modeled on it (Haas, 1990).

9.4. THE POLAR REGIONS[4]

The polar regions, the Arctic and the Antarctic, share some common features with the oceanic "global commons." The Arctic is literally an ocean, although covered by an ice shelf; Antarctica is a land mass, also covered by ice, and like the seabed still largely unexplored and inaccessible. The Arctic is a host for submarines and is therefore involved in international security issues as well as environmental resource concerns. Antarctica is a demilitarized zone, but both its nonmilitary status and its environmental security may be endangered if, as is expected, its mineral resources prove to be large and exploitable. In both polar regions, conflicts arise among the claims and activities of competing users, and in Antarctica the "common heritage of mankind" issue arises as well.

9.4.1 The Arctic

The major conflicts to date over the use of the Arctic have been between the US and Canada; however, the interests of Russia, European countries, and others are also involved. Setting aside the international security aspects, the principal issues involve the use of the Arctic for transit shipping and the likelihood that Arctic seabeds will become important future sources of oil and natural gas. (Fisheries and wildlife protection also pose difficult issues; cf. Young, 1994, chapter 3.) Sea transit concerns include not only physical access to shipping lanes (i.e., distinctions between high seas and territorial waters) but also the environmental protections that may be required for both shipping and exploration or extraction activities. There is also some concern on the Canadian side with the impact of any type of modern economic activity on native populations and wildlife.

Canada attempted to obtain an extension of national authority over the ice-covered area of the Arctic in UNCLOS III, and when this effort was unsuccessful (and the US did not sign the agreement anyway) declared unilaterally all waters of the Canadian Arctic Archipelago to be *internal waters* (i.e., not open seas) in 1985. Many Canadian authorities favor even more extensive claims, all of which are rejected by the US. Additional disputes involving both navigation and fisheries involve Norway, Russia, Denmark/Greenland, and Iceland.

Young (1989a, pp. 182–187) argues that the time is ripe for creation of a North American Arctic shipping regime negotiated in terms of the intended uses and values of all involved parties rather than on formal "jurisdictional" principles. He notes that Denmark/Greenland should certainly be included along with the US and Canada, and possibly other potential Arctic shippers as well. The knowledge and interests of native peoples should also be taken into account. Since tanker design and other technical aspects of Arctic shipping are still under development, establishment of standards and criteria in these areas should, in his view, come more easily now than after investments and technical arrangements have been put in place.

9.4.2 Antarctica

Various and often overlapping portions of Antarctica are claimed by seven nations: Argentina, Australia, Chile, France, New Zealand, Norway, and the UK. Most of these nations, plus the US, Russia, and Poland, also maintain scientific stations on the continent. In spite of this activity, along with the additional theoretical claims of other states (Brazil, Peru, Germany), large portions of Antarctica remain unexplored, and some parts of the continent are still unclaimed.

The notion that a special international regime should be established for Antarctica was accepted by the seven territorial claimants plus five cooperating powers (Belgium, Japan, South Africa, the then USSR, and the US) in 1959. The Antarctic Treaty among these twelve nations, which came into effect in 1961, rejected all other territorial claims and declared Antarctica to be a demilitarized zone. This treaty (which currently has twenty-six signatories), along with its subsequent emendations and satellite agreements, contains provisions for environmental protection (for both living organisms and physical conditions), freedom for scientific research, and open access and inspection of all research facilities to all nations similarly engaged. Nuclear explosions and storage of radioactive materials are barred. An attempt in 1975 by nontreaty states to declare Antarctica an international nature park (with guaranteed freedom for research) were defeated in the UN, as was a 1983 proposal by LDCs to establish a UN regime, analogous to the International Seabed Authority (ISA), for the continent.

Nevertheless, in response to these pressures, proposals for the creation of an Antarctic mineral regime reflecting a broad range of international interests continue to be made. There is no formal UN presence in Antarctica, but the territorial waters of the unclaimed portion of the continent would logically fall under the control of the ISA under any circumstance. The International Commission on Antarctica and its satellite agencies currently regulate prospecting, exploration, and development in the Arctic in much the same way that is contemplated for the ISA in the seabed. During the 1990–1991 treaty renewal negotiations, New Zealand and five European countries indicated support for a "world park" with a permanent prohibition on commercial mining activity; the UK, Germany, and Japan favored establishment of a set of rules to govern future mining activity. In the ultimate compromise, treaty signatories agreed to a moratorium on mining that is subject to review and removal in fifty years. Kratochwil, Rohrlich, and Mahajan note that although "the Antarctic regime has often been celebrated for its innovative solution to otherwise seemingly insoluble problems ...," this arrangement could change very quickly in response to resource scarcities and availabilities, LDC pressures for inclusion within the regime, and international political developments (1985, pp. 111–112).

9.5 OUTER SPACE[5]

In terms of both human access and legal status, the air and atmosphere surrounding the earth are divisible into three distinct regions. The immediate airspace enclosing the planet (out to an unspecified level) is considered to be an extension of the underlying land/water territory on the earth's surface. Thus, nation states have jurisdiction of the air space above their respective territories, and airspace above the high seas and unclaimed land areas is part of the "global commons." The next broad band, approximately 150–500 miles outward from the earth, is the so-called *low earth orbit (LEO)*, the location of numerous commercial and scientific satellites. (Navigational and military satellites operate just above or below this band.) Finally, a narrow band of space some 22,300 miles directly above the equator defines the *geostationary* (or *geosynchronous*) *orbit* (GSO). Satellites placed in this orbit remain positioned in a fixed location with respect to the equator at all times.

The rotation of the earth alters the relationship between terrestrial locations and specific sectors of the LEO. Hence, extension of national jurisdiction outward to include this domain is not feasible. In recognition of this fact, the first article of the 1967 Outer Space Treaty declared outer space to be "the province of all mankind." However, any point within the GSO is uniquely linked with a specific equatorial ground location. The Bogota Declaration of 1976 argued that the twenty-seven equatorial countries, all of them LDCs, should have authority to control the sites above their respective locations. This proposition has not been accepted by others, and the countries involved are thus far powerless to take action to assert their claims (Soroos, in Papp and McIntyre, eds., 1987, pp. 147–149). Issues involving the allocation of GSO positions, as well as the reservation of orbital "slots" for future assignment, are being addressed in the ongoing "Space-WARC" being conducted under International Telecommunications Union (ITU) auspices (see chapter 8 above).

The space age began with the flight of the Soviet Sputnik in 1957 and remained a US-USSR duopoly for more than a decade thereafter. Other nations, including Japan, China, and the European Space Agency (ESA), gradually entered the field, but satellite launching was a state monopoly within each jurisdiction until the 1980s. This picture has now changed dramatically. During 1981–1985, ESA launched twelve Ariane satellites and NASA an additional thirty. China and the former USSR began to offer commercial launching services in 1985, and in the following year the US began to encourage private companies to enter the space-launch business. Four US companies (Martin-Marietta, General Dynamics, McDonnell Douglas, Hughes/Boeing) have done so, and others are making plans in this direction. Hence, it seems clear that commercial space operations are, or will soon become, highly competitive among both nations and enterprises.

The legal status of space operations under these rapidly changing circumstances has been described by one authority as a "transition of confusion" (Goldman, in Papp and McIntyre, eds., 1987, pp. 157–177). The Committee on the Peaceful Uses of Outer Space (COPUOS) was created by the UN immediately after the initial Sputnik flight, and this organization has been the primary source of "space law" up to the present. The most recent work of this Committee, the Moon Treaty of 1979, did not receive its necessary ratifications until 1985 and is not recognized by any of the nations with large space programs. Other recent issues have fared little better; and problems of liability, safety, sovereignty, and privacy (associated with remote sensing activity), etc., generate controversy and tension rather than cooperation and agreement. Potential military uses of space expand the areas of international concern and conflict. Goldman believes that national space law will expand, particularly in the US, to deal with problems for which there is no established international consensus, with the likelihood of increased conflict and fragmentation on this most "global" of environmental use issues.

9.6 CONCLUSION: UNRESOLVED AND EMERGING ISSUES

This review of the recent evolution of international policy regimes for environmental and natural resource issues indicates that the concerns motivating these developments are far from resolved. Widespread acceptance of the "global commons" concept does not by itself reduce important scientific uncertainties about optimal usage rates and undesirable secondary effects. Moreover, even where there is both scientific and policy agreement about the need to "take thought for the morrow," feasible and appropriate institutional arrangements and procedures are by no means obvious. The principal concerns of the 1992 Earth Summit, in addition to climate change, were global biodiversity and deforestation, but minimal "framework" agreements were not produced in either of these areas, and a host of other issues raised in the Rio Declaration of Principles ("Agenda 21") remain untouched. (For an overall evaluation of the Earth Summit, see Haas, Levy, and Parson, 1992.)

On the one hand, it seems unarguable that the most efficient way to avoid "the tragedy of the commons" (unrestricted use that reduces long-range benefits) is to allocate property rights and responsibilities among users in such a way that they themselves will try to follow socially optimal usage patterns. However, this approach is not feasible for many important "common" domains: ambient air, water, and climate; high seas; and outer space. Regional regimes based on the common interests of closely involved parties are effective mechanisms in some instances, but truly "global" issues are outside their scope. In any event, even where feasible, the "property rights/responsibilities" approach eliminates the "commons" itself and has serious distributional consequences. Hence, it seems quite likely that environmental and natural resource issues will be major foci of international regime development activity and controversy for the foreseeable future.

The problem of dealing with the "global commons" illustrates at least two significant points about international regime formulation. The first point is that national and regional regimes, even when effective within their jurisdictions, do not necessarily promote global policy objectives. In fact, they may permit, and even encourage, spillovers beyond their boundaries, just as private property rights regimes often do. The second point is that international consensus on these matters is seriously hampered by current differences in national status and by distributional considerations. The LDCs have been very active in pushing for greater international control of, or at least more equitable sharing in, the use of various global natural resources. The advanced industrial countries, acting in their own immediate interests, have generally resisted such efforts. Absent a clearly perceived global ecological crisis, these fundamental differences in viewpoints and objectives make it very unlikely that significant new international environmental and natural resource regimes will evolve in the near future.

Benedick's analysis of the evolution of international policy for protection of the ozone layer highlights situations and problems common to many contemporary environmental issues (Benedick, 1991; see also Haas, 1993.) He traces the evolving scientific consensus that there is a connection between chlorofluorocarbon (CFC) use and the integrity of the ozone layer from the initial introduction of the hypothesis in 1974 to its general acceptance by the end of the decade. Although there was widespread agreement that any successful response to this situation would require a global context, there was no existing forum for consideration of the matter and no obvious vehicle for implementation of any policy that might be adopted. Formal negotiations under UNEP auspices began in 1982 and eventually led to the Vienna Convention (1985), which included a commitment to subsequent negotiation of a *legally binding* agreement. In this period of heightened interest, private sector groups (affected industries, citizen organizations, and the media) played active and often adversarial roles. After considerable discussion and compromise, the 1987 Montreal Protocol on Substances That Deplete the Ozone Layer emerged; it has now been signed by more than one hundred countries (see Getz, 1995). Although this agreement was hailed by the principal US negotiator as "the most significant international environmental agreement in history" (Benedick, 1991, p. 1), it has proved difficult to enforce. Global CFC production in advanced countries has indeed fallen, but production in LDCs has expanded dramatically and a substantial international black market has emerged. On the other hand, the 1990 London Meeting of Parties led to the creation of a $240 million "Multilateral Ozone Fund" to be used to meet the incremental costs of implementing control requirements in Third World countries (UNCED, 1992b, pp. 137–143). In this area, as in so many others, the ultimate success of an international agreement appears to require a judicious combination of sticks and carrots, rigorous enforcement by local and national authorities on the one hand and economic inducements on the other hand.

Notes

1. The classic collection of papers on environmental "commons" issues is Hardin and Baden, eds., 1977. See also Young, 1989a&b, 1994; Ostrom, Gardner, and Walker, 1994; Cooper, 1994.

2. Coucri, 1993; Harvey and Rothe, 1995; Mahon and Kelley, 1988; Pearson, ed., 1987; Schmidheiny, 1992; UNCTAD, 1993.

3. This section is based primarily on the collection of papers edited by Pontecorvo, 1986, particularly the contributions of Pontecorvo and Schachter, together with Brown et al., 1977; Cuyvers, 1984; Krasner, 1985; Miles, ed., 1989; Sanger, 1986; Smith, 1988; Young 1989a; and papers by Sahrhage and Floistad in Andresen and Ostreng, eds., 1989.

4. This section is based primarily on Young, 1989a, chapter 7, and 1994, chapter 3; see also Krasner, 1985, chapter 9, especially pp. 250–264; Kratochwil, Rohrlich, and Mahajan, 1985, pp. 101–114, Young and Osherenko, eds., 1993.

5. This section is based on the collection of papers published in Papp and McIntyre, eds., 1987. Policy issues concerned with the use of space for communications purposes are discussed in chapter 8 above.

References

American Assembly. 1990. *Preserving the Global Environment*. Final Report of the 77th American Assembly. New York: American Assembly.

Andresen, Steinar, and Willy Ostreng, eds. 1989. *International Resource Management: The Role of Science and Politics*. London: Belhaven.

Benedick, Richard E. 1991. *Ozone Diplomacy: New Directions in Safeguarding the Planet*. Cambridge, MA: Harvard University Press.

Brown, Lester R., et al. 1990. *The State of the World*. New York: W.W. Norton for Worldwatch Institute.

Brown, Seyom, Nina W. Cornell, Larry L. Fabian, and Edith Brown Weiss. 1977. *Regimes for the Ocean, Outer Space, and Weather*. Washington, DC: Brookings Institution.

Brubaker, Douglas. 1993. *Marine Pollution and International Law*. London: Belhaven Press.

Choucri, Nazli. 1993. "Multinational Corporations and the Global Environment," in Nazli Choucri, ed., *Global Accord*. Cambridge, MA: MIT Press, pp. 206–253.

Choucri, Nazli, ed.. 1994. "Special Issue: Global Environmental Accords: Implications for Technology, Industry and International Relations," *Business and the Contemporary World*, vol. 6, no. 2 (Spring).

Cooper, Richard N. 1994. *Environment and Resource Policies for the World Economy*. Washington, DC: Brookings Institution.

Cuyvers, Luc. 1984. *Ocean Uses and Their Regulation.* New York: Wiley.

Douglass, Christopher, and Murray Weidenbaum. 1996. *The Quiet Reversal of U.S. Global Climate Change Policy.* Center for the Study of American Business, Washington University, St. Louis, MO.

French, Hilary F. 1990. *Clearing the Air: A Global Agenda.* Washington, DC: Worldwatch Institute.

Getz, Kathleen A. 1995. "Implementing Multilateral Regulation: A Preliminary Theory and Illustration," *Business and Society*, vol. 34, no. 3 (December), pp. 280–316.

Global 2000 Report to the President. 1980. Washington, DC: US Government Printing Office.

Haas, Peter M. 1990. *Saving the Mediterranean: The Politics of International Environmental Cooperation.* New York: Columbia University Press.

Haas, Peter M. 1993. "Stratospheric Ozone: Regime Formation in Stages," in Young and Osherenko, eds., *Polar Politics.* Ithaca, NY: Cornell University Press, pp. 152–185.

Haas, Peter M., Marc Levy, and Edward Parson. 1992. "Appraising the Earth Summit," *Environment*, vol. 34 (October), pp. 6–12.

Hahn, Robert W., and Kenneth R. Richards. 1989. "The Internationalization of Environmental Regulation," *Harvard International Law Journal*, vol. 30, no. 2 (Spring), pp. 422–445.

Hardin, Garrett, and John Baden, eds. 1977. *Managing the Commons.* San Francisco, CA: W.H. Freeman.

Harvey, Michael G., and James T. Rothe. 1995. "Environet: Monitoring MNC's Global Environmental Behavior," *Business and the Contemporary World*, vol. 7, no. 4, pp. 114–133.

Hufbauer, G.C., and J.J. Schott. 1992. *North American Free Trade.* Washington, DC: Institute for International Economics.

Kahler, Miles. 1995. *International Institutions and the Political Economy of Integration.* Washington, DC: Brookings Institution.

Kennan, George. 1970. "To Prevent a World Wasteland: A Proposal," *Foreign Affairs*, vol. 48, no. 3 (April), pp. 401–413.

Krasner, Stephen D. 1985. *Structural Conflict: The Third World Against Global Liberalism.* Berkeley and Los Angeles, CA: University of California Press.

Kratochwil, Friedrich, Paul Rohrlich, and Harpreet Mahajan. 1985. *Peace and Disputed Sovereignty.* Lanham, MD: University Press of America.

Lang, Winfried. 1994. "UN Framework Convention on Climate Change," *Business and the Contemporary World*, vol. 6, no. 2, pp. 20–24.

Low, Patrick, ed. 1992. *International Trade and the Environment.* Washington, DC: World Bank, Discussion Papers No. 159.

MacNeill, Jim, Pieter Winsemius, and Taizo Yakushiji. 1991. *Beyond Interdependence: The Meshing of the World's Economy and the Earth's Ecology.* New York: Oxford University Press.

Mahon, John F., and Patricia C. Kelley. 1988. "The Politics of Toxic Waste: Multinational Corporations as Facilitators of National Policy," in Lee E. Preston, ed., *Research in Corporate Social Performance and Policy*, vol. 10, pp. 59–86. Greenwich, CT: JAI.

Miles, Edward L., ed. 1989. *Management of World Fisheries: Implications of Extended Coastal State Jurisdiction.* Seattle, WA: University of Washington Press.

Mitchell, Ronald B. 1994. *International Oil Pollution at Sea.* Cambridge, MA: MIT Press.

Ostrom, Elinor, Roy Gardner, and James Walker. 1994. *Rules, Games and Common-Pool Resources.* Ann Arbor, MI: University of Michigan Press.

Papp, Daniel S., and John R. McIntyre, eds. 1987. *International Space Policy.* New York: Quorum. See particularly "Introduction" and articles by Soroos and Goldman.

Pearson, Calres S., ed. 1987. *Multinational Corporations, Environment, and the Third World.* Durham, NC: Duke University Press for World Resources Institute.

Pirages, Dennis. 1989. *Global Technopolitics: The International Politics of Technology and Resources.* Pacific Grove, CA: Brooks/Cole.

Pontecorvo, Guilio, ed. 1986. *The New Order of the Oceans.* New York: Columbia University Press.

Sanger, Clyde. 1986. *Ordering the Oceans: The Making of the Law of the Sea.* London: Zed Books Ltd.

Schmidheiny, Stephan. 1992. *Changing Course: A Global Business Perspective on Development and Environment.* Cambridge, MA: MIT Press.

Simon, Julian, and Herman Kahn, eds. 1984. *The Resourceful Earth.* Oxford, England: Basil Blackwell.

Smith, B.D. 1988. *State Responsibility and the Marine Environment.* Oxford, England: Clarendon Press.

Solsten, Eric, and David E. McClave, eds. 1994. *Austria: A Country Study.* Washington, DC: US Government Printing Office. US Department of the Army DA Pam 550-176, second edition.

United Nations. 1993. *The Global Partnership for Environment and Development.* New York: UN.

UN Conference on Environment and Development (UNCED). 1992a. *Agenda 21: The United Nations Programme of Action from Rio.* New York: UN.

UN Conference on Environment and Development (UNCED). 1992b. *The Effectiveness of International Environmental Agreements.* London: Grotius.

UN Conference on Trade and Development (UNCTAD). 1993. *Environmental Management in Transnational Corporations*. New York: UN.

Young, Oran R. 1989a. *International Cooperation*. Ithaca, NY: Cornell University Press.

Young, Oran R. 1989b. "The Politics of International Regime Formation: Managing Natural Resources and the Environment," *International Organization*, vol. 43, no. 3 (Summer), pp. 349–376.

Young, Oran R. 1994. *International Governance: Protecting the Environment in a Stateless Society*. Ithaca, NY: Cornell University Press.

Young, Oran R., and Gail Osherenko, eds. 1993. *Polar Politics*. Ithaca, NY: Cornell University Press.

THE FUTURE OF
INTERNATIONAL POLICY REGIMES

The idea that international policy regimes might be needed to facilitate or control business activities that involve multiple national jurisdictions is scarcely more than a century old. First appearing in response to the global expansion of trade and technology in the late nineteenth century, this idea now embraces a wide range of international macroeconomic, financial, trade, and environmental issues and the associated regimes have taken on diverse organizational forms. This epilogue presents a summary overview of some of the frontier issues in the major regime areas discussed in the previous chapters, and examines some critical aspects of two topics of great current interest: the taxation of international investment income and international business bribery of government officials. The epilogue concludes with brief comments on a theme that has been present throughout the volume: the implications of policy regime development for international business management.

E.1 FRONTIER ISSUES FOR REGIME EVOLUTION

The data and analysis presented in part I of this book clearly document the contemporary growth and increasing integration of the world economy. It is also argued there that these developments have led to the creation and evolution of policy regimes concerned with various aspects of international business activity; and that these regimes have, in turn, both stimulated and directed the growth and integration processes themselves. Although the scope, goals, and operating arrangements of individual regimes remain subject to continuing controversy and evolutionary change, there seems to be general agreement that such regimes are likely to become more numerous, more complex, and more important in the future.

The most widely held current view, however, is that comprehensive global regimes embracing diverse aspects of international business activity are *not* likely to evolve in the near future or perhaps ever. On the contrary, the more popular scenario anticipates the growth of regimes with limited membership and/or limited functions that promise specific benefits and problem-solving capabilities for their participants, both governments and enterprises. According to this scenario, policy regimes concerned with international business will become more numerous and more complex in response to diverse and not necessarily related specific circumstances in various industries and regions. However, this predicted pattern of evolution raises a further question: What will be the impact of these fragmented developments upon each other and on the evolution of the total system of international policy regimes over time? The possibility of interregime conflicts, analogous to the conflicts among regulatory jurisdictions that have plagued the US economy in recent decades, is readily apparent.

E.1.1   Global and Comprehensive Regimes

Although the UN does not in itself constitute a comprehensive global regime for international business, it serves as an organizational "home" and information node for a broad array of international organizations and consultative bodies. Virtually all of the globally functional international economic and business regimes have some kind of UN status or connection.

The single most ambitious UN-centered effort to address international business issues is the draft UNCTC Code of Conduct on Transnational Corporations, first developed during the 1970s. It could well be argued that the actual complex of regimes in place, both within and outside the UN framework, has long since evolved beyond the scope of any single integrative concept or document. Indeed, the environment of international business in the 1990s is quite different from that in the 1970s that gave initial stimulus to the UN proposals, and the proposed content of the Code of Conduct has changed substantially as a result. The current draft document (published as appendix A in the 1992 edition of this book) is addressed to both enterprises and governments, and might be more appropriately titled "Statement of Principles Relating to International Business." The argument favoring formal adoption of this (or some similar) version of the code is not that such an action will actually change arrangements and behaviors that have become established over the last couple of decades, nor even that there is a great need for change in current practices. Instead, the argument is that the formal code is a summary statement of mutually understood principles, and hence that reference to the code in this form should encourage anticipatory behavior on the part of both enterprises and governments and perhaps contribute to the avoidance of problems and misunderstandings in the future (UNCTC, 1990).

E.1.2 Regional and Associative Regimes

The single most dramatic contemporary development remains, as predicted in our first edition, the growth of regional regimes, particularly the now fifteen-nation European Union (EU) and the North American Free Trade Area (NAFTA, composed of the US, Canada, and Mexico). There have been more recent, still developing trade arrangement efforts in South America (Mercosur) and the Pacific Rim (Asia Pacific Economic Cooperation, or APEC). Counterdevelopments were the collapse of the Soviet-dominated Council for Mutual Economic Assistance (CMEA or COMECON) and the continuing weakness and instability of regional collaborations in most of the developing regions of the globe. The benefits expected from the EU and NAFTA regimes in particular are likely to maintain and strengthen their development over time. There remain even today, however, several critical questions about the future evolution and impact of these regional regimes:

1. How, and how rapidly, will the new regional regimes expand to embrace satellite economies (Eastern Europe for the EU and Latin America for NAFTA), and how will these developments affect less developed countries (LDCs) in Asia and Africa that are unlikely to be included in these arrangements?

2. Will the policies of the two major economic blocs bordering the North Atlantic (the EU and NAFTA), particularly including agreements and understandings between them, lead to increasingly open and unrestricted worldwide trade and investment, or will their policies become increasingly restrictive over time? The evidence is beginning to point now in the direction of greater cooperation and harmonization.

3. In the light of developments suggested by the first two questions, will the two currently evolving regional regimes inevitably lead to the creation of a third, centered on Japan, or to a new global consensus, particularly among advanced countries?

Asia Pacific Economic Cooperation (APEC) is an associative initiative intended to bring Japan and the US, along with developing Pacific Rim countries, into a broader and more cooperative framework. However, US–Japan trade relations remain problematic, and the APEC structure as a whole shows signs of stress. The Organization for Economic Cooperation and Development (OECD), consisting of the "Triad" countries of the

North Atlantic and the Pacific Rim, is an consultative body, not a functioning regime; and economic warfare among the "Triad" countries, although unlikely to occur, remains a viable negotiating threat. The Group of 7 (G7) is arguably a better forum for certain types of collaboration and cooperation among key Triad countries than the OECD, but the G7 consultative process remains ad hoc and unstable.

These detailed questions involve the evolution of particular regional and associative regimes; but what are the implications of subglobal regime developments, whatever their specific form, for the operation of global regimes, whether comprehensive or functional? On the one hand, the various regional blocs may adopt stronger protectionist measures against foreign imports and investment, although this development now seems less likely than it did earlier. On the other hand, the evolution of large and prosperous regional economic systems may provide a favorable environment for growth of multinational enterprises (MNEs) and for interregional, and ultimately global, cooperation and integration. As the data presented in chapter 3 clearly show, global growth and integration trends are much stronger among the Triad countries than elsewhere. Expansion of any elements of the Triad through accretion and/or through the development of additional centers of regional growth and prosperity (e.g., Latin America), would seem more likely to stimulate than to retard worldwide economic development and hence to promote the development of global regimes. In any event, many critical issues (from agricultural production and prices to environmental protection) are too broad for comprehension within even very extensive regional regimes. If the World Trade Organization (WTO) can maintain emphasis on "global" issues and arrangements and not become overwhelmed with bilateral disputes, the gradual strengthening of worldwide policy systems can be anticipated.

E.1.3 Trade, Monetary, and Investment Regimes

The postwar international economic regimes intended to promote stable currency exchange and a liberal trade environment have undergone substantial change over the last couple of decades and continue to experience severe strains. However, there is universal agreement that an international "bank" to provide an underlying framework for the international currency market and an international "forum" for discussion of trade-related issues are essential elements of the global policy framework. Moves by the former USSR and Eastern European states to join the International Monetary Fund (IMF) and General Agreement on Tariffs and Trade/World Trade Organization (GATT/WTO) show the strength of these economic regimes. Whatever specific agreements and rules may govern these institutions at any point in time, their critical feature is the *process* of mutual consultation and collaboration that they embody and toward which international commitment remains strong. Of necessity, the leading economic powers (the US, the EU, and Japan) have dominant roles in these regimes. At the same time, these regimes are committed to recognition of the special concerns of middle-income countries and LDCs and to collaborative responses to their problems.

The missing element in the postwar arrangements is an identifiable global regime for foreign direct investment (FDI). Historically, the OECD countries have attempted to gain greater freedom for foreign investment activity (both among themselves and in other "host" countries) and to provide some measure of protection against expropriation or other form of loss. Some host countries (as illustrated by the Andean Code, Canada's Foreign Investment Review Agency, or FIRA, process, and France's efforts to control US investment activity) have attempted to restrict foreign investment. Other host countries, as illustrated by the efforts of the Association of Southeast Asian Nations (ASEAN) group, have attempted to encourage it. Generally, both types of efforts have tended to fail; investment tends to be driven by market dynamics. (FDI in Japan, however, continues to be both discouraged and restricted.)

US bilateral agreements with Canada, Israel, and Mexico and the NAFTA arrangements probably signal the future pattern. Those efforts all address reduction of restrictions of investment (largely from the US into the other country). The Canada–US agreement eliminated most barriers to both goods and investment flows; the same reductions will occur in due course between Mexico and other countries. Formal barriers to capital movements within the EU disappeared at the end of 1992. Regional efforts will probably tend to support the evolution of a truly international regime for foreign investment, a goal that is also embodied in initial WTO policies. (See further discussion of the taxation of foreign investment income in section E.2 below.)

E.1.4 Sea and Air Transport

International transport cannot take place at all without some kind of mutual understanding between origin and destination jurisdictions, and policy regimes for air and sea transport have been in place for many decades. The major trend within both regimes is toward increasing liberalization, both with respect to formal arrangements (so that the regimes themselves become less and less restrictive) and with respect to enterprise-level evolution. Cooperative alliances among airlines (most of which are both heavily regulated and subsidized, and many of which are state-owned) have become the characteristic enterprise structure. The result is increasing flexibility in rates and fares and in service performance, which in turn increases the importance of the informational and consultative functions of the policy regimes.

E.1.5 Telecommunications and Services

Communication is the "transport service" for information, and communication contacts are both generators of and substitutes for physical movements of both people and goods. International communications is becoming the freest of international business functions, partially because some of the technology in use is simply beyond the control of regulatory bodies, whether national or international. The international telecommunications regime, dating back to 1865, is one of the oldest formal multilateral policy systems affecting business; it is also one of the most clearly "global." The International Telecommunications Union (ITU) is now a specialized agency of the UN. Nevertheless, there is at the present time no set of coherent international policies in place governing interconnections, access, investment, or trade in this important arena. Technological change, changing national regulatory policies, and the emergence of new forms and forces of competition (including privatization of public monopolies and crossborder investments or acquisitions) place considerable stress on a century-old approach to international cooperation.

International protection of intellectual property is closely related to communications and service activities and has been a major concern in US trade policy since the early 1980s. In response to strong US pressure, increased emphasis on protection of intellectual property was included within the WTO agreement, along with initial efforts to create an international regime for services.

International trade and investment in financial services, insurance, tourism, and other professional and business services have grown rapidly in recent decades. And monitoring, to say nothing of regulating, these activities presents peculiar difficulties. Services are invisible, often nebulous, and may take place without any contact with geographic borders: through telecommunications, for example. They may also occur through the movement of *persons* who subsequently receive services (e.g., tourism) or provide services (e.g., professional work) in another jurisdiction. Services may have substantial effects on the incomes and international accounts of the enterprises, individuals, and countries involved, and services are the lubricants of international trade and investment and a major vehicle for the transfer of intellectual property, such as technology and management processes, among countries. Hence, it seems likely that international attention to policy issues related to telecommunications and service industries will continue, although probably with limited impact.

E.1.6 Environment

International environmental regimes are not new phenomena, although earlier historic examples were primarily regional in scope. The shift toward a global perspective on the environment has come about in part because of increasing knowledge about the planet and its characteristics and in part because increased worldwide resource use gives rise to problems that can only be addressed on a global basis. Since the 1960s, there has been a virtual explosion of environmental regime initiatives, some rather tentative and noncontroversial (e.g., the Moon Treaty) and some involving sharp differences in scientific judgment and clashes of interests (e.g., undersea mining). The Framework Convention on Climate Change was the most important achievement of the 1992 Rio Earth Summit; however, implementation of this agreement will extend over decades. Global issues of biodiversity and deforestation were approached even more tentatively. Regulatory advances in these areas clearly depend heavily on the evolution of scientific knowledge and consensus as well as on national and regional political and economic negotiations.

With respect to the other most conspicuously "global" environmental issue (the use of outer space), it seems most likely that events will proceed at the national policy level, with leadership by some countries establishing patterns for others (as in the historic cases of air transport and telecommunications, for example).

E.2 TAXATION OF INTERNATIONAL INCOME[1]

Increasing international economic integration and increasing facilitation and harmonization of international contacts through the growth of international policy regimes inevitably draws attention to the fact that there are large and persistent differences in the taxation of income, both individual and corporate, in various national jurisdictions, and no significant multinational effort to reduce, or even to clarify, their effects. There is no question that legitimate governments have a sovereign right to levy taxes on *all* economic interests and activities within their borders. However, most national tax systems developed, and remain primarily focused, within a domestic context. And, since different polities will have different views about the appropriate role of the state, as well as different economic and social development goals, it is no surprise that national tax systems vary considerably. Now that increasing amounts of income in many countries are arising from international sources, these differences may affect the choice of country of residence by individuals free to move from one location to another and may also affect the attractiveness of various markets to international traders, both buyers and sellers. Their most important effects, however, are probably on international investment, and particularly on FDI.

International investment income gives rise to potentially taxable events in two different places, one where the income is generated (the "source") and the other where it is received (the "tax residence" of the recipient). And it may be taxed at either or both places. In the "source" location, foreign investment may be subject to special benefits (e.g., "tax holidays") or penalties (e.g., restrictions on repatriation and/or reinvestment.) And, if any taxes are paid at the source, they may be treated as "tax credits" (i.e., deductible against any further taxes that may be due) in the taxpayer's country of residence, or may simply be considered a "cost of doing business" (i.e., deductible only in the process of calculating net, or taxable, income). Moreover, in the country of residence, foreign investment income may be taxed exactly like domestic income, may be taxed only when repatriated (i.e., returned to the home country in the form of interest or dividends), or may receive other distinctive treatment.

As noted above, the international business environment is increasingly open to investment; indeed, international capital flows have become almost impossible to regulate directly, even by countries that might wish to do so. However, even within this open market framework, differential tax policies can be used to enhance the attractiveness of investment flows or, alternatively, to discourage them. A theoretically "ideal" tax system is one that collects the desired amount of revenue without altering the relative attractiveness/unattractiveness of different investments (or occupations, etc.) A developing country, however, may specifically wish to attract foreign investors by granting special privileges (e.g., "tax holidays"); or may wish to provide protection for local enterprises through discriminatory tax treatment against MNEs. And domestic goals in any country may favor the promotion of certain industries (such as high-technology or export-oriented activities) or certain types of investment over others. Within this complex set of national policy situations, motivations, and technical options, countries differ considerably with respect to all critical dimensions of their tax systems, viz.:

1) tax base — what types of income are and are not subject to domestic taxation (see further discussion of the "unitary tax" concept, below);
2) tax structure — what distinctions are made among income sources and/or taxpayers, and what exceptions, subsidies, and penalties are in force; and
3) tax rates — what stated percentages of income, in various categories, are due to be paid in taxes.

These critical dimensions, and many ancillary features as well, vary greatly both within and between tax jurisdictions. As a result, comparison of the actual effective rates of taxation in various jurisdictions is a difficult task. For example, corporate tax rates within the major industrial countries appear to vary from 34%–35% to over 50% (Tanzi, 1995, p. 105). However, econometric research shows that in 1990 marginal effective tax rates on corporate income (which would be the critical elements in *new* investment decisions) ranged from only 6% (Japan) to 28% (UK), and two countries (France and Italy) actually had *negative* marginal rates due to special investment incentives then in force (Tanzi, 1995, p. 113).

An extensive OECD study (1991) found that pretax rates of return necessary to justify a *domestic* investment decision with 5% annual cost of capital varied from 5% in Sweden to 7.1% in Australia; for *foreign* investment from other countries into the named country, the range was 6.4% in Sweden to 9.7% in New Zealand. The difference between each of these figures and the 5% cost of capital (i.e., minimum aftertax rate of return) used in this analysis is generally referred to as the "tax wedge." Thus, according to this analysis, there is no "tax wedge" on domestic investment income in Sweden, and there is a 1.4% "tax wedge" on international investment income from Swedish sources. (There is also a 1.8% "tax wedge" on foreign investment income earned by Swedish taxpayers.) It appears that the "tax wedge" on income from international investment in all OECD countries is significant (2.5%, on average, on a 5% base), and substantially higher than the 0.9% average "tax wedge" on domestic investment income (OECD, 1991, table 5.8, p. 141).

There are also considerable differences both within and between countries in the *way* in which the income of large, multilocation corporations is taxed. Within the US, most states use some variation of the "Massachusetts formula," according to which the total US taxable income of a multistate corporation is allocated among states in proportion to their shares of its sales, assets, and labor costs. California and a few other states have applied this "unitary" formula to the entire global earnings of MNEs for purposes of state-level tax computations, and the US government itself taxes MNEs on the basis of their global operations. These practices have become highly controversial and subject to intense pressures from both MNEs and foreign governments. Their actual impact on effective tax rates is, however, difficult to ascertain.

In summary, there is no question that there are nontrivial differences in the tax treatment of investment income, both domestic and international, among countries. However, there is considerable uncertainty as to the exact magnitude of these differences in any specific case; and there is even more uncertainty as to the impact of such differences (whatever their magnitude) on international investment behavior.

An initial hypothesis might be that "all differences matter." Tanzi cites an argument that reductions in taxes on capital during the Reagan

Administration, beginning in 1981, brought about a major shift (and a misallocation) of capital toward the US and eventually led to a rise in the value of the dollar in foreign exchange markets (1995, p. 15, citing Sinn, 1989). He also notes evidence that investors from countries that do not offer tax credit for foreign tax payments tend to invest relatively more heavily in lower-tax states within the US (1995, p. 25, citing Hines, 1993). On the other hand, international tax competition among countries is notably strong, and tax arrangements among major countries are governed by an intricate web of bilateral tax treaties and agreements, so that the actual magnitudes of apparent differences are extremely difficult to discern. Moreover, many other considerations (investment costs, labor costs, productivity, market access, etc.) may offset or overwhelm apparent tax advantages or penalties. Hence, although there is some movement of wealthy individuals and finance capital holdings to tax havens such as the Bahamas, there is no mass exodus of MNEs to such locations. A dispassionate analyst is inclined to conclude that actual "tax competition" is much more effective than apparent rates and structures indicate, and/or that nontax factors typically overwhelm any genuine tax impact differences that may persist.

In any event, there is no worldwide movement toward greater harmonization of internationally important tax principles at the present time. The 1991 OECD study notes a considerable number of national-level policy changes during the 1980s with respect to double taxation of corporate income, but these changes were evenly split between reducing and increasing such practices. EU and NAFTA arrangements certainly move in the direction of harmonization, but special investment incentives and penalties abound even within these frameworks and certainly outside them. The greatest force favoring harmonization may be the actual investment behavior of MNEs, which demand "competitive" tax treatment from individual countries and hence stimulate them to consult with and monitor each other for self-protection.

E.3 CORRUPTION OF FOREIGN GOVERNMENT OFFICIALS[2]

Another major issue not addressed in the case study chapters of this book is the integrity and responsibility of multinational enterprises in dealing with foreign officials. There is no doubt that customary government-business relationships vary in different parts of the world. Corporate political contributions are legal in some countries, illegal in others; bribery is commonplace in some cultures, morally repugnant (as well as illegal) elsewhere; banking records are secret in one place, routinely available to government inspectors in another; etc. The first attempts to establish some explicit international standards in these areas occurred in 1996, in both the OECD and the Organization of American States (OAS); US leadership was a major force in both cases. The OECD action was endorsed by the law ministers of the British Commonwealth countries; the International Chamber of Commerce (ICC) urged its members to adopt enforceable antibribery codes. Corruption and bribery in all forms, and including all ancillary practices (e.g., extradition of persons accused of crimes), is clearly a "hot" topic in international business circles.

The various and complex aspects of international business ethics are beyond the scope of this book, but in very broad terms, there are two opposing schools of thought about these matters. One school advocates universal moral standards. The other school defends cultural relativism on the basis of variations in local standards and practices. A reasonable intermediate position anticipates universal consensus about a minimum core of global norms (e.g., thou shalt not kill), but with considerable local variation beyond core limits (Donaldson and Dunfee, 1994).

Our discussion here focuses on the bribery of foreign government officials in order to obtain business opportunities within their jurisdictions. There is little question that such bribery, whatever its moral status, falls outside the realm of legitimate business competition and undermines the development of markets based on product/service quality, price, efficiency, etc. At the same time, there is no doubt whatsoever that bribery, in both overt and disguised forms, is endemic in the international business environment. Pastin (1986) reported that the legal department head of a major oil company kept a list of customary levels of bribes in each country of the Middle East for ready reference; and the Watergate investigation brought to light established patterns of questionable foreign payments in certain industries in the US. Over the past couple of decades, bribery scandals have broken out in several OECD countries (e.g., Belgium, Germany, Italy, Japan, the Netherlands) as well as in the Philippines, South Korea, and other newly industrialized or developing countries.

In 1977, the US adopted the Foreign Corrupt Practices Act (FCPA) which imposed both civil and criminal penalties on foreign bribery by US companies. (The act exempted "facilitating payments" or "grease" from its definition of bribery.)[3] The FCPA reflects a history of intense public concern in the US about the moral conduct of business managers. According to Pastin, "The primary motivation for the FCPA was neither economic nor legal. The motivation was ethical and political. ... In fact, bribes may promote our individual or collective best interests. We oppose bribes because they violate our fundamental ethical principles" (1986, pp. 470 and 472). Only one other country, Sweden, has adopted a similar prohibitory statute.

There is no reliable study of the economic effects of the FCPA; only indirect indicators, opinion, and anecdotal evidence are available. A 1976 SEC study predicted no substantial competitive effect, but a Reagan

Administration task force later estimated an annual loss in foreign business revenues of $1 billion (Ramsey and Alkhafaji, 1990), about 1% of the 1993 US current account deficit. In 1996, US Special Trade Representative Mickey Kantor stated that US companies lose sales of some $45 billion annually to foreign companies using bribes (Cooper, 1996).

The FCPA imposes two economic losses on US enterprises: 1) exclusion from specific opportunities dependent on bribery; and 2) costs of compliance with accounting and internal control standards, which would occur to some degree even under a disclosure statute. Although many business executives complain about the costs and immorality of bribery, business interests generally did not support passage of the FCPA and argued that its detailed record keeping should be reduced (Kim, 1981; *Business Week*, September 19, 1983). Business support for international anticorruption activities has not been conspicuous.

The US has long campaigned for an international anticorruption agreement in order, as expressed by the US representative to the OECD, to "level the playing field for international business" (*Wall Street Journal*, April 15, 1996). The FCPA explicitly called for the US president "to obtain international agreements in as many forums as appropriate concerning the reporting and exchange of ... information and the establishment of international standards and codes of conduct for the operations of companies" as well as "international rules and regulations for international government procurement and sales" (section 11). The US has undertaken such multilateral efforts through the UN, the OECD, and the OAS.

The draft UN Code of Conduct on Transnational Corporations includes specific language modeled on the FCPA prohibiting corrupt payments to public officials by MNEs and requiring them to maintain and make available to competent authorities accurate records of any payments made to public officials or intermediaries. The relevant language is as follows:

(a) Transnational corporations shall refrain, in their transactions, from the offering, promising or giving of any payment, gift or other advantage to or for the benefit of a public official as consideration for performing or refraining from the performance of his duties in connection with those transactions.
(b) Transnational corporations shall maintain accurate records of any payments made by them to any public official or intermediary. They shall make available these records to the competent authorities of the countries in which they operate, upon request, for investigations and proceedings concerning those payments ("Activities of Transnational

Corporations," section A, "General," paragraph 20, "Abstention from corrupt practices").

The thirty-four member OAS agreed in principle at the "Summit of the Americas" held in Miami in December 1994 to work toward crossborder cooperation in suppressing graft and drug trafficking. In early April 1996, twenty-one of the member countries signed a twenty-eight article agreement intended to encourage development of national anticorruption laws and crossborder cooperation (*The Economist*, 1996). The other member countries, including Canada and the US, must consider the agreement internally before signing. The signatories agreed to exchange information on banking accounts. Extradition of fugitives remains dependent on national laws and bilateral agreements. The OAS accord is the first international agreement against corruption.

Recent OECD action has focused on the tax deductibility of bribes, which constitutes a home-country subsidy for foreign corrupt practices. Fourteen OECD countries, including Germany, currently permit such deductions (*USA Today*, 1996; Cooper, 1996), although in some instances "Euphemisms are used on tax returns to disguise the practice" (*Wall Street Journal*, April 15, 1996). In April 1996, the OECD countries agreed to repeal all deduction privileges for corrupt payments. Two official reasons were offered for this change in tax policy: 1) corrupt payments raise "serious moral and political concerns;" and 2) corrupt payments hinder international investment by "increasing transaction costs and distorting competitive conditions" (*Wall Street Journal*, April 15, 1996). The European Union has left the matter entirely in the hands of its member states. Some of the smaller nations in the OECD regarded the change in tax policy as unfair since it would hinder them in international business. Their view of a level playing field is quite different from that of the US government. It can be argued that, in terms of their interest in maintaining domestic employment, bribery to obtain foreign business opportunities is economically sensible policy (*Wall Street Journal*, April 19, 1996).

These international accords lack any enforcement authority or mechanisms other than good-faith compliance by each member nation and ultimately depend on moral authority. The strongest argument against corrupt practices in international business is that they tend to spread to the home country; they also cause conflict among political and economic allies. However, many countries do not see a moral obligation to contribute to the international common good and can in any case "free ride" on the efforts of other countries, such as the US, which bear the economic and political costs of maintaining a legitimate international business climate while others reap the economic benefits through corrupt practices. The negative impact of bribery in terms of official corruption, increased costs and prices, inferior products and services, etc., may appear, and may in fact *be*, "absent or minimal" from the viewpoint of certain participants (Pastin, 1986, p. 471). Velasquez (1992) concludes that an international enforcement agency is desirable, but such an enforcement agency is difficult to create, since most multilateral agreements rely primarily on domestic enforcement. A pertinent consideration in this regard is that extortion by foreign government officials may be as important an element of the situation as deliberate bribery by MNEs (Kotchian, 1977).

E.4 IMPLICATIONS OF REGIME DEVELOPMENT FOR INTERNATIONAL MANAGEMENT

The enterprise manager of the future will operate within a complex web of international policy regimes. The basic functions of international business (trade in goods and services, currency exchange, investment, transportation, and communication) would be impossible without the existence of supportive agreements and understandings among enterprises and governments. Indeed, the network of formal regimes and looser arrangements forms part of the institutional infrastructure for the global economy. This infrastructure does not consist, for the most part, of a set of *regulations* governing international business. It is more appropriately understood as a reflection of mutual agreement among participating parties about norms and patterns of desirable and acceptable (and undesirable and unacceptable) behavior.

The notion of operating within a network of policy regimes is, however, new and strange to most international managers. Perhaps the most difficult, but also most fundamental, point to grasp is that industries and enterprises are active participants in the formation and operation of regimes, not simply impacted parties. Some regimes originate primarily in response to the specific concerns of industries and enterprises; the air transport regime is perhaps the most conspicuous example. Whatever their origins, effective regimes require collaborative and adaptive behavior on the part of enterprise, and often of several different *kinds* of enterprises operating in various political jurisdictions.

Another feature of regimes that is particularly problematic for managers is their highly *dynamic* character. Although most important regimes contain significant institutional elements (formal agreements or organizations) that persist over time, the understandings and norms of behavior that are of primary importance tend to change in response to changing circumstances and often in very subtle ways. These changes are driven ultimately by the dynamism of international business itself, as well as by domestic and international political developments. The international manager's difficult task is to monitor, anticipate, and even participate in these processes in order to protect and advance enterprise objectives.

From the perspective of international managers, the most conspicuous policy restrictions on business activities are probably those relating to foreign direct investment, services trade, intellectual property rights, and such specific MNE activities as transfer pricing and corrupt payments. In general, attempts to limit FDI and restrict MNE activities have not been particularly successful in market-oriented economies. Even where the restrictions themselves have been effective (as in the old CMEA and occasionally in Latin America), they have not typically improved economic conditions within the target environments and have often had perverse effects. Managers confronted with these kinds of issues may need to familiarize themselves with the dismal record of past experience and then use that information in their negotiations with other involved parties.

A final, and particularly troubling, consideration for managers is the fact that the complex network of policy regimes does not constitute a single, integrated whole and, in fact, contains many inconsistent and conflicting elements. Hence, it is often the case that one principle (say, special consideration for a particular group of countries or interests) prevails in one type of activity, while another principle (say, equal treatment of all participants) prevails elsewhere. This state of affairs is not surprising, since there is no overarching concept or idea uniting the diverse elements of the international policy network, nor is it likely that a comprehensive global regime covering all important aspects of international business activity will appear in the near future. The proposed UN Code of Conduct on Transnational Corporations, even if adopted, does not have such a unifying character; and, in any event, the more important policy regimes now in place and evolving tend to be functional or regional in focus. Hence, the problems of diversity, and perhaps direct conflict, among the multiple regimes that affect the operations of individual managers and enterprises are likely to become greater, rather than less, in the future. The general trend is nevertheless toward a global economy with fewer restrictions on mobility of capital, goods and services, resources, and profits.

Notes

1. This section is based primarily on Eden, forthcoming; Hines, 1994; OECD, 1991; and Tanzi, 1995.

2. Key references include Donaldson, 1989; Greanias and Windsor, 1982; Houck and Williams, eds., 1996; and *Wall Street Journal*, May 5, 1996. A good source of current information on corruption worldwide is

Transparency International, based in Berlin and available on the World Wide Web at http://www.transparency.de/.

3. The FCPA language, statutorily an amendment of the 1934 Securities Exchange Act, and the Ford Administration's proposed disclosure, rather than criminalization, bill are available in Greanias and Windsor (1982, pp. 153–170). The Omnibus Trade and Competitiveness Act of 1988 eliminated the "reason to know" standard of the FCPA in favor of liability only for specific authorization so that responsibility for foreign agents or middlemen was lessened and excluded facilitating payments, payments or gifts lawful in country of operation, courtesy payments or gifts, selling or purchasing expenditures, and ordinary expenditures of contract performance.

References

Cooper, Helene. 1996. "Kantor Suggests Using Trade Sanctions As a Way to Fight Foreign Corruption," *Wall Street Journal*, March 7.

Donaldson, Thomas. 1989. *The Ethics of International Business*. New York: Oxford University Press.

Donaldson, Thomas, and Thomas W. Dunfee. 1994. "Towards a Unified Conception of Business Ethics: Integrative Social Contracts Theory," *Academy of Management Review*, vol. 19, no. 2 (April), pp. 252–284.

The Economist. 1996. "Cleaning up Latin America," April 6, p. 41.

Eden, Lorraine. Forthcoming. *Taxing Multinationals*. Toronto, Canada: University of Toronto.

Greanias, George C., and Duane Windsor. 1982. *The Foreign Corrupt Practices Act: Anatomy of a Statute*. Lexington, MA: Lexington Books.

Hines, James R. 1993. *Altered States: Taxes and the Location of Foreign Direct Investment in America*. Cambridge, MA: National Bureau of Economic Research.

Hines, James R. 1994. "International Taxation," *NBER Reporter* (Fall), pp. 10–15.

Houck, John W., and Oliver F. Williams, eds. 1996. *Is the Good Corporation Dead? Social Responsibility in a Global Economy*. Lanham, MD: Rowman & Littlefield.

Kim, S.H. 1981. "On Repealing the Foreign Corrupt Practices Act: Survey and Assessment," *Columbia Journal of World Business*, vol. 16, no. 3 (Fall), pp. 16–21.

Kotchian, A.C. 1977. "The Pay-Off: Lockheed's 70-Day Mission to Tokyo," *Saturday Review* (July 9), pp. 6–12.

Organization for Economic Cooperation and Development (OECD). 1991. *Taxing Profits in a Global Economy*. Paris: OECD.

Pastin, Mark. 1986. "Managing the Rules of Conflict: International Bribery," in William M. Hoffman et al., eds., *Ethics and the Multinational Enterprise*. Washington, DC: University Press of America, pp. 463–476.

Ramsey, Richard D., and Abbass F. Alkhafaji. 1990. "Foreign Corrupt Practices Act," in Abbass F. Alkhafaji, ed., *International Management Challenge*. Acton, MA: Copley Publishing Group, pp. 137–149.

Sinn, Hans-Werner. 1989. "The Policy of Tax-Cut-Cum-Base Broadening: Implications for International Capital Movements," in Manfred Neumann and Karl W. Roskamp, eds., *Public Finance and Performance of Enterprises*. Detroit, MI: Wayne State University Press, pp. 153–176.

Tanzi, Vito. 1995. *Taxation in an Integration World*. Washington, DC: Brookings Institution.

UN Centre on Transnational Corporations (UNCTC). 1990. *The New Code Environment*. No. 16, Series A. New York: UNCTC.

USA Today. 1996. "Bribery Threatens Trade," March 7.

Velasquez, Manuel. 1992. "International Business, Morality, and the Common Good," *Business Ethics Quarterly*, vol. 2, no. 1, pp. 27–40.

Wall Street Journal. 1996. "OECD Asks Repeal of Tax Deductions for Bribe Payments," April 15.

Wall Street Journal. 1996. "Competitive Bidding," April 19.

Wall Street Journal. 1996. "Is Corruption an Asian Value?" May 5.

NOTE ON DATA AND SOURCES

This book relies primarily on official data sources, especially trade, investment, enterprise, economic, and population information provided by the World Bank, the UN Conference on Trade and Development (UNCTAD), the UN Centre on Transnational Corporations (UNCTC), and the International Monetary Fund (IMF). Other data sources, especially the US Department of Commerce, have also been used where appropriate. All the data sources on international economic activity include significant omissions and defects. Fortunately, these data deficiencies do not materially affect the basic patterns of international economic activity reported here.

Chapter 3 above explains the general scheme for classification of types of economies employed in this book. The purpose of this note is to provide amplification concerning our data and sources. In chapter 3, we group economies into the five types recognized by UNCTAD, modified in certain respects to our purposes. The country composition of the five types of economies is as follows:

1. Developed (or industrial) market economies: US, Canada, Japan, European Union (EU 15), European Free Trade Area (EFTA 4), and Australia and New Zealand (typically grouped together). The US and Canada are grouped with Mexico (in "Other" below) to constitute the North American Free Trade Area (NAFTA). Western Europe (or Europe) is the EU and EFTA, often combined in UNCTAD sources with Turkey (an associate member of the EU). The Organization for Economic Cooperation and Development (OECD), the set of advanced industrial countries (AICs), is roughly the same as this category. Greece, Portugal, and Turkey are basically still developing countries, although most sources include them in this category. Although Eastern European states are beginning to join the OECD, we have left these countries in the Eastern Europe category below. UNCTAD includes South Africa, Israel, Faeroe Islands, and Gibraltar in this category; we generally place these countries

in the "Other" category below (which includes Malta); the statistical effect is small.

a. EU 15: Austria, Belgium, Denmark, Finland, France, Germany (unified in 1991), Greece, Ireland, Italy, Luxembourg, Netherlands, Portugal, Spain, Sweden, United Kingdom. EU 12 where used excludes Austria, Finland, and Sweden, which all joined the EU from the EFTA in 1993. Turkey is an associate member of the EU.

b. EFTA 4: Iceland, Liechtenstein (data often combined with Austria), Norway, and Switzerland. Liechtenstein, not a member of OECD, is entering the European Economic Area (EEA), in which all EU and EFTA members now participate with the exception of Switzerland. Prior to 1993, the EFTA 7 included Austria, Finland, and Sweden, which then joined the EU.

2. Eastern Europe: Albania, Bulgaria, Czechoslovakia, East Germany (to 1991 when unified with West Germany), Hungary, Poland, Romania, and the former USSR, now the 15-country Commonwealth of Independent States (CIS). These economies (with the exception of Albania) were the European members of the now defunct Council for Mutual Economic Assistance (CMEA or COMECON for "Communist Economies"); CMEA also included Cuba, Mongolia, and North Korea (in "Other"). For geographical reasons, we include where possible Yugoslavia, classified by UNCTAD as a developing country; Yugoslavia had special observer status with CMEA and the OECD. Yugoslavia disintegrated in 1993 into a set of states not all of which were recognized officially by the US.

3. Asian Socialist: People's Republic of China (PRC), Mongolia, North Korea, Vietnam. Statistically China dominates this category (Cambodia and Laos are in "Other").

4. Organization of Petroleum Exporting Countries (OPEC): Algeria, Ecuador (until 1993), Gabon, Indonesia, Iran, Iraq, Kuwait, Libya, Nigeria, Qatar, Saudi Arabia, United Arab Emirates (UAR), and Venezuela. The UNCTAD category of "major oil exporters" consists of OPEC plus Angola, Bahrain, Brunei, Congo, Oman, Syria, and Trinidad/Tobago. There are other oil exporting countries.

5. Other: includes all countries, both "newly industrialized countries" (NICs) and "less developed countries" (LDCs), not members of the previous categories. We place certain other countries from the developed market category here in order to focus on the OECD. We use in chapter 3 a selected set of seven NICs: Argentina, Brazil, Hong Kong, Mexico (a member of NAFTA), Singapore, South Korea, and Taiwan. Other coun-

tries often classified as NICs include Chile, China, India, Israel, Malaysia, South Africa, and Turkey (an associate member of the EU). UNCTAD classifies developing economies into low-, middle-, and high-income subcategories. UNCTAD (since 1990) classifies countries, in addition to major petroleum exporters, into major exporters of manufactures (Brazil, Hong Kong, Mexico, Singapore, South Korea, Taiwan, and Yugoslavia)— a category which is close to the NIC notion, least developed countries, and other developing countries. Sources vary on the handling of data for Hong Kong and Taiwan ("provinces" of China by convention).

The World Bank and IMF now use a somewhat different approach that recognizes developed market economies, developing economies, and oil exporters. The World Bank organizes countries into three income categories: low, middle, and high, the latter including an OECD subcategory. The three institutions may include somewhat different sets of countries in particular categories. Membership in the IMF is a prerequisite for World Bank membership. Russia (the Russian Federation) and other Eastern European states are now seeking entry into the IMF/World Bank and OECD; the EU is examining the issue of how to handle economic integration with these states.

In contrast to both UNCTAD and the World Bank, the UNCTC does not generally publish country-by-country data. Its tabulations utilize three principal categories:

a. Developed market economies;
b. Developing economies (including both OPEC countries and Asian Socialist states);
c. Eastern European economies, including the former USSR.

References

Choi, Frederick D.S. 1988. "International Data Sources for Empirical Research in Financial Management," *Financial Management*, vol. 17, no. 2 (Summer), pp. 80–98.

Graham, Edward M., and Paul R. Krugman. 1989. "Appendix A: US Government Data on Foreign Direct Investment," *Foreign Direct Investment In the United States*. Washington, DC: Institute for International Economics, pp. 135–147.

Rice, Gillian, and Essam Mahmoud. 1985. "Forecasting and the Database: An Analysis of Databases for International Business," *Journal of Forecasting*, vol. 4, no. 1 (January-March), pp. 89–97.

Thomsen, Stephen. 1990. "Appendix: FDI Data Sources and Uses," in DeAnne Julius, *Global Companies and Public Policy: The Growing Challenge of Foreign Direct Investment*. New York: Council on Foreign Relations for The Royal Institute of International Affairs, pp. 109–122.

Table A-1. Growth in World Exports by Type of Economy, 1970–1990 (current US$ in billions, f.o.b., "free on board")

Origin of Exports by Type of Economy	Year	World $ Volume	% of World Volume	Period Growth in $ Volume	% Share of World Growth in Volume
World	1970	311.91	100.00		
	1975	872.06	100.00	560.16	100.00
	1980	2000.95	100.00	1128.89	100.00
	1985	1929.54	100.00	79.38	100.00
	1990	3391.91	100.00	1464.40	100.00
Developed	1970	222.56	71.35		
Market	1975	573.11	65.72	350.55	62.58
	1980	1258.94	62.92	685.83	60.75
	1985	1262.10	65.41	3.16	3.98
	1990	2445.21	72.09	1183.11	80.79
CIS (former USSR)	1970	30.53	9.79		
and Eastern Europe	1975	77.36	8.87	46.83	8.36
	1980	155.12	7.75	77.76	6.89
	1985	173.97	9.02	18.85	23.74
	1990	171.94	5.07	-2.03	-100.00
Asian	1970	2.31	0.74		
Socialist	1975	7.26	0.83	4.95	0.88
	1980	20.38	1.02	13.12	1.16
	1985	30.06	1.56	9.68	12.19
	1990	65.81	1.94	35.75	2.44
OPEC	1970	17.99	5.77		
	1975	113.18	12.98	95.19	16.99
	1980	306.77	15.33	193.60	17.15
	1985	155.96	8.08	-150.81	-100.00
	1990	164.51	4.85	8.55	0.58
Other	1970	38.53	12.35		
	1975	101.16	11.60	62.63	11.18
	1980	259.75	12.98	158.59	14.05
	1985	307.45	15.93	47.70	60.09
	1990	544.44	16.05	236.99	16.18

Sources: UNCTAD, *Handbook of International Trade and Development Statistics* (New York: 1989, 1992), table 1, and *Supplement* (1984, 1987), table A.1.
  Notes: Source includes some data restatement over time.
  1985 and 1990 figures for "Period Growth in $ Volume" exclude the declines in dollar value reported for OPEC or Commonwealth of Independent States (CIS) groups.
Percentage shares for growth also exclude OPEC and CIS (which are 100% of decline).
  "Developed Market" as defined by UNCTAD rather than as in table 3-1.

Table A-2. Origin and Destination of Exports by Type of Economy, 1970–1990 (current US$ in billions, f.o.b., "free on board")

| | | Destination of Exports | | | | | |
| | | | Developed | Developing Countries | | Communist or Formerly So | |
Origin of Exports	Year	World	Market	OPEC	Non-OPEC	Eastern Europe	Asia
World	1970	311.91	218.16	9.58	49.56	28.63	3.65
	1975	872.06	567.69	57.25	147.99	82.60	8.91
	1980	2,000.95	1,335.99	127.67	353.54	143.96	22.83
	1985	1,929.54	1,274.79	97.76	341.36	151.14	43.40
	1990	3,391.91	2,429.66	111.87	604.08	142.94	56.77
Developed	1970	222.56	169.99	7.70	35.03	6.40	2.01
Market	1975	573.11	396.26	47.22	94.87	26.00	5.89
	1980	1,258.94	891.46	99.89	201.84	42.24	14.43
	1985	1,262.10	932.94	68.59	187.24	33.72	24.97
	1990	2,445.21	1,894.31	80.18	375.57	49.91	21.96
CIS (former USSR)	1970	30.53	6.98	0.67	3.42	18.39	1.02
and Eastern Europe	1975	77.36	20.20	2.64	7.73	44.37	1.96
	1980	155.12	43.27	4.94	23.28	78.71	4.19
	1985	173.97	43.61	4.28	26.03	92.00	6.53
	1990	171.94	65.81	2.96	27.87	64.98	8.67

	Year					
Asian Socialist	1970	2.31	0.73	0.11	0.97	0.49	n.a.
	1975	7.26	2.89	0.51	2.61	1.24	n.a.
	1980	20.38	8.86	1.35	7.49	2.68	n.a.
	1985	30.06	11.79	0.81	13.15	3.79	n.a.
	1990	65.81	21.89	1.51	34.75	5.92	0.503
OPEC	1970	17.99	13.50	0.13	3.38	0.28	0.02
	1975	113.18	83.44	0.80	23.94	2.10	0.08
	1980	306.77	231.10	3.97	65.78	3.72	0.32
	1985	155.96	96.53	4.56	51.01	2.62	0.16
	1990	164.51	105.12	4.51	36.07	3.05	1.13
Other	1970	38.53	26.95	0.98	6.76	3.09	0.60
	1975	101.16	64.89	6.09	18.84	8.89	0.98
	1980	259.75	161.31	17.53	55.14	16.62	3.90
	1985	307.45	189.92	19.52	63.93	19.01	11.21
	1990	544.44	342.53	22.71	129.82	19.09	24.51

Source: UN Conference on Trade and Development (UNCTAD), *Handbook of International Trade and Development Statistics* or *Supplement* (New York: 1984, 1987, 1992), table A.1, Total Exports. Some data restated over time.
Notes: Yugoslavia classified a developing country ("Other") from 1980 on. "Asian Socialist" intratrade excluded prior to 1988.

Table A-3. Origin and Destination of Manufactured Exports by Type of Economy, 1970–1990

	Origin of Exports							
	World Total		Developed Market Economies		Developing Economies		Rest of World	
	1970	1990	1970	1990	1970	1990	1970	1990
Destination of Exports (current US$ in millions)								
World Total	189,913	2,412,350	128,490	1,752,139	39,947	518,225	20,573	129,190
Developed Market	160,352	1,907,567	119,512	1,476,633	33,608	366,949	6233	55,393
Developing	10,455	382,634	6212	240,815	3402	109,196	957	29,513
Other	19,106	122,149	2762	34,691	2939	42,079	13,381	44,283
Percentage Distribution by Destination								
World Total	100	100	100	100	100	100	100	100
Developed Market	84	79	93	84	84	71	30	43
Developing	6	16	5	14	9	21	5	23
Other	10	5	2	2	7	8	65	34

Source: UNCTAD, *Handbook of International Trade and Development Statistics, 1992* (New York: UN, 1993), table A.13.
Notes: "Developed Market" is basically OECD plus South Africa; "Developing" includes OPEC (minor manufactured exports) and most other oil exporters. "Other" is CIS (former USSR), Eastern Europe, and Asian Socialist.

Table A-4. Changes in Origin and Destination of Manufactured Exports by Type of Economy, 1970–1990

		Destination of Exports		
	World Exports by Origin	Developed Market Economies	Developing Economies	Other Economies
1970–1990 $ Increase in Exports (current US$ in millions)				
World Total	2,222,437	1,623,649	478,278	108,617
Developed Market	1,747,215	1,357,121	333,341	49,160
Developing	372,179	234,603	105,794	28,556
Other	103,043	31,929	39,140	30,902
1970–1990 % Increase in Exports				
World Total	1170	1264	1197	528
Developed Market	1090	1136	992	789
Developing	3560	3777	3110	2984
Other	539	1156	1332	231
1970–1990 Average Annual % Increase in Exports				
World Total	59	63	60	26
Developed Market	54	57	50	39
Developing	178	189	155	149
Other	27	58	67	12

Source: UNCTAD, *Handbook of International Trade and Development Statistics, 1992* (New York: UN, 1993), table A.13.

Notes: "Developed Market" is basically OECD plus South Africa; "Developing" includes OPEC (minor manufactured exports) and most other oil exporters. "Other" is Commonwealth of Independent States (CIS, formerly USSR), Eastern Europe, and Asian Socialist.

Table A-5. Foreign Direct Investment (FDI) by the US Abroad and in the US by Country and Industry, 1994 (current US$)

	US FDI Abroad by Country or Industry of Destination $ Millions	%	FDI in the US by Country or Industry of Origin $ Millions	%	US FDI Net Position Abroad $ Millions
Total by Region	612,109	100	504,401	100	107,708
Europe and Turkey	300,177	49	312,876	62	-12,699
Western Hemisphere	187,793	31	67,245	13	120,548
Canada	72,808	12	43,223	9	29,585
Mexico	16,375	3	2187	0	14,188
Other	98,610	16	21,835	4	76,775
Asia and Pacific	108,402	18	117,835	23	-9,433
Japan	37,027	6	103,120	20	-66,093
Other and International	15,736	3	6,445	1	9,291
Addendum: EU 12	251,149	41	273,732	54	-22,583
Addendum: OPEC	12,586	2	3214	1	9,372
Total by Industry	612,109	100	504,401	100	107,708
Petroleum	65,711	11	34,048	7	31,663
Manufacturing	220,328	36	184,484	37	35,844
Wholesale Trade	67,303	11	79,542	16	-12,239
Banking	29,529	5	36,734	7	-7,205
Finance, Insurance, Real Estate	175,045	29	104,437	21	70,608
Services	22,994	4	*	*	*
Other (including Retail Trade)	31,200	5	65,158	13	-33,958

Source: US Department of Commerce, Survey of Current Business (June 1995). Source contains more detailed breakdown by country.
Notes: EU 12 and OPEC overlap other categories; Ecuador left OPEC at end of 1993. "Services" not broken out separately for FDI into US. *Included in "Other."

Table A-6. Industry Composition of the *Fortune* Industrial "Global 500," 1995 (current US$)

Industry by Sales Volume	Number of Enterprises	Sales ($ Billions)	% of Total Sales	Employees (Thousands)	% of Total Employees
Trading	21	1378	12.1	558	1.6
Insurance	56	1224	10.8	1655	4.7
Banks and Savings	67	1213	10.7	2500	7.1
Motor Vehicles and Parts	26	1087	9.6	3471	9.9
Electronics and Electrical Equipment	30	889	7.8	4008	11.4
Petroleum Refining	29	849	7.5	1063	3.0
Telecommunications	22	513	4.5	2425	6.9
Food and Drug Stores	25	429	3.8	2243	6.4
General Merchandisers	17	386	3.4	2349	6.7
Food, Beverages, Food Services	19	330	2.9	1913	5.4
Chemicals	18	323	2.8	1123	3.2
Electric and Gas Utilities	16	322	2.8	700	2.0
Metals and Metal Products	18	271	2.4	860	2.4
Transportation	18	237	2.1	1294	3.7
Computers and Office Equipment	8	217	1.9	749	2.1
Engineering and Construction	13	210	1.8	608	1.7
Delivery	8	169	1.5	2331	6.6
Wholesalers and Retailers	12	164	1.4	519	1.5
Pharmaceuticals	10	131	1.2	542	1.5
Industrial and Farm Equipment	8	128	1.1	482	1.4
Aerospace	8	123	1.1	727	2.1
Financial and Brokerage	8	123	1.1	183	0.5
Tobacco	3	98	0.9	344	1.0
Scientific and Photographic Equipment	5	71	0.6	318	0.9
Forest and Paper Products	5	71	0.6	239	0.7
All Others	30	422	3.7	1916	5.5
Total	500	11,378	100.0	35,120	100.0

Source: Fortune "Global 500" (August 5, 1996). Note: Industries ordered by volume of sales and combined.

Table A-7. US Ownership of Nonbank Foreign Affiliates by Country of Operation, 1993

	Total Affiliates	% Distribution by Location	Majority Owned	% Majority Owned	Wholly Owned	% Wholly Owned
			Number of Affiliates			
All Countries	18,698	100	16,484	88	14,834	79
Europe	9202	49	8496	92	7802	85
Western Hemisphere	4865	26	4337	89	3913	80
Canada	1941	10	1837	95	1699	88
Mexico	624	3	458	73	402	64
Other	2300	12	2042	89	1812	79
Asia/Pacific	3672	20	2891	79	2470	67
Australia	777	4	672	86	630	81
Japan	842	5	523	62	413	49
Singapore	348	2	321	92	310	89
Other and Unassigned	959	5	760	79	649	68
			Employment in Thousands			
All Countries	6731.1	100	5259.9	78	4299.8	64
Europe	2733.1	41	2418.5	88	2085.1	76
Western Hemisphere	2295.2	34	1836.6	80	1477.5	64
Canada	874.9	13	830.2	95	676.2	77
Mexico	666.1	10	411.7	62	338.5	51
Other	754.2	11	594.7	79	462.8	61
Asia/Pacific	1518	23	876.9	58	653.2	43
Australia	371.5	6	189.8	51	150.3	40
Japan	411.3	6	157.5	38	112.3	27
Singapore	100.7	1	93.5	93	92.2	92
Other and Unassigned	184.9	3	128.0	69	84.1	45

Source: US Department of Commerce, *Survey of Current Business* (June 1995).

Note: Source states that employment is the best measure of relative size.

Index

Abu Dhabi, 90 (see UAE)
accounting records and
standards, 81, 216ff.
acquisitions and mergers (see
mergers and acquisitions)
Adelman, Carol C., 9, 12, 179
advanced industrial countries
(AICs), 3, 9, 11, 31, 33,
34, 37, 38, 51, 58, 70,
80, 83, 88, 105, 109,
140, 171, 175, 199, 207,
223–225 (see First
World, industrial market
economies, OECD,
Triad)
Aeppel, Timothy, 108, 118
affiliates, foreign, 48, 50, 54–58
Afghanistan, 118
Africa, 32, 88, 113–114, 207
(see Central Africa, East
Africa, South Africa,
West Africa)
Agenda 21, 182, 198 (see UN
Declaration on the
Human Environment)
Agreement on Trade–Related
Aspects of Intellectual
Property Rights (TRIPS),
127
agriculture, 127, 129, 136, 208
air pollution agreements (see
regimes, ambient
environment)
air transport regimes (see
regimes, air transport)
Albania, 118, 224

Algeria, 90, 224
Alkhafaji, Abbass F., 216, 221
alliances, 43, 48–51, 101 (EU),
161, 209 (see coalitions,
networks)
allocative efficiency, 23
Alpine environment, 186–187
ambient environment (air, water,
climate) regimes (see
regimes, ambient
environment)
America, Central (see Central
America)
America, Developing (see
Developing America)
America, Latin (see Latin
America)
America, North (see North
America)
Americas, The, 88, 110
American Assembly, 183, 184,
188, 200
The Americas initiative (see US
Enterprise for the
Americas initiative
Amtrak, 47, 48
Amuzegar, Jahangir, 113, 118
anarchy, 26
Anastassopoulos, Jean-Pierre,
58
Andean Code for Foreign
Investment (Declaration
24), 116, 209
Andean Common Market
(ANCOM), 89, 90, 111
Andean Group, 90, 111,